LI
in
GRACE

Experiencing God's Peace and Protection

ANGELS

PEACE WITH GOD

BILLY GRAHAM

THOMAS NELSON
Since 1798

NASHVILLE DALLAS MEXICO CITY RIO DE JANEIRO BEIJING

Published in Nashville, Tennessee, by Thomas Nelson. Thomas Nelson is a registered trademark of Thomas Nelson, Inc.

Thomas Nelson, Inc., titles may be purchased in bulk for educational, business, fund-raising, or sales promotional use. For information, please e-mail SpecialMarkets@ThomasNelson.com.

ISBN: 978-0-8499-2146-9

Printed in the United States of America

09 10 11 12 QWF 6 5 4 3 2 1

ANGELS

The angels are the dispensers and administrators of the divine beneficence toward us; they regard our safety, undertake our defense, direct our ways, and exercise a constant solicitude that no evil befall us.

JOHN CALVIN

Institutes of the Christian Religion, I

Contents

Publisher's Note

If ever there was a time when people needed the special power and blessings of heaven in their lives, that time is now. We live in troubled times. Political, social, and economic issues loom so large in our daily lives, we often seem to be in danger of losing any sense of happiness or peace. And many people have lost touch with basic values and beliefs. For many people, life is so difficult and serious that they simply don't pause to discover the inner strength that comes through the supernatural. We trust that Dr. Graham's personal insights into this fascinating subject will help each reader achieve a new level of happiness and a dynamic, new hope for the future.

1

Are Angels God's Secret Agents?

My wife, who was born and raised in China, recalls that in her childhood days tigers lived in the mountains. One day a poor woman went up to the foothills to cut grass. To her back was tied a baby, and a little child walked beside her. In her hand she carried a sharp sickle to cut grass. Just as she reached the top of a hill, she heard a roar. Frightened almost speechless, she looked around to see a mother tigress springing at her, followed by two cubs.

This illiterate Chinese mother had never attended school or entered a church. She had never seen a Bible. But a year or two earlier a missionary had told her about Jesus, "who is able to help you when you are in trouble." As the claws of the tigress tore her arm and shoulder, the woman cried out in a frenzy, "O Jesus, help me!" The ferocious beast, instead of attacking again to get an easy meal, suddenly turned and ran away.

The Bible says, "He will give his angels charge of you, to guard you in all your ways" (Psalm 91:11 RSV). Had God sent an angel to help this poor ignorant Chinese woman? Are there supernatural beings today who are able to influence the affairs of men and nations?

In *A Slow and Certain Light*, Elizabeth Elliot told about her father's experiences with angelic helpers:

> My father, when he was a small boy, was climbing on an upper story of a house that was being built. He walked to the end of a board that was not nailed at the other end, and it slowly began to tip. He knew that he was doomed, but inexplicably the board began to tip the other way, as though a hand had pushed it down again. He always wondered if it was an angel's hand.

HELP FROM ANGELS

A celebrated Philadelphia neurologist had gone to bed after an exceptionally tiring day. Suddenly he was awakened by someone knocking on his door. Opening it he found a little girl, poorly dressed and deeply upset. She told him her mother was very sick and asked him if he would please come with her. It was a bitterly cold, snowy night, but though he was bone tired, the doctor dressed and followed the girl.

As *Reader's Digest* reports the story, he found the mother desperately ill with pneumonia. After arranging for medical care, he complimented the sick woman on the intelligence and persistence of her little daughter. The woman looked at him strangely and then said, "My daughter died a month ago." She added, "Her shoes and coat are in the clothes closet there." Amazed and perplexed, the doctor went to the closet and opened the door. There hung the very coat worn by the little girl who had brought him to tend to her mother. It was warm and dry and could not possibly have been out in the wintry night.

Could the doctor have been called in the hour of desperate need by an angel who appeared as this woman's young daughter? Was this the work of God's angels on behalf of the sick woman?

The Reverend John G. Paton, pioneer missionary in the New Hebrides Islands, told a thrilling story involving the protective care of angels. Hostile natives surrounded his mission headquarters one night, intent on burning the Patons out and killing them. John Paton and his wife prayed all during that terror-filled night that God would deliver them. When daylight came they were amazed to see that, unaccountably, the attackers had left. They thanked God for delivering them.

A year later, the chief of the tribe was converted to Jesus Christ, and Mr. Paton, remembering what had happened, asked the chief what had kept him and his men from burning down the house and killing them. The chief replied in surprise, "Who were all those men you had with you there?" The missionary answered, "There were no men there; just my wife and I." The chief argued that they had seen many men standing guard—hundreds of big men in shining garments with drawn swords in their hands. They seemed to circle the mission station so that the natives were afraid to attack.

Only then did Mr. Paton realize that God had sent His angels to protect them. The chief agreed that there was no other explanation. Could it be that God had sent a legion of angels to protect His servants, whose lives were being endangered?

A Persian colporteur was accosted by a man who asked him if he had a right to sell Bibles. "Why, yes," he answered, "we are allowed to sell these books anywhere in the country!" The man looked puzzled and asked, "How is it, then, that you are always surrounded by soldiers? I planned three times to attack you, and each time, seeing the soldiers, I left you alone. Now I no longer want to harm you." Were these soldiers heavenly beings?

During World War II, Captain Eddie Rickenbacker and the rest of the crew of the B-17 in which he was flying ran out of fuel and "ditched" in the Pacific Ocean. For weeks nothing was heard of him. The newspapers reported his disappearance, and across the country thousands of people prayed. Mayor LaGuardia asked the whole city of New York to pray for him. Then he returned. The Sunday papers headlined the news, and in an article, Captain Rickenbacker himself told what had happened. "And this part I would hesitate to tell," he wrote, "except that there were six witnesses who saw it with me. A gull came out of nowhere, and lighted on my head—I reached up my hand very gently—I killed him and then we divided him equally among us. We ate every bit, even the little bones. Nothing ever tasted so good." This gull saved the lives of Rickenbacker and his companions. Years later I asked him to tell me the story personally, because it was through this experience that he came to know Christ. He said, "I have no explanation except that God sent one of His angels to rescue us."

During my ministry I have heard or read literally thousands of stories. Could it be that these were all hallucinations or accidents or fate or luck? Or were real angels sent from God to perform certain tasks?

THE CURRENT CULT OF THE DEMONIC

Just a few years ago such ideas would have been scorned by most educated people. Science was king, and science was tuned in to believe only what could be seen or measured. The idea of supernatural beings was thought to be nonsense, the ravings of the lunatic fringe.

All this has changed. Think, for example, of the morbid fascination modern society has for the occult. Walk into a bookstore; visit any newsstand at a modern airport; go to a university library. You will be confronted by shelves and tables packed with books about the devil, Satan worship, and demon possession. A number of Hollywood films, television programs and as many as one in four hard-rock pop songs are devoted to, or thematically make reference to, the devil. Years ago the Rolling Stones sang their "Sympathy for the Devil" to the top of the popularity chart; another group answered back with a symphony to the devil.

The Exorcist proved to be one of the biggest money-makers of any film in history. Arthur Lyons gave his book a title that is frighteningly accurate: *The Second Coming: Satanism in America.* This theme, which intellectuals would have derided a generation ago, is now being dealt with seriously by such people as noted author John Updike and Harvard professor Harvey Cox. Some polls indicate that 70 percent of Americans believe in a personal devil. Some years ago Walter Cronkite announced a poll over his CBS network news showing that the number of Americans who believe in a personal devil has increased 12 percent. This was in the mid-1970s. What would the figure be today? It is ironic that a generation ago, scientists, psychologists, sociologists, and even some theologians were predicting that by the late 1970s there would be a sharp decline in belief in the supernatural. The reverse is true!

Some years ago, in a medium-sized metropolitan area, I turned out of curiosity to the entertainment pages of the local newspaper and studied them carefully. I was unprepared for the shock I received as I read the descriptions of the themes and content of the feature motion pictures being shown in the theaters in that area. They focused on sadism, murder, demon possession and demonism, devil worship and horror, not to mention those that depicted erotic sex. It seemed that each advertisement tried to outdo the others in the degree of shock, horror and mind-bending emotional devastation. The picture hasn't changed. If anything, the movies are even worse today!

Even in the Christian world the presses have turned out a rash of books on the devil by both Catholic and Protestant writers. I myself have thought about writing a book on the devil and his demons.

THE REALITY AND POWER OF SATAN

The Bible does teach that Satan is a real being who is at work in the world together with his emissaries, the demons. In the New

Testament they intensified their activities and bent every effort to defeat the work of Jesus Christ, God's Son. The apparent increase in satanic activity against people on this planet today may indicate that the second coming of Jesus Christ is close at hand. Certainly, the activity of Satan is evident on every side. We can see it in the wars and other crises that affect all people daily. We can also see it in the attacks of Satan against individual members of the body of Christ.

Some years ago I had dinner with several senators and congressmen in a dining room in the Capitol building. We began discussing the rising interest in the occult with special reference to *The Exorcist.* One of the senators, who had recently passed through a deep religious experience, said that due to his past experience with the occult, whenever he knew of a theater that was showing *The Exorcist* he would drive a block around it. He was afraid even to go near it. He said, "I know that both angels and demons are for real."

Several years ago the late Pope Paul said he was sure that the evil forces attacking every level of society had behind them the work of a personal devil with a whole kingdom of demons at his command. The Roman Catholic Church has been rethinking its position on the reality of the spirit world; and interest in this subject has revived among both theological liberals and evangelicals in Protestant churches everywhere.

UNIDENTIFIED FLYING OBJECTS

The renewed interest in the occult and satanism is not the only evidence of the new openness to the supernatural. It also was revealed in the widespread revival of speculation about the so-called "unidentified flying objects"—UFOs—some years ago. Even some of today's popular movies center on visitors from outer space.

Some reputable scientists deny and others assert that UFOs do appear to people from time to time. Some scientists have reached the place where they think they can prove that these are possibly visitors from outer space. Some Christian writers have speculated that UFOs could very well be a part of God's angelic host who preside over the physical affairs of universal creation. While we cannot assert such a view with certainty, many people are now seeking some type of supernatural explanation for these phenomena. Nothing can hide the fact, however, that these unexplained events are occurring with greater frequency around the entire world and in unexpected places.

Some years ago, Japan witnessed a typical example of unexplained objects that appeared in the night skies. On January 15, 1975, a squadron of UFO-like objects, resembling a celestial string of pearls, soared silently through the evening skies over half the length of Japan. As government officials, police, and thousands of curious citizens stared at the sky in wonder, from fifteen to twenty glowing objects, cruising in straight formation, flew over Japan inside a strange misty cloud. Further, they were sighted and reported in cities seven hundred miles apart in less than an hour.

Hundreds of frantic telephone calls jammed switchboards of police stations and government installations as the spectacular formation sped south. "All the callers reported seeing a huge cloud passing over the city."

They said they saw strange objects inside the cloud moving in a straight line, recalled Duty Officer Takeo Ohira. Were they planes? "No," said Hiroshi Mayazawa, "because no planes or natural phenomena appeared on my radar. It was an exceptionally clear night. To me the whole thing is a mystery."

Professor Masatoshi Kitamura watched the dazzling display in the night sky from the control room of Tokyo's Meteorological Bureau station near the airport. He said, "I was mystified. Nothing showed up on my radar. I reported my sighting to the airport control tower, and they told me nothing showed on their radar either."

OTHER EXPLANATIONS

Erich von Daniken's *Chariots of the Gods?*, published many years ago, was reissued in paperback by Berkeley in 1984. It theorizes that in prehistory astronauts from distant stars visited earth in spaceships. From these visits grew man's idea of gods and many of his conceptions of them. Immanuel Velikovsky, in his equally popular *Worlds in Collision* and *Ages in Chaos* put forward the notion that the turbulent history of the Middle East in the second millennium B.C. can be traced to a violent scattering of the solar system that caused ruin on earth. The knowledge of the intense suffering of those times was soon repressed but lies buried in man's racial memory, explaining his modern self-destructive behavior.

Men would dismiss these grandiose cosmologies lightly if it were not that they, along with a number of other theories, have been put forward with such frequency and serious import that no one can shrug them off. They are being studied seriously at many of our universities. As a theme for talk shows, hardly anything or anyone can top concerns like this.

Some sincere Christians, whose views are anchored in a strong commitment to Scripture, contend that these UFOs are angels. But are they? These people point to certain passages in Isaiah, Ezekiel, Zechariah, and the book of Revelation, and draw parallels to the reports of observers of alleged UFO appearances. They take the detailed descriptions, for example, of a highly credible airline crew and lay them alongside Ezekiel 10, and put forward a strong case. In Ezekiel 10 we read, "Each of the four cherubim had a wheel beside him—'The Whirl-Wheels,' as I heard them called, for each one had a second wheel crosswise within, sparkled like chrysolite, giving off a greenish-yellow glow. Because of the construction of these wheels, the cherubim could go straight forward in each of four directions; they did not turn when they changed direction but could go in any of the four ways their faces looked. . . And when they rose into the air the wheels rose with them, and stayed beside them as they flew. When the cherubim stood still, so did the wheels, for the spirit of the cherubim was in the wheels" (verses 9-13, 16-17 TLB).

Any attempt to connect such passages with the visits of angels may, at best, be speculation. Nor should we become too preoccupied or overly fascinated with trying to identify contemporary theories and speculations about UFOs or similar phenomena with biblical passages. Secular speculations often, in fact, run counter to the Bible's teaching concerning the origin of life on this planet. What is interesting, however, is that such theories are now being given serious attention even by people who make no claim to believe in the God of the Bible.

A further evidence of the renewed interest in the supernatural is the widespread fascination with extrasensory perception—ESP. The subjective science of parapsychology is now one of the fastest-growing fields of academic research in our universities today.

At Duke University, Dr. Joseph B. Rhine took up the study of extrasensory perception in the 1930s and championed it to the point where a department of parapsychology was established at the university. He became its pioneering professor. Today scientists are probing every conceivable frontier for ESP possibilities. Its line-up of protagonists reads like a Who's Who. Not only is serious intellectual and scientific study being carried on, but the subject is immensely popular because many of its aggressive proponents profess to be nonreligious. It has gained even more widespread respectability in communist societies (such as in the Soviet Union) than here in the United States. It plays a role of a "substitute religion" in some cases, although it has been used primarily as a technique to influence people.

Notice also the reaction on network talk shows. When a celebrity steps through the grand entrance and strolls to the guest chair, he is asked, "Do you believe in ESP?" To say, "No," in the middle 1980s would be as unfashionable as to have said, "Yes," a generation ago.

WHY I WROTE THIS BOOK

But why write a book on angels? Isn't talking about angels merely adding to the speculation about supernatural phenomena? What possible value is there in such a discussion? Didn't the fascination with angels vanish with the Middle Ages?

Because all the powers of the evil world system seem to be preying on the minds of people already disturbed and frustrated in our generation, I believe the time has come to focus on the positives of the Christian faith. John the apostle said, "Greater is he that is in you, than he that is in the world" (1 John 4:4). Satan is indeed capable of doing supernatural things—but he acts only by the permissive will of God; he is on a leash. It is God who is all powerful. It is God who is omnipotent. God has provided Christians with both offensive and defensive weapons. We are not to be fearful; we are not to be distressed; we are not to be deceived; nor are we to be intimidated. Rather, we are to be on our guard, calm and alert, "lest Satan should get an advantage of us, for we are not ignorant of his devices" (2 Corinthians 2:11).

One of Satan's sly devices is to divert our minds from the help God offers us in our struggles against the forces of evil. However, the Bible testifies that God has provided assistance for us in our spiritual conflicts. We are not alone in this world! The Bible teaches us that God's Holy Spirit has been given to empower us and guide us. In addition, the Bible—in nearly three hundred different places—also teaches that God has countless angels at His command. Furthermore, God has commissioned these angels to aid His children in their struggles against Satan. The Bible does not give as much information about them as we might like, but what it does say should be a source of comfort and strength for us in every circumstance.

I am convinced that these heavenly beings exist and that they provide unseen aid on our behalf. I do not believe in angels because someone has told me about a dramatic visitation from an angel, impressive as such rare testimonies may be. I do not believe in angels because UFOs are astonishingly angel-like in some of their reported appearances. I do not believe in angels because ESP experts are making the realm of the spirit world seem more and more plausible. I do not believe in angels because of the sudden worldwide emphasis on the reality of Satan and demons. I do not believe in angels because I have ever seen one—because I haven't.

I believe in angels because the Bible says there are angels; and I believe the Bible to be the true Word of God.

I also believe in angels because I have sensed their presence in my life on special occasions.

So what I have to say in the chapters that follow will not be an accumulation of my ideas about the spirit world, nor even a reflection of my own spiritual experiences in the spirit realm. I propose to put forward, at least in part, what I understand the Bible to say about angels. Naturally, this will not be an exhaustive study of the subject. I hope, however, that it will arouse your curiosity sufficiently for you to dig out from the Bible all that you can find on this subject after you have read this book. More than that, it is my prayer that you will discover the reality of God's love and care for you as evidenced in the ministry of His angels on your behalf, and that you would go forth in faith each day trusting God's constant watch-care over you.

Spiritual forces and resources are available to all Christians. Because our resources are unlimited, Christians will be winners. Millions of angels are at God's command and at our service. The hosts of heaven stand at attention as we make our way from earth to glory, and Satan's BB guns are no match for God's heavy artillery. So don't be afraid. God is for you. He has committed His angels to wage war in this conflict of the ages—and they will win the victory. The apostle Paul has said in Colossians 2:15, "And having spoiled principalities and powers, he made a show of them openly, triumphing over them." Victory over the flesh, the world, and the devil is ours now! The angels are here to help, and they are prepared for any emergency.

As you read this book, therefore, I pray that God will open your eyes to the resources He has provided for all who turn to Him for strength. I pray also that God will use it to show you your constant need of Him, and how He has sent His Son, Jesus Christ, into the world to deliver you from both the guilt and power of sin.

The British express train raced through the night, its powerful headlight piercing the darkness. Queen Victoria was a passenger on the train.

Suddenly the engineer saw a startling sight. Revealed in the beam of the engine's light was a strange figure in a black cloak standing in the middle of the tracks and waving its arms. The engineer grabbed for the brake and brought the train to a grinding halt.

He and his fellow trainmen clambered down to see what had stopped them. But they could find no trace of the strange figure. On a hunch the engineer walked a few yards further up the tracks. Suddenly he stopped and stared into the fog in horror. The bridge had been washed out in the middle and ahead of them it had toppled into a swollen stream. If the engineer had not heeded the ghostly figure, his train would have plummeted down the stream.

While the bridge and the tracks were being repaired, the crew made a more intensive search for the strange flagman. But not until they got to London did they solve the mystery.

At the base of the engine's headlamp, the engineer discovered a huge dead moth. He looked at it a moment, then on impulse wet its wings and pasted it to the glass of the lamp.

Climbing back into his cab, he switched on the light and saw the "flagman" in the beam. He knew the answer now: the moth had flown into the beam seconds before the train was due to reach the washed-out bridge. In the fog, it appeared to be a phantom figure waving its arms.

When Queen Victoria was told of the strange happening, she said, "I'm sure it was no accident. It was God's way of protecting us."

No, the figure the engineer saw in the headlight's beam was not an angel, yet God, quite possibly through the ministry of His unseen angels, had placed the moth on the headlight lens exactly when and where it was needed. Truly "he will command his angels concerning you to guard you in all your ways" (Psalm 91:11 NIV).

2

Angels Are for Real

Speculation about the nature of angels has been around since long before Queen Victoria's time, and it continues down to the present time. Yet through revelation in the Bible God has told us a great deal about them. For this reason, theologians through the ages have universally agreed about the importance of "angel-ology" (the orderly statement of biblical truth about angels). They judged it worthy of treatment in any book of systematic theology. They wrote at length, distinguishing between good angels and satanology (the study of fallen and thus evil angels). But today we have neglected the theme of good angels, although many are giving the devil and all of his demons rapt attention, even worshiping them.

Angels belong to a uniquely different dimension of creation that we, limited to the natural order, can scarcely comprehend. In this angelic domain the limitations are different from those God has imposed on our natural order. He has given angels higher knowledge, power, and mobility than humans. Have you ever seen or met one of these superior beings called angels? Probably not, for both the Bible and human experience tell us visible appearances by angels are very rare—but that in no way makes angels any less real or powerful. They are God's messengers whose chief business is to carry out His orders in the world. He has given them an ambassadorial charge. He has designated and empowered them as holy deputies to perform works of righteousness. In this way they assist Him as their creator while He sovereignly controls the universe. So He has given them the capacity to bring His holy enterprises to a successful conclusion.

ANGELS ARE CREATED BEINGS

Don't believe everything you hear (and read!) about angels! Some would have us believe that they are only spiritual will-o'-the-wisps. Some view them as only celestial beings with beautiful wings and bowed heads. Others would have us think of them as effeminate weirdos.

The Bible states that angels, like men, were created by God. At one time no angels existed; indeed there was nothing but the Triune God: Father, Son, and Holy Spirit. Paul, in Colossians 1:16, says, "For by him were all things created, that are in heaven, and that are in earth, visible and invisible." Angels indeed are among the invisible things made by God, for "all things were created by him, and for him." This creator, Jesus, "is before all things, and by him all things consist" (Colossians 1:17), so that even angels would cease to exist if Jesus, who is Almighty God, did not sustain them by His power.

It seems that angels have the ability to change their appearance and shuttle in a flash from the capital glory of heaven to earth and back again. Although some interpreters have said that the phrase "sons of God" in Genesis 6:2 refers to angels, the Bible frequently makes it clear that angels are nonmaterial; Hebrews 1:14 calls them ministering "spirits." Intrinsically, they do not possess physical bodies, although they may take on physical bodies when God appoints them to special tasks. Furthermore, God has given them no ability to reproduce, and they neither marry nor are given in marriage (Mark 12:25).

The empire of angels is as vast as God's creation. If you believe the Bible, you will believe in their ministry. They crisscross the Old and New Testaments, being mentioned directly or indirectly nearly three hundred times. Some biblical scholars believe that angels can be numbered potentially in the millions since Hebrews 12:22 speaks of "an innumerable [myriads—a great but indefinite number] company of angels." As to their number, David recorded twenty thousand coursing through the skyways of the stars. Even with his limited vision, he impressively notes, "The chariots of God are twenty thousand, even thousands of angels" (Psalm 68:17). Matthew Henry says of this passage, "Angels are 'the chariots of God,' his chariots of war, which he makes use of against his enemies, his chariots of conveyance, which he sends for his friends, as he did for Elijah . . . , his chariots of state, in the midst of which he shows his glory and power. They are vastly numerous: 'Twenty thousands,' even thousands multiplied."

Ten thousand angels came down on Mount Sinai to confirm the presence of God as He gave the Law to Moses (Deuteronomy 33:2). An earthquake shook the mountain. Moses was held in speechbound wonder at this mighty cataclysm attended by the visitation of heavenly beings. Furthermore, in the New Testament John tells us of having seen ten thousand times ten thousand angels ministering to the Lamb of God in the throne room of the universe (Revelation 5:11). The book of Revelation also says that armies of angels will appear with Jesus at the Battle of Armageddon when God's foes gather for their final defeat. Paul says in 2 Thessalonians, "The Lord Jesus shall be revealed from heaven with his mighty angels" (1:7).

Think of it! Multitudes of angels, indescribably mighty, performing the commands of heaven! More amazingly, even one angel is indescribably mighty, as though an extension of the arm of God. Singly or corporately, angels are for real. They are better organized than were the armies of Alexander the Great, Napoleon, or Eisenhower. From earliest antiquity, when the angels guarding the gates of Eden sealed its entrance, angels have manifested their presence in the world. God placed angelic sentinels called cherubim at the east of the Garden of Eden. They were commissioned not only to bar man's return into Eden, but with "a flaming sword flashing back and forth to guard the way to the tree of life" (Genesis 3:24 NIV) lest Adam by eating of its fruit should live forever. If Adam had lived in his sin forever—this earth would long ago have been hell. Thus, in one sense, death is a blessing to the human race.

ANGELS SERVE GOD AND REGENERATE MEN

Witness the unprecedented and unrepeated pageantry at Mount Sinai. When God moves toward man, it is an event of the first magnitude and can include the visitation of angelic hosts. In the billowing clouds that covered Sinai, an angelic trumpeter announced the presence of God. The whole mountain seemed to pulsate with life. Consternation gripped the people below. The earth seemed convulsed with a nameless fear. As God came to the mountaintop, He was accompanied by thousands of angels. Moses, the silent, lone witness, must have been overcome with even a limited vision of the forces of God. It staggers the imagination to wonder what kind of a headline would be prompted in the daily press for even a man-sided view of such a heavenly visitation. "And so terrible was the sight, that Moses said, I exceedingly fear and quake" (Hebrews 12:21).

The appearance of God was glorious. He shone like the sun when it goes to its strength. In his commentary, Matthew Henry says, "Even Seir and Paran, two mountains at some distance, were illuminated by the divine glory which appeared on Mount Sinai, and reflected some of the rays of it, so bright was the appearance, and so much taken notice to set forth the wonders of the divine providence (Habakkuk 3:3, 4; Psalm 18:7–9). The Jerusalem Targum has a strange gloss [note of explanation] upon this, that, 'when God came down to give the law, he offered it on Mount Seir to the Edomites, but they refused it, because they found in it, *Thou shalt not kill.* Then he offered it on Mount Paran to the Ishmaelites, but they also refused it, because they found in it, *Thou shalt not steal*;

and then he came to Mount Sinai and offered it to Israel, and they said *All that the Lord shall say we will do*.'" This account by the Jerusalem Targum is, of course, fictional, but it throws an interesting light on how some Jews later regarded this extraordinary and spectacular event.

BELIEF IN ANGELS: A GENERAL PHENOMENON

The history of virtually all nations and cultures reveals at least some belief in angelic beings. Ancient Egyptians made the tombs of their dead more impregnable and lavish than their homes because they felt angels would visit there in succeeding ages. Islamic scholars have proposed that at least two angels are assigned to each person: one angel records the good deeds and the other the bad. In fact, long before Islam arose, and even apart from contact with Scripture, some religions taught the existence of angels. But no matter what the traditions, our frame of reference must be the Scripture as our supreme authority on this subject.

Today some hard-nosed scientists lend credence to the scientific probability of angels when they admit the likelihood of unseen and invisible intelligence. Increasingly, our world is being made acutely aware of the existence of occult and demonic powers. People pay attention as never before to sensational headlines promoting films and books concerning the occult. News accounts of strange happenings around the world fascinate readers and TV viewers everywhere. Ought not Christians, grasping the eternal dimension of life, become conscious of the sinless angelic powers who are for real, and who associate with God Himself and administer His works in our behalf? After all, references to the holy angels in the Bible far outnumber references to Satan and his subordinate demons.

COSMIC POWERS

If the activities of the devil and his demons seem to be intensifying in these days, as I believe they are, should not the incredibly greater supernatural powers of God's holy angels be even more indelibly impressed on the minds of people of faith? Certainly the eye of faith sees many evidences of the supernatural display of God's power and glory. God is still in business too.

Christians must never fail to sense the operation of angelic glory. It forever eclipses the world of demonic powers, as the sun does the candle's light.

If you are a believer, expect powerful angels to accompany you in your life experiences. And let those events dramatically illustrate the friendly presence of "the holy ones," as Daniel calls them.

Angels speak. They appear and reappear. They are emotional creatures. While angels may become visible by choice, our eyes are not constructed to see them ordinarily any more than we can see the dimensions of a nuclear field, the structure of atoms, or the electricity that flows through copper wiring. Our ability to sense reality is limited: The deer of the forest far surpass our human capacity in their keenness of smell. Bats possess a phenomenally sensitive built-in radar system. Some animals can see things in the dark that escape our attention. Swallows and geese possess sophisticated guidance systems that appear to border on the supernatural. So why should we think it strange if men fail to perceive the evidences of angelic presence? Could it be that God granted Balaam and his ass a new optical capacity to view the angel? (See Numbers 22:23, 31.) Without this special sense, they might have thought him to be only a figment of their imagination.

Reports continually flow to my attention from many places around the world telling of visitors of the angelic order appearing, ministering, fellowshiping, and disappearing. They warn of God's impending judgment; they spell out the tenderness of His love; they meet a desperate need; then they are gone. Of one thing we can be sure: angels never draw attention to themselves but ascribe glory to God and press His message upon the hearers as a delivering and sustaining word of the highest order.

Demonic activity and Satan worship are on the increase in all parts of the world. The devil is alive and more at work than at any other time. The Bible says that since he realizes his time is short, his activity will increase. Through his demonic influences he does succeed in turning many away from true faith; but we can still say that his evil activities are countered for the people of God by His ministering spirits, the holy ones of the angelic order. They are vigorous in delivering the heirs of salvation from the stratagems of evil men. They cannot fail.

Believers, look up—take courage. The angels are nearer than you think. For after all (as we have already noted), God has given "his angels charge of you, to guard you in all your ways. On their hands they will bear you up, lest you dash your foot against a stone" (Psalm 91:11–12 RSV).

3

ANGELS—VISIBLE OR INVISIBLE?

The spirit world and its activities are big news today. And the idea of the supernatural is not only seriously regarded, but is accepted as a fact. Many of the most recent books on the subject border on the sensational, or are purely speculative, or have been dreamed up in somebody's imagination. But those who take the Bible at full value cannot discount the subject of angels as speculation or hollow conjecture. After all, the Scriptures mention their existence almost three hundred times.

HAVE YOU EVER SEEN AN ANGEL?

I have already said that the angels are created spirit beings who can become visible when necessary. They can appear and disappear.

They think, feel, will, and display emotions. But some people have questions about them that ought not concern us. The old debate about how many angels can dance on the head of a pin is foolish. And to ask how many angels can be crowded into a telephone booth or into a Volkswagen hardly merits our attention. On the other hand, we should know what the Bible teaches about them as oracles of God who give divine or authoritative decisions and bring messages from God to men. To fulfill this function, angels have not infrequently assumed visible, human form. The writer to the Hebrews asks, "Are they [angels] not all ministering spirits?" (1:14). Now, have you ever seen a pure spirit? I can't say that I have. Yet I do know that down through the ages God has chosen to manifest His own spiritual presence in different ways. At the baptism of Jesus, God the Holy Spirit was present in the form of a dove. So God has chosen also to manifest His presence through His angels, who are lesser beings to whom He has given the power to assume forms that occasionally make them visible to men.

ARE ANGELS TO BE WORSHIPED?

It is no mere accident that angels are usually invisible. Though God in His infinite wisdom does not, as a rule, permit angels to take on physical dimensions, people tend to venerate them in a fashion that borders on worship. We are warned against worshiping the creature rather than the Creator (Romans 1:24–25). It is no less than heretical, and indeed is a breach of the first commandment, to worship any manifestation of angelic presence, patron, or blesser.

Paul has pointed out that while unusual manifestations may be deeply significant, Jesus Christ the incarnate God, the second person of the Trinity, who is creator of all things and by whom all things exist, is worthy of our worship (Colossians 2:18). We are not to pray to angels. Nor are we to engage in "a voluntary humility and worshiping" of them. Only the Triune God is to be the object of our worship and of our prayers.

Moreover, we should not confuse angels, whether visible or invisible, with the Holy Spirit, the third person of the Trinity and Himself God. Angels do not indwell men; the Holy Spirit seals them and indwells them when he has regenerated them. The Holy Spirit is all-knowing, all-present, and all-powerful. Angels are mightier than men, but they are not gods and they do not possess the attributes of the Godhead.

Not angels, but the Holy Spirit convicts men of sin, righteousness, and judgment (John 16:7). He reveals and interprets Jesus Christ to men, while angels remain messengers of God who serve men as ministering spirits (Hebrews 1:14). So far as I know, no Scripture says that the Holy Spirit ever manifested Himself in human form to men. Jesus did this in the incarnation. The glorious Holy Spirit can be everywhere at the same time, but no angel can be in more than one place at any given moment. We know the Holy Spirit as spirit, not flesh, but we can know angels not as spirits alone but sometimes also in visible form.

At the same time, both angels and the Holy Spirit are at work in our world to accomplish God's perfect will. Frankly, we may not always know the agent or means God is using—the Holy Spirit or the angels—when we discern God's hand at work. We can be sure, however, that there is no contradiction or competition between

God the Holy Spirit and God's command of the angelic hosts. God Himself is in control to accomplish His will—and in that we can rejoice!

God uses angels to work out the destinies of men and nations. He has altered the courses of the busy political and social arenas of our society and directed the destinies of men by angelic visitation many times over. We must be aware that angels keep in close and vital contact with all that is happening on the earth. Their knowledge of earthly matters exceeds that of men. We must attest to their invisible presence and unceasing labors. Let us believe that they are here among us. They may not laugh or cry with us, but we do know they delight with us over every victory in our evangelistic endeavors. Jesus taught that "there is joy in the presence of the angels of God when one sinner repents" (Luke 15:10 TLB).

ANGELS VISIBLE? INVISIBLE?

In Daniel 6:22 we read, "My God hath sent his angel, and hath shut the lions' mouths." In the den, Daniel's sight evidently perceived the angelic presence, and the lions' strength more than met its match in the power of the angel. In most instances, angels, when appearing visibly, are so glorious and impressively beautiful as to stun and amaze men who witness their presence.

Can you imagine a being, white and dazzling as lightning? General William Booth, founder of the Salvation Army, described a vision of angelic beings, stating that every angel was surrounded with an aura of rainbow light so brilliant that were it not withheld, no human being could stand the sight of it.

Who can measure the brilliance of the lightning flash that illuminates the countryside for miles around? The angel who rolled away the stone from the tomb of Jesus was not only dressed in white, but shone as a flash of lightning with dazzling brilliance (Matthew 28:30). The keepers of the tomb shook and became as dead men. Incidentally, that stone weighed several times more than a single man could move, yet the physical power of the angel was not taxed in rolling it aside.

Abraham, Lot, Jacob and others had no difficulty recognizing angels when God allowed them to manifest themselves in physical form. Note, for example, Jacob's instant recognition of angels in Genesis 32:1, 2. "And Jacob went on his way, and the angels of God met him. And when Jacob saw them, he said, This is God's host: and he called the name of that place Mahanaim."

Further, both Daniel and John described the glories of the angels (Daniel 10:6 and Revelation 10:1) visibly descending from heaven with immeasurable beauty and brilliance, shining like the sun. Who has not thrilled to read the account of the three Hebrew children, Shadrach, Meshach, and Abednego? They refused to fall in line with the music of obeisance and worship the king of Babylon. They learned that the angel presence can be observed on occasion by people in the unbelieving world on the outside. After they had refused to bow, the angel preserved them from being burned alive or even having the smell of smoke on their garments from the seven-times-hotter fire. The angel came to them in the midst of the flame without harm and was seen by the king who said, "I see four men . . . in the midst of the fire" (Daniel 3:25).

On the other hand, the Bible indicates angels are more often invisible to human eyes. Whether visible or invisible, however, God causes His angels to go before us, to be with us, and to follow after us.

All of this can be fully understood only by believers who know that angelic presences are in control of the battlefield about us, so that we may stand with complete confidence in the midst of the fight. "If God be for us who can be against us?" (Romans 8:31).

WHAT DO YOU SEE WHEN YOU SEE AN ANGEL?

God is forever imaginative, colorful, and glorious in what He designs. Some of the descriptions of angels, including the one of Lucifer in Ezekiel 28, indicate that they are exotic to the human eye and mind. Apparently angels have a beauty and variety that surpass anything known to men. Scripture does not tell us what elements make up angels. Nor can modern science, which is only beginning to explore the realm of the unseen, tell us about the constitution or even the work of angels.

The Bible seems to indicate that angels do not age, and never says that one was sick. Except for those who fell with Lucifer, the ravages of sin that have brought destruction, sickness, and chaos to our earth have not affected them. The holy angels will never die.

The Bible also teaches that angels are sexless. Jesus said that in heaven men "neither marry, nor are given in marriage, but are as the angels of God in heaven" (Matthew 22:30). This may indicate that angels enjoy relationships that are far more thrilling and exciting than sex. The joy of sex in this life may be only a foretaste of something that believers will enjoy in heaven which is far beyond anything man has ever known.

How are we to understand "theophanies"? (This is a theological term for the visible appearances of Jesus Christ in other forms prior to His incarnation.) Some passages in the Old Testament tell us that the second person of the Trinity appeared and was called either "the Lord" or "the angel of the Lord." Nowhere is it clearer than in Genesis 18 where three men appear before Abraham. Their leader is clearly identified with the Lord, whereas the other two are merely angels. There are no grounds for questioning the very early and traditional Christian interpretation that in these cases there is a preincarnation manifestation of the second person of the Trinity, whether He is called "the Lord" or "the Angel of the Lord" (*Zondervan Pictorial Encyclopedia of the Bible*).

We must remember, then, that in some cases in the Old Testament God Himself appeared in human form as an angel. This reinforces the idea of the relationship between God and His angels. Nevertheless, in almost all of the cases where angelic personages appear, they are God's created angelic beings and not God Himself.

Yes, angels are real. They are not the product of our imagination, but were made by God Himself. Think of it! Whether we see them or not, God has created a vast host of angels to help accomplish His work in this world. When we know God personally through faith in His Son, Jesus Christ, we can have confidence that the angels of God will watch over us and assist us because we belong to Him.

4

Angels—How They Differ from Man

The Bible tells us that God has made man "a little lower than the angels." Yet it also says angels are "ministering spirits, sent forth to minister for them who shall be heirs of salvation" (Hebrews 2:5–7; 1:13–14). This sounds like a contradiction: man lower—but eventually higher through redemption. How can we explain this?

First we must remember that this Scripture is speaking both of Jesus Christ and men. Jesus did "stoop" when He became man. And as a man He was a little lower than the angels in His humanity—although without losing in any sense His divine nature. But it also speaks about men other than Jesus. God has made men head over all the creatures of our earthly world, but they are lower than angels with respect to their bodies and to their place while here on earth. In his *Institutes*, John Calvin said, "The angels are the dispensers and administrators of the Divine beneficence toward us; they regard our safety, undertake our defense, direct our ways, and exercise a constant solicitude that no evil befall us."

God commands angels to help men since they will be made higher than the angels at the resurrection. So says Jesus in Luke 20:36. God will alter the temporary lower position of man when the kingdom of God has come in its fullness.

Now let us examine in detail how God says angels differ from men. Although angels are glorious beings, the Scriptures make it clear that they differ from regenerated men in significant ways. How can the angels who have never sinned fully understand what it means to be delivered from sin? How can they understand how precious Jesus is to those for whom His death on Calvary brings light, life, and immortality? Is it not stranger still that angels themselves will be judged by believers who were once sinners? Such judgment, however, apparently applies only to those fallen angels who followed Lucifer.

Thus Paul writes in 1 Corinthians 6:3, "Know ye not that we shall judge angels?" But even the holy angels have limitations, though the Bible speaks of them as being superior to men in many ways.

IS GOD "FATHER" TO ANGELS?

God is not called "Father" by the holy angels because, not having sinned, they need not be redeemed. All the fallen angels cannot call God "Father" because they cannot be redeemed. The latter case is one of the mysteries of Scripture: God made provision for the salvation of fallen men, but He made no provision for the salvation of fallen angels. Why? Perhaps because, unlike Adam and Eve, who were enticed toward sin by sinners, the angels fell when there were no sinners, so no one could entice them to sin. Thus, their sinful state cannot be altered; their sin cannot be forgiven; their salvation cannot be achieved.

The wicked angels would never want to call God "Father," though they may call Lucifer "father," as many Satan worshipers do. They are in revolt against God and will never voluntarily accept His sovereign lordship, except in that Day of Judgment when every knee will bow and every tongue confess that Jesus Christ is Lord (Philippians 2:9–10). Yet even holy angels who might like to call God "Father" could do so only in the looser sense of that word. As Creator, God is the Father of all created beings; since angels are created beings, they might think of Him this way. But the term is normally reserved in Scripture for lost men who have been redeemed. So in a real sense, even ordinary men cannot call God "Father" except as their Creator God—until they are born again.

ANGELS ARE NOT HEIRS OF GOD

Christians are joint heirs with Jesus Christ through redemption (Romans 8:17), which is made theirs by faith in Him based on His death at Calvary. Angels who are not joint heirs must stand aside when the believers are introduced to their boundless, eternal riches. The holy angels, however, who are ministering spirits, have never lost their original glory and spiritual relationship with God. This assures them of their exalted place in the royal order of God's creation. By contrast, Jesus identified Himself with fallen men in the incarnation when He was "made a little lower than the angels for the suffering of death" (Hebrews 2:9). That He chose to taste the death we deserve also shows that the holy angels do not share our sinfulness—nor our need of redemption.

ANGELS CANNOT TESTIFY OF SALVATION BY GRACE THROUGH FAITH

Who can comprehend the overwhelming thrill of fellowship with God and the joy of salvation that even angels do not know? When the local church assembles as a group of Christian believers, it represents in the human sphere the highest order of the love of God. No love could go deeper, rise higher, or extend farther than the amazing love that moved Him to give His only begotten Son. The angels are aware of that joy (Luke 15:10), and when a person accepts God's gift of eternal life through Jesus Christ, angels set all the bells of heaven to ringing with their rejoicing before the Lamb of God.

Yet although the angels rejoice when people are saved and glorify God who has saved them, they cannot do one thing: testify personally to something they have not experienced. They can only point to the experiences of the redeemed and rejoice that God has saved them. This means that throughout eternity we humans alone will give our personal witness to the salvation that God achieved by grace and that we received through faith in

Jesus Christ. The man who has never married cannot fully appreciate the wonders of that relationship. The person who has never lost a father or mother cannot understand what the loss means. So angels, great as they are, cannot testify to salvation the same way as those who have experienced it.

ANGELS HAVE NO EXPERIENTIAL KNOWLEDGE OF THE INDWELLING GOD

Nothing in the Bible indicates that the Holy Spirit indwells angels as He does redeemed people. Since He seals believers when they accept Christ, such sealing would be unnecessary for the angels who never fell and who therefore need no salvation.

But there is a second reason for this difference. Redeemed men on earth have not yet been glorified. Once God has declared them just and given them life, He embarks on a process of making them inwardly holy while they live here below. At death, He makes them perfect. So the Holy Spirit takes His abode in the hearts of all believers while they are still on earth, to perform His unique ministry, one that angels cannot perform. God the Father sent Jesus the Son to die; Jesus performed His unique ministry as His part of God's saving process. Likewise, the Holy Spirit has a role, one different from the Son's. Sent by the Father and the Son, He not only guides and directs believers, but also performs a work of grace in their hearts, conforming them to the image of God to make them holy like Christ. Angels cannot provide this sanctifying power.

Furthermore, angels themselves do not need the ministry of

the Holy Spirit the way believers do. The angels have already been endowed with authority by virtue of their relationship to God through creation and continuing obedience. They are unspoiled by sin. People, however, are not yet perfect and therefore need what the Holy Spirit alone can give. Someday we will be as perfect as angels are now.

ANGELS DO NOT MARRY OR PROCREATE

I have already said that angels do not marry. In Matthew 22:30, Jesus points out that "in the resurrection they [men] neither marry, nor are given in marriage, but are as the angels of God in heaven." Because of this we can make a deduction: the number of angels remains constant. For the obedient angels do not die. The fallen angels will suffer the final judgment at the time God finishes dealing with them. While we cannot be certain, some scholars estimate that as many as one-third of the angels cast their lot with Satan when he mysteriously rebelled against his Creator. In any event, the book of Hebrews says the angels constitute an "innumerable company," vast hosts that stagger our imagination. A third of them would likely be counted in the hundreds of thousands—ones who are now desperate demons.

Just as angels differ from people with respect to marriage, so they differ in other important ways. Nothing in Scripture says that angels must eat to stay alive. But the Bible says that on certain occasions angels in human form did indeed eat. David refers to the manna eaten by the children of Israel in the wilderness as the bread of angels. In Psalm 78:25, Asaph says, "Man did eat angels' food." We can hardly disregard what happened to Elijah after he won a great victory over the priests of Baal on Mount Carmel. Because Jezebel threatened his life, he needed help from God. So God's angel came to the tired, discouraged prophet and set before him food and drink. When he had eaten twice he was sent on his journey; the food he had eaten was enough to keep him for forty days and forty nights (1 Kings 19:5). Not without reason some have concluded that Elijah indeed ate angels' food.

When Abraham was encamped in the plains of Mamre, three angels visited him, of whom one may have been the Lord Jesus (Genesis 18:1–2). These heavenly beings ate and drank what he provided for them by way of customary entertainment. Shortly thereafter, when God decided to destroy Sodom and Gomorrah, two angelic beings came to save backslidden Lot and his family. Lot made them a feast, and there again they ate food, including unleavened bread (Genesis 19).

It is interesting that after His resurrection, Jesus ate with His disciples. Luke's account says that the disciples "gave him a piece of a broiled fish, and of an honeycomb. And he took it, and did eat before them" (Luke 24:42–43).

THE KNOWLEDGE OF ANGELS

Angels excel humankind in their knowledge. When King David was being urged to bring Absalom back to Jerusalem, Joab asked a woman of Tekoah to talk to the king. She said: "My lord is wise, according to the wisdom of an angel of God, to know all things that are in the earth" (2 Samuel 14:20). And angels possess knowledge that men do not have. But however vast is their knowledge, we can be sure they are not omniscient. They do not know everything. They are not like God. Jesus bore testimony to the limited knowledge of the angels when He was speaking of His second coming. In Mark 13:32, He said, "But of that day and that hour knoweth no man, no, not the angels which are in heaven."

Angels probably know things about us that we do not know about ourselves. And because they are ministering spirits, they will always use this knowledge for our good and not for evil purposes. In a day when few men can be trusted with secret information, it is comforting to know that angels will not divulge their great knowledge to hurt us. Rather, they will use it for our good.

THE POWER OF ANGELS

Angels enjoy far greater power than men, but they are not omnipotent or "all powerful." In 2 Thessalonians 1:7, Paul refers to the "mighty angels of God." From the word translated "mighty" here we get the English word *dynamite*. In material power, angels are God's dynamite! In 1 Peter we read, "Angels who are greater in might and power [than men] do not bring a reviling judgment against them before the Lord" (2 Peter 2:11 NASB). Peter's testimony here reinforces Paul's. We should also note that it took only one angel to slay the firstborn of Egypt in Moses' day, and one to shut the lions' mouths for Daniel.

In Psalm 103:20, David speaks about [God's] "angels that excel in strength." Nowhere in Scripture is that strength manifested more dramatically than in the climax of this age. Following the

Battle of Armageddon, Scripture pictures what will happen to Satan: He is to be bound and cast into a bottomless pit. But what power, apart from God Himself, can do this to Satan, whose power we all know about and whose evil designs we have experienced? The Bible says that one angel will come from heaven. He will have a great chain in his hand. He will lay hold of Satan and bind him with that chain. And then he will cast him into the pit. How great is the power of one of God's mighty angels.

DO ANGELS SING?

There has been much conjecture about angel choirs. We at least assume that angels can and do sing, even if the Scriptures do not pointedly say so. In *Hamlet*, William Shakespeare seemed to underscore the possibility that angels sing when he stated, "Now cracks a noble heart, Good night, sweet prince: / and flights of angels sing thee to thy rest."

Some Bible students insist that angels do not sing. This seems inconceivable. Angels possess the ultimate capacity to offer praise, and their music from time immemorial has been the primary vehicle of praise to our all-glorious God. Music is the universal language. It is likely that John saw a massive heavenly choir (Revelation 5:11–12) of many millions who expressed their praise of the heavenly Lamb through magnificent music. I believe angel choirs will sing in eternity to the glory of God and the supreme delight of the redeemed.

While it is partly speculative, I believe that angels have the capacity to employ heavenly celestial music. Many dying believers have testified that they have heard the music of heaven. Most of my close friends tease me because I cannot carry a tune. When I am singing beside people in a congregation, I usually throw them off-key. But from years of listening I recognize good music when I hear it—even if I can't produce it myself. And there have been times when I have seriously tried to understand and appreciate music I did not like, whether it was a difficult opera or rock. I think that before we can understand the music of heaven, we will have to go beyond our earthly concept of music. I think most earthly music will seem to us to have been in the "minor key" in comparison to what we are going to hear in heaven.

The Bible tells us of many who sang: Moses (Exodus 15:1), Miriam (Exodus 15:20–21), David (Psalms), and many others. Thousands of worshipers at the temple continually sang, praising the Lord (2 Chronicles 5:12). Thousands of singers preceded the ark of the covenant (1 Chronicles 15:27–28). We all think of Psalms as the hymnbook of the Bible.

New Testament believers also sang with rapturous joy. Though the Bible does not say it, it implies that angels, who are of a higher creative order, are tuned to sing with no discordant note to God and the Lamb. Paul reminds us that there is a language of man and a language of angels (1 Corinthians 13:1). Angels have a celestial language and make music that is worthy of the God who made them. I believe in heaven we will be taught the language and music of the celestial world. The wonderful hymn "Holy, Holy Is What the Angels Sing" by Johnson Oatman, Jr., and J. Sweney expresses this thought in verse 4:

So, altho' I'm not an angel,
yet I know that over there
I will join the blessed chorus
that the angels cannot share;
I will sing about my Saviour,
who upon dark Calvary
Freely pardoned my transgressions,
died to set a sinner free.

ANGELS WORSHIP BEFORE THE THRONE

Unquestionably angels ascribe honor and glory to the Lamb of God. But angels do not spend all their time in heaven. They are not omnipresent (everywhere present at the same time), so they can be in only one place at a given time. Yet, as God's messengers, they are busy around the world carrying out God's orders. Is it not, therefore, obvious that when they are engaged in their ministry here they cannot stand before God's throne? But when angels do stand before the throne of God, indeed they worship and adore their Creator.

We can look for that future day when angels will have finished their earthly ministry. Then they will gather with all the redeemed before the throne of God in heaven. There they will offer their praise and sing their songs. In that day the angels who veiled their faces and stood mute when Jesus hung on the cross will then ascribe glory to the Lamb whose work is finished and whose kingdom has come. The angels may also stop to listen as the redeemed children of God express their own thanksgiving for salvation. It may well be true as the hymn writer has said in verse 3 of, "Holy, Holy Is What the Angels Sing:"

Then the angels stand and listen,
for they cannot join that song,
Like the sound of many waters,
by that happy, blood-washed throng.

But the children of God will also stop to listen to the angels. They have their own reasons for singing, ones that differ from ours. They have given themselves to the service of God Almighty. They have had a part in bringing in the kingdom of God. They have helped the children of God in difficult circumstances. So theirs shall be a shout and a song of victory. The cause they represent has been victorious; the fight they fought is finished; the enemy they met has been conquered; their wicked companion angels who fell shall vex them no more. The angels sing a different song. But they sing; my, how they sing! And I believe that angels and those of us who have been redeemed will compete with each other for the endless ages of eternity to see who can best ascribe glory and praise to our wonderful God!

Do you have that hope of eternity in your heart right now? Do you know—beyond doubt—that some day you will join the angels in heaven in singing praises to God? If not, make your commitment to Christ today. Without Christ you are separated from God and without hope of eternal life. You need to have your sins forgiven, and you need to be renewed and cleansed by the power of God. And this can happen if you will give your life to Christ and trust Him as your personal Lord and Savior. Christ came to take away your sins by His death on the cross. You deserved to die—but He died in your place! "For Christ died for sins once for all, the righteous for the unrighteous, to bring you to God" (1 Peter 3:18 NIV). Right now by a simple prayer of faith you can know that some day you will join with the angels and with millions of believers from across the ages in singing praises to God in heaven. Take that step of faith today.

5

Angelic Organization

We cannot study the subject of angels in the Bible without becoming aware of ranks among angelic beings. The evidence shows that they are organized in terms of authority and glory.

Though some see the ranking of celestial powers as conjectural, it seems to follow this pattern: archangels, angels, seraphim, cherubim, principalities, authorities, powers, thrones, might, and dominion (Colossians 1:16; Romans 8:38).

Medieval theologians divided angelic beings into ten grades. Some people, however, have asked whether some of these grades—the principalities, authorities, powers, thrones, might, and dominion—could not refer to human institutions and human beings. To answer, we must understand Colossians 1:16. Paul is speaking about creation of things both seen and unseen. On this verse Matthew Henry says that Christ "made all things out of nothing, the highest angel in heaven as well as men upon earth. He made the world, the upper and lower world, with all the inhabitants of both. . . . He [Paul] speaks here as if there were several orders of angels: 'Whether thrones, or dominions, or principalities, or powers,' which must signify either different degrees of excellence or different offices and employments." Perhaps any list that ranks angelic beings will err, but we can be sure they differ in power, some having authority others do not possess. While I do not wish to be dogmatic, I think there are different ranks of angels and that the list given in Colossians does refer to these celestial personalities. Let's look at four of them:

ARCHANGEL

While Scripture designates only Michael as an archangel (Jude 9), we have biblical grounds for believing that before his fall Lucifer was also an archangel, equal or perhaps superior to Michael. The prefix "arch" suggests a chief, principal, or great angel. Thus, Michael is now the angel above all angels, recognized in rank to be the first prince of heaven. He is, as it were, the prime minister in God's administration of the universe, and is the "angel administrator" of God for judgment. He must stand alone, because the Bible never speaks of archangels, only *the* archangel. His name means "who is like unto the Lord."

In the Old Testament, Michael seems to be identified primarily with Israel as a nation. Thus, God speaks of Michael as prince of His chosen people, "the great prince which standeth for the children of thy people" (Daniel 12:1). He especially protects and defends God's people whoever they are.

Further, in Daniel he is referred to as "Michael, your prince" (Daniel 10:21). He is God's messenger of law and judgment. In this capacity he appears in Revelation 12:7–12 leading the armies that battle Satan, the great dragon, and all of his demons. Michael with his angels will be locked in the titanic struggle of the universe at the last conflict of the age, which will mark the defeat of Satan and all forces of darkness. Scripture tells us in advance that Michael will finally be victorious in the battle. Hell will tremble; heaven will rejoice and celebrate!

Bible students have speculated that Michael cast Lucifer and his fallen angels out of heaven, and that Michael enters into conflict with Satan and the evil angels today to destroy their power and to give to God's people the prospect of their ultimate victory.

Michael, the archangel, will shout as he accompanies Jesus at His second coming. Not only does he proclaim the matchless and exciting news that Jesus Christ returns, but he speaks the word of life to all who are dead in Christ and who await their resurrection. "For the Lord himself shall descend from heaven with a shout, with the voice of the archangel . . . and the dead in Christ shall rise first" (1 Thessalonians 4:16).

THE ANGEL GABRIEL

Gabriel is one of the most prominent angels mentioned in Scripture.

Gabriel, in Hebrew, means "God's hero," or "the mighty one," or

"God is great." Scripture frequently refers to him as "the messenger of Jehovah" or "the Lord's messenger." However, contrary to popular opinion and to the poet John Milton, it never calls him an archangel. Yet it refers to his work more often than to Michael's.

Ministry of Gabriel

Gabriel is primarily God's messenger of mercy and promise. He appears four times in the Bible, always bearing good news (Daniel 8:16; 9:21; Luke 1:19, 26). We may question whether he blows a silver trumpet, since this idea arises from folk music and finds only indirect support in Scripture. But the announcements of Gabriel in unfolding the plans, purposes, and verdicts of God are of monumental importance.

In Scripture we gain our first glimpse of Gabriel in Daniel 8:15–16. There he announces the vision of God for the "end time." God has charged him to convey the message from the "situation room" of heaven that reveals God's plan in history. In verse 17 Gabriel says, "Understand, . . . the vision belongs to (events that shall occur in) the time of the end" (AMP).

Daniel, while in prayer, records Gabriel's second appearance to him: "While I was speaking in prayer, the man Gabriel, whom I had seen in the former vision, being caused to fly swiftly, came near to me and touched me about the time of the evening sacrifice" (Daniel 9:21 AMP). To Daniel he said, "Understand the vision" (9:23), and then revealed to him the magnificent sequence of events at the end time. Gabriel, sketching panoramically the procession of earthly kingdoms, assured Daniel that history would culminate in the return of Christ, "the prince of princes" (Daniel 8:25

AMP) and conqueror of the "king of fierce countenance" (Daniel 8:23 AMP). The prophetic announcement by Daniel in his prayer to God is twofold. He expressly refers to the more immediate judgment upon Israel (Daniel 9:16) and then to the awesome portent of "end-time judgment" and "tribulation," which shall be for "seven years" (Daniel 9:27). In a later chapter, "Angels in Prophecy," we will trace how the angels supervise the fearsome events of the end time.

Gabriel in the New Testament

Gabriel first appears in the New Testament in Luke 1. He identifies himself to Zacharias (verse 19), announces the birth of John the Baptist, and describes his life and ministry as the forerunner of Jesus.

But in his most important appearance, Gabriel informs the Virgin Mary about Jesus, the incarnate God! What a message to deliver to the world through a teenage girl! What a wonderfully holy girl she must have been, to be visited by the mighty Gabriel. He declares:

> Fear not, Mary: for thou hast found favour with God. And, behold, thou shalt conceive in thy womb, and bring forth a son, and shalt call his name Jesus. . . . And he shall reign over the house of Jacob for ever; and of his kingdom there shall be no end. (Luke 1:30–33)

Throughout all time, this divine declaration of Gabriel shall be the Magna Charta of the incarnation and the foundation stone of the world to come: God became flesh to redeem us.

SERAPHIM

It would appear from the Bible that celestial and extraterrestrial beings differ in rank and authority. The seraphim and cherubim follow in order after the archangel and angels. These may possibly define the angelic authority to which Peter refers when he speaks of Jesus, "who is gone into heaven, and is on the right hand of God; angels and authorities and powers being made subject unto him" (1 Peter 3:22).

The word *seraphim* may come from the Hebrew root meaning "love" (though some think the word means "burning ones" or "nobles"). We find the seraphim only in Isaiah 6:1–6. It is an awe-inspiring sight as the worshiping prophet beholds the six-winged seraphim above the throne of the Lord. We can assume that there were several seraphim, since Isaiah speaks about "each one" and "one cried unto another."

The ministry of the seraphim is to praise the name and character of God in heaven. Their ministry relates directly to God and His heavenly throne, because they are positioned above the throne—unlike the cherubim, who are beside it. Students of the Bible have not always agreed on the duties of the seraphim, but we know one thing: they are constantly glorifying God. We also learn from Isaiah 6:7 that God can use them to cleanse and purify His servants.

They were indescribably beautiful. "With two [wings] he covered his face, and with two he covered his feet, and with two he did fly" (implying that some angelic beings fly). The Scriptures do not, however, support the common belief that all angels have wings. The traditional concept of angels with wings is drawn from their ability to move instantaneously and with unlimited speed from place to place, and wings were thought to permit such limitless movement. But here in Isaiah 6 only two of the seraphim's wings were employed for flying.

The glory of the seraphim reminds us of Ezekiel's description of the four living creatures. He did not call them seraphim, but they too performed their service for God. Like seraphim they acted as both agents and spokesmen of God. In both cases, the glory displayed was a witness to God, though only the seraphim, of course, hovered over the heavenly throne as functionaries and attendants, with a chief duty of praising God. In all these manifestations, we see God willing that men should know of His glory. He determines to maintain an adequate witness to that glory in both terrestrial and celestial realms.

CHERUBIM

Cherubim are real, and they are powerful. But the cherubim in the Bible were often symbolic of heavenly things. "At God's direction they were incorporated into the design of the Ark of the Covenant and the Tabernacle. Solomon's temple utilized them in its decoration" (*Zondervan Pictorial Encyclopedia*). They had wings, feet, and hands. Ezekiel 10 pictures the cherubim in detail as having not only wings and hands, but being "full of eyes," encompassed by "wheels within wheels."

But Ezekiel sounds a somber note in chapter 10 also, and the cherubim provide the clue. The prophet presents his vision that prophesies the destruction of Jerusalem. In Ezekiel 9:3, the Lord has descended from His throne above the cherubim to the threshold of the temple, while in 10:1 He returns again to take His seat above them. In the calm before the storm, we see the cherubim stationed on the south side of the sanctuary. Being stationed in position toward the city, they witness the beginning of the gradual withdrawal of God's glory from Jerusalem. The fluttering of their wings indicates immensely important events to follow (10:5). Then the cherubim rise up in preparation for the departure.

While Ezekiel 10 is difficult to understand, one point comes across clearly. The cherubim have to do with the glory of God. This chapter is one of the most mysterious and yet descriptive passages of the glory of God to be found in the Bible, and it involves angelic beings. It should be read carefully and prayerfully. The reader gets a sense of God's greatness and glory as in few other passages in the Bible.

While the seraphim and the cherubim belong to different orders and are surrounded by much mystery in Scripture, they share one thing. They constantly glorify God. We see the cherubim beside the throne of God. "Thou that dwellest between the cherubim, shine forth" (Psalm 80:1). He sitteth between the cherubim" (Psalm 99:1). God's glory will not be denied, and every heavenly being gives silent or vocal testimony to the splendor of God. In Genesis 3:24, we see cherubim guarding the tree of life in Eden. In the tabernacle in the wilderness, designs representing the guardian cherubim formed a part of the mercy seat and were made of gold (Exodus 25:18).

The cherubim did more than guard the most holy place from

those who had no right of access to God. They also assured the right of the high priest to enter the holy place with blood as the mediator with God on behalf of the people. He, and he alone, was permitted to enter into the inner sanctuary of the Lord. By right of redemption and in accordance with the position of believers, each true child of God now has direct access as a believer-priest to the presence of God through Jesus. Cherubim will not refuse the humblest Christian access to the throne. They assure us that we can come boldly—because of Christ's work on the cross! The veil in the temple has been rent. As Paul says, "Ye are no more strangers and foreigners, but fellow citizens with the saints, and of the household of God" (Ephesians 2:19). Further, Peter assures, "Ye are a chosen generation, a royal priesthood, an holy nation, a peculiar people; that ye should show forth the praises of him who hath called you out of darkness into his marvelous light" (1 Peter 2:9).

The inner sanctuary of God's throne is always open to those who have repented of sin and trusted Christ as Savior.

Many believe that the "living creatures" often mentioned in the book of Revelation are cherubim. But as glorious as the angelic and heavenly beings are, they become dim beside the inexpressible glory resident in our heavenly Lamb, the Lord of glory, to whom all powers in heaven and on earth bow in holy worship and breathless adoration.

6

Lucifer and the Angelic Rebellion

Few people realize the profound part angelic forces play in human events. It is Daniel who most dramatically reveals the constant and bitter conflict between the holy angels faithful to God and the angels of darkness allied with Satan (Daniel 10:11–14). This Satan, or the devil, was once called "Lucifer, the son of the morning." Along with Michael, he may have been one of the two archangels, but he was cast from heaven with his rebel forces, and continues to fight. Satan may appear to be winning the war because sometimes he wins important battles, but the final outcome is certain. One day he will be defeated and stripped of his powers eternally. God will shatter the powers of darkness.

Many people ask, "How could this conflict come about in

God's perfect universe?" The apostle Paul calls it "the mystery of iniquity" (2 Thessalonians 2:7). While we have not been given as much information as we might like, we do know one thing for certain: The angels who fell, fell because they had sinned against God. In 2 Peter 2:4 the Scripture says, "God spared not the angels that sinned but cast them down to hell, and delivered them into chains of darkness, to be reserved unto judgment." Perhaps the parallel passage in Jude 6 puts the onus of responsibility more directly on the shoulders of the angels themselves. "The angels," wrote Jude quite deliberately, "kept not their first estate, but left their own habitation."

Thus, the greatest catastrophe in the history of the universal creation was Lucifer's defiance of God and the consequent fall of perhaps one-third of the angels who joined him in his wickedness.

When did it happen? Sometime between the dawn of creation and the intrusion of Satan into the Garden of Eden. The poet Dante reckoned that the fall of the rebel angels took place within twenty seconds of their creation and originated in the pride that made Lucifer unwilling to await the time when he would have perfect knowledge. Others, like Milton, put the angelic creation and fall immediately prior to the temptation of Adam and Eve in the Garden of Eden.

The important question is not, "When were angels created?" but, "When did they fall?" It is difficult to suppose that their fall occurred before God placed Adam and Eve in the garden. We know for a fact that God rested on the seventh day, or at the end of all creation, and pronounced everything to be good. By implication, up to this time even the angelic creation was good. We might then ask, "How long were Adam and Eve in the garden before the angels fell and before Satan tempted the first man and woman?" This question must remain unanswered. All we can say positively is that Satan, who had fallen before he tempted Adam and Eve, was the agent and bears a greater guilt because there was no one to tempt him when he sinned; on the other hand, Adam and Eve were faced with a tempter.

Thus, we pick up the story where it began. It all started mysteriously with Lucifer. He was the most brilliant and most beautiful of all created beings in heaven. He was probably the ruling prince of the universe under God, against whom he rebelled. The result was insurrection and war in heaven! He began a war that has been raging in heaven from the moment he sinned and was brought to earth shortly after the dawn of human history. It sounds like a modern world crisis!

Isaiah 14:12–14 records the conflict's origin. Prior to his rebellion, Lucifer, an angel of light, is described in scintillating terms in Ezekiel 28:12–17 (NASB): "You had the seal of perfection, full of wisdom and perfect in beauty. . . . You were the anointed cherub who covers, and I placed you there. You were on the holy mountain of God. You walked in the midst of the stones of fire. You were blameless in your ways from the day you were created, until unrighteousness was found in you. . . . Your heart was lifted up because of your beauty; you corrupted your wisdom by reason of your splendor." When the angel Lucifer rebelled against God and His works, some have estimated that as many as one-third of the angelic hosts of the universe may have joined him in his rebellion. Thus, the war that started in heaven continues on earth and will see its climax at Armageddon with Christ and His angelic army victorious.

Leslie Miller, in his excellent little book *All About Angels*, points out that Scripture sometimes refers to angels as stars. This explains why prior to his fall Satan was called "the star of the morning." And to this description John adds a qualifying detail: "His tail swept a third of the stars out of the sky and flung them to the earth" (Revelation 12:4 NIV).

REBELLION IN HEAVEN

The apostle Paul understood and spoke of the war of rebellion in the heavens when he referred to the former Lucifer, now Satan, as "the prince of the power of the air, the spirit that now worketh in the children of disobedience" (Ephesians 2:2). He also says that in fighting the organized kingdom of satanic darkness, we struggle against "the world forces of this darkness . . . the spiritual forces of wickedness in the heavenly places" (Ephesians 6:12 NASB).

We can describe all unrighteousness and transgression against God as "self-will" against the will of God. This definition applies to human beings today as well as to angels.

LUCIFER'S FIVE "I WILLS"

Lucifer, the son of the morning, was created, as were all angels, for the purpose of glorifying God. However, instead of serving God and praising Him forever, Satan desired to rule over heaven and creation in the place of God. He wanted supreme authority!

Lucifer said (Isaiah 14), "I will ascend into heaven." "I will exalt my throne above the stars of God." "I will sit also upon the mount of the congregation." "I will ascend above the heights of the clouds." "I will be like the most high." I . . . I . . . I . . . I . . . I.

Lucifer was not satisfied with being subordinated to his creator. He wanted to usurp God's throne. He exulted at the thought of being the center of power throughout the universe—he wanted to be the Caesar, the Napoleon, the Hitler of the entire universe. The "I will" spirit is the spirit of rebellion. His was a bold act to dethrone the Lord Most High. Here was a wicked schemer who saw himself occupying the superlative position of power and glory. He wanted to be worshiped, not to worship.

Satan's desire to replace God as ruler of the universe may have been rooted in a basic sin that leads to the sin of pride I have already mentioned. Underneath Satan's pride lurked the deadliest of all sins, the sin of covetousness. He wanted what did not belong to him. Virtually every war ever fought began because of covetousness. The warfare in heaven and on earth between God and the devil certainly sprang from the same desire—the lust for what belonged to God alone.

Today, as always in the past, virtually no one can sin alone. The influences of sin are contagious. The Bible speaks of "the dragon . . . and his angels" (Revelation 12:7), indicating that along with Lucifer, myriads of angels also chose to deny the authority of God and subsequently lost their high position. They chose to participate in the "war program" of Lucifer. As a result of their fall, those angels have been "reserved unto judgment" (2 Peter 2:4) and have their part with Lucifer in the "everlasting fire, prepared for the devil and his angels" (Matthew 25:41). But until this happens, they constitute a mighty force—capable of wreaking havoc among individuals, families, and nations! Watch out for, they are dangerous, vicious and deadly. They want you under their control, and they will pay any price to get you!

Satan, the fallen prince of heaven, has made his decision to battle against God to the death. He is the master craftsman who has plotted destruction during all the ages since he first rebelled. His "I will" spirit has worked through his consuming hatred of God to write his tragic story in the annals of human history. In his warfare against God, Satan uses the human race, which God created and loved. So God's forces of good and Satan's forces of evil have been engaged in a deadly conflict from the dawn of our history. Unless world leaders and statesmen understand the true nature of this warfare, they will continue to be blind leaders of the blind. They can only patch a little here and patch a little there. We will find no final solution to the world's great problems until this spiritual warfare has been settled. And it will be settled in the last war of history—Armageddon. Then Christ and His angelic armies will be the victors!

PAST, PRESENT, AND FUTURE IN PERSPECTIVE

Lucifer became Satan, the devil, the author of sin; and it is sin that has always deceived, disturbed, betrayed, depraved, and destroyed all that it has touched.

Will there never be an end to this battle of the ages, this war against God lustfully conceived in Lucifer and perpetrated on earth?

Not only does the battle rage on earth, but it rages in heaven. "And there was war in heaven: Michael and his angels fought against the dragon; and the dragon fought and his angels . . . and the great dragon was cast out" (Revelation 12:7, 9).

Satan and his demons are known by the discord they promote, the wars they start, the hatred they engender, the murders they initiate, the opposition to God and His commandments. They are dedicated to the spirit of destruction. On the other hand the holy angels obey their Creator. No discordant note sounds among the angels of heaven. They are committed to fulfill the purpose for which all true children of God pray, "Thy kingdom come. Thy will be done . . . as it is in heaven" (Matthew 6:10).

The Bible refers to Lucifer and the fallen angels as those who sinned and did not keep their first position (Jude 6). They committed the sins of consummate pride and covetousness. The sin of pride particularly has caused the downfall of Lucifer in heaven; most certainly it can bring mortal man down too. We must be on guard against pride, or we are headed for a fall patterned after the fall of Lucifer and his angels, who turned into demons.

Could it be that God wanted to be sure that men would not question the existence of Satan and his demon-hosts? Perhaps He had this in mind when He inspired the writing of Ezekiel 28, which sets forth the typology of Satan in the earthly sense. This account by the prophet Ezekiel speaks of an earthly prince of the city of Tyre. He seems to be an earthly symbol of Satan. It is clear from the passage that the king of Tyre became a devil incarnate and an earthly illustration of the heavenly Lucifer who became the devil.

We live in a perpetual battlefield—the great war of the ages continues to rage. The lines of battle press in ever more tightly about God's own people. The wars among nations on earth are merely popgun affairs compared to the fierceness of battle in the spiritual, unseen world. This invisible spiritual conflict is waged around us incessantly and unremittingly. Where the Lord works, Satan's forces hinder; where angel beings carry out their divine directives, the devils rage. All this comes about because the powers of darkness press their counterattack to recapture the ground held for the glory of God.

Were it not for the angel hosts empowered by God to resist the demons of Satan, who could ever hope to press through the battlements of the fiendish demons of darkness to the Lord of eternal liberty and salvation? Paul speaks the truth when he says that the forts of darkness are impregnable. Yet they yield to the warfare of faith and light as angel hosts press the warfare to gain the victory for us (2 Corinthians 10:4–5).

SATAN ON THE ATTACK

Revelation 12:10 speaks of Satan as "the accuser of the brethren" and Ephesians 6:12 (NIV) describes the "rulers . . . authorities . . . the powers of this dark world . . . the spiritual forces of evil in the heavenly realms." Although Satan and his evil followers press their warfare in the heavens, it seems that their primary endeavor is to destroy faith in the world.

Isaiah 13:12–14 clearly points up Satan's objectives: he works to bring about the downfall of nations, to corrupt moral standards, and to waste human resources. Corrupting society's order, he wants to prevent the attainment of order and to shake the kingdoms of our God. He uses his destructive power to create havoc, fire, flood, earthquake, storm, pestilence, disease, and the devastation of peoples and nations. The description of Satan's great power ends with the words, "who opened not the house of his prisoners" (Isaiah 14:17). This undoubtedly refers to the prison house of Satan, Hades or the abode of the dead so clearly pictured in Luke 16:19–31.

Satan has great power. He is cunning and clever, having set himself against God and His people. He will do everything in his power to hold people captive in sin and to drag them down to the prison of eternal separation from God.

Since the fall of Lucifer, that angel of light and son of the morning, there has been no respite in the bitter battle of the ages. Night and day Lucifer, the master craftsman of the devices of darkness, labors to thwart God's plan of the ages. We can find inscribed on every page of human history the consequences of the evil brought to fruition by the powers of darkness with the devil in charge. Satan never yields an inch, nor does he ever pause in his opposition to the plan of God to redeem the "cosmos" from his control. He forever tries to discredit the truthfulness of the Word of God; he coaxes men to deny the authority of God; and he persuades the world to wallow in the deluding comforts of sin. "He was a murderer from the beginning, not holding to the truth, for there is no truth in him. When he lies, he speaks his native language, for he is a liar and the father of lies" (John 8:44 NIV). Sin is the frightful fact in our world. It writes its ruin in vice and lust, in the convulsions of war, in selfishness and sorrow, and in broken hearts and lost souls. It remains as the tragedy of the universe and the tool of Satan to blunt or destroy the works of God.

SATANIC INTRIGUE

God cannot tolerate sin forever if He is just. He will not permit the perversions of Lucifer to mock Him, for the inescapable answer to the evil of the world is found in the unalterable law of the Word of God that "the wages of sin is death; but the gift of God is eternal life through Jesus Christ our Lord" (Romans 6:23). Satan's attacks, which began at the dawn of history, will continue until God begins to bring down the curtain on this frightening drama at Armageddon.

Satan's ideology is based on the little word "if." Through all time he has sought to discredit God by making Him out a liar in the eyes of man. He never ceases trying to discredit the claims of the Word of God and to rob mankind of the strength and comfort of faith. The all-time tool of Lucifer is an "if," but God declares that there are no "ifs," "buts," or "ands" about His program for salvation. God's plan is unalterable; His antidote for the satanic "if" works and is unchangeable. God assures us that through the work of Christ and the labors of His angelic deputies, we can look for the triumphant and victorious warfare over the armies of Lucifer.

It is not surprising that the fallen Lucifer hatched his plot to usurp the preeminence of God in His creation. In the first conversation in the garden, the serpent embodying Lucifer asked, "Hath God said, Ye shall not eat of every tree of the garden?" (Genesis 3:1). To this question Eve replied, "But God did say, You must not eat fruit from the tree that is in the middle of the garden, and you must not touch it, or you will die" (Genesis 3:3 NIV).

Hear Lucifer reply, if you eat of the fruit of this tree "ye shall not surely die" (Genesis 3:4). He says in effect that God does not know what He is talking about.

Satan often works by interjecting a question to raise doubts. It is deadly to doubt God's Word! Satan's strategy is to persuade us to rationalize. Eve probably began to reason with the enemy: Is it possible that God would be so unjust and unkind as to forbid this seemingly innocent thing?—"It was pleasant to the eyes" (Genesis 3:6).

Eve foolishly parleyed with the tempter. In her own mind she began to doubt the truth and the wisdom of God. How easily Satan covers with a light color ideas that are dark. His intrigue comes to us colored in the light of our own desires. Time after time he injects his subtle "ifs." "This tree is to be desired to make one wise." Eve listened; she reasoned with herself, she took, she tasted. Satan never fails to appeal to the appetites of the flesh and to the seeming sensual satisfactions that come from the inventions of sin. Our senses are inlets through which Satan can work, prod, and inject his deadly "ifs."

The Genesis account states that Eve ate first and then gave some to Adam to eat. If they had fixed their minds on God and trusted His wisdom, recognizing the danger that lurked in the fruit He had forbidden, all history would have been radically different and had another ending. Had they only realized the consequences of disobedience, had they only seen the danger of the satanic "if," had they only envisioned the flaming sword barring them forever from the garden! Had they only realized the terrible consequences of a single "innocent" moment, they would not have had to stand over the silent, lifeless form of their son Abel. His tragic death was the fruit of the seductive power of sin in their own lives. Apart from it our world would have been paradise today!

Had Adam and Eve resisted the devil, he would have fled, forever defeated. But they fell, and thus death passed upon all men (Genesis 3:13). This is where death began! Sin works the same with all of us, whatever our condition, nature, or environment. We are depraved by nature because we inherited it from our parents (Romans 3:19). The stream has been polluted. We must bear the sentence of guilt and the stain of sin. Each must give account of himself to God.

Listen to Satan's "ifs" of death being injected into the minds of people today: "if" you live a good life, "if" you do what is right, "if" you go to church, "if" you work for the benefit of others—if, if, if. But the Bible teaches that these "ifs" are not enough to meet God's requirements for salvation. Our good works and intentions are not enough. Jesus said, "Ye must be born again" (John 3:7). Only when we turn to Christ in faith and trust, confessing our sins to Him and seeking His forgiveness, can we be assured of our salvation. Satan will do all in his power to make us trust ourselves instead of Christ. But only Christ can save us—and He will, if we will commit our lives to Him and trust His work on the cross for our salvation. "For God so loved the world that he gave his one and only Son, that whosoever believes in him shall not perish but have eternal life" (John 3:16 NIV).

These are Satan's approaches today. The hiss of the serpent is the "if" of death. The stench of death is everywhere today! As C. S. Lewis points out, "War does not increase death—death is total in every generation." But we can find eternal life when we believe in Jesus Christ.

Have you made your personal commitment to Christ, and are you trusting Him alone for your salvation? If you have never taken that step of faith, or if you are unsure about your relationship to Christ, turn to Him today and receive Him as your personal Lord and Savior. "To all who received him, to those who believed in his name, he gave the right to become children of God" (John 1:12 NIV). This can be your experience today if you will ask Christ to come into your heart by faith.

7

Angels as Messengers of God

Angels minister to us personally. Many accounts in Scripture confirm that we are the subjects of their individual concern. In his book *Table Talk*, Martin Luther said, "An angel is a spiritual creature created by God without a body, for the service of Christendom and the church."

We may not always be aware of the presence of angels. We can't always predict how they will appear. But angels have been said to be our neighbors. Often they may be our companions without our being aware of their presence. We know little of their constant ministry. The Bible assures us, however, that one day our eyes will be unscaled to see and know the full extent of the attention angels have given us (1 Corinthians 13:11–12).

Many experiences of God's people suggest that angels have been ministering to them. Others may not have known they were being helped, yet the visitation was real. The Bible tells us that God has ordered angels to minister to His people—those who have been redeemed by the power of Christ's blood.

DANIEL AND THE ANGEL

In the Old Testament, Daniel vividly describes the bitter conflict between the angelic forces of God and the opposing demons of darkness. Before the angel came to him, he had spent three weeks mourning (Daniel 10:3). He ate no bread, meat, or wine, nor did he anoint himself. As he stood by the Tigris River, a man appeared clothed in linen. His face looked like lightning and his eyes like flaming torches. His voice sounded like the roar of a crowd.

Daniel alone saw the vision. The men who were with him did not. Yet a great dread came upon them, and they ran away to hide. Left alone with the heavenly visitor, Daniel's strength departed from him, so great was the effect of this personage on him.

Daniel was held in the bonds of a great sleep, yet he heard the voice of the angel. A hand touched him, and the angel described an experience he himself had just had. The angel had started to come to Daniel from the moment he began to pray but enroute was waylaid by a demon prince who engaged him in conflict and delayed him. Then Michael came to help this subordinate angel, freeing him to fulfill his mission to Daniel.

The angel had a message. He was to show Daniel what God foresaw would befall the world—especially Israel in the latter days. Daniel then found himself weak and unable to speak, so the angel touched his lips and also restored his strength. Having finished his mission, the angel told Daniel he was returning to fight with the demon prince in the unending struggle of the forces of good versus the forces of evil. In all this Daniel was having no hallucination or dream. It was a genuine experience with a real person, and no one ever could have persuaded Daniel otherwise.

He had pleaded with God for the sons of Israel. His prayer session, accompanied by fasting, had lasted for three weeks. At that moment he received the news from the "angel visitor" sent from heaven that his prayer had been heard. This incident makes it clear that delays are not denials, and that God's permissive will is involved in all of life.

UNSEEN FORCES AT WORK

During several world crises I have had the privilege of talking with some heads of state or secretaries of state. During the 1967 War in the Middle East, for example, Secretary of State Dean Rusk, who was visiting my home town of Montreat, North Carolina, invited me to his room. While we were discussing the war that had just broken out, I told him I believed "supernatural forces are at work."

On the eve of one of his missions abroad during the Ford Administration, Secretary of State Kissinger briefed me on some of the staggering problems facing the world. I told him I believed the world was experiencing an unseen spiritual war in which the powers of darkness were attacking the forces of God. As we have moved through the turbulent events of the past decade, I have become more convinced than ever that the activities of the unseen demonic forces are increasing. A well-known television newscaster said to me in his office, "The world is out of control." It seems incredible that such a warfare is taking place—but the Bible says it is!

Dr. A. C. Gaebelein has called it "the conflict of the ages." It will be resolved only when Jesus Christ returns to earth. This is why the world is crying for "a leader." The Antichrist, who will be Satan's "front," will arrive on the scene for a brief time and seemingly be "The Answer." But after only a few months, the world will be thrown back into chaos and conflict. He will prove to be "The Lie" (2 Thessalonians 2:3–10). Then the One whom God chose and anointed before time began will return to earth with His mighty, holy angels. At the end of the age, He will throw the devil and his demons into the lake of fire. Thus, for the true believer the conflict now raging will end as God intends. Righteousness will prevail.

JACOB'S EXPERIENCE

The experience of Jacob with angels is a splendid illustration of their ministry for God to men. In some ways Jacob was a cheat. He had stolen the birthright from his brother. He lied to his father and deceived him when his sight was almost gone. He fled from his brother, who would have killed him. He married his Uncle Laban's two daughters, and when their father and brothers no longer looked on him with favor, he took his family and flocks back to Canaan.

Though Jacob was a cunning schemer and skilled in deception,

God was concerned for him as the one who was in "the line of promise." From him the twelve tribes of Israel were to come. While he was en route home, the Scripture tells us that "the angels of God met him." So overcome was he by what happened that he said, "This is God's army!" (Genesis 32:2 AMP), and called the place Mahanaim, meaning "two camps." He called the angels "God's hosts." But the story does not end there. Having formerly cheated his brother Esau, he now feared him, not knowing whether he would be welcomed or killed. So Jacob prayed, admitting he was not worthy of the least of God's mercies. He asked to be delivered from the hand of his brother Esau.

The night before Jacob met Esau he was alone, his family and servants having gone ahead. Suddenly a man appeared and wrestled with him until daybreak, when he finally touched Jacob's thigh, "and the hollow of the thigh was out of joint." At this, Jacob realized the man was a heavenly visitor and would not let him go until the man had blessed him. When he had told the stranger his name, the man said, "Thy name shall be called no more Jacob, but Israel: for as a prince hast thou power with God and with men and hast prevailed." When Jacob asked the man to identify himself, he received no reply. But the man blessed him there. Jacob called the place Peniel, meaning "face of God," saying, "I have seen God face to face, and my life is preserved" (Genesis 32:24–30).

It may well be that the wrestler was Jesus, appearing fleetingly in human form. In the former part of the story, many angels were surrounding Jacob. Through the two experiences, God revealed His will for Jacob's life more fully and promised that he would be a prince. The next day he therefore went forward cheerfully to meet Esau; everything turned out well for him and his family. Centuries later Hosea testified to this incident, saying that the God of heaven had appeared to Jacob, ministering to him in the person of an angel (Hosea 12:3–6).

Moses and Abraham are perhaps the two greatest Old Testament characters; angels were involved in their lives on important occasions. We have already seen how angels ministered to Abraham. We must look at the experience of Moses at the burning bush (Exodus 3).

MOSES MEETS AN ANGEL

The background is important. For forty years Moses had lived amid the splendors of Egypt, coming to know its language, customs, and laws. He lived a life of luxury and occupied an important position in the social structure. Then, because of the misadventure of slaying an Egyptian, he fled to the desert. For forty years more he was tutored as a sheepherder in the "university of solitude." Scripture says little about that period, but it represented a great change in circumstances to go from the court of Pharaoh to a field of grazing sheep. It was not exactly an occupation that ranked high in the social order. He was an outcast, a lonely figure compared to his former life. And it took God forty years to bring him to the place where he was serviceable for the job God had in mind for him. So it was that at eighty years of age when the life work of most people has already been completed, Moses was ready for God's call.

One day as he was going about his duties, Moses saw a bush burning. It struck him as peculiar because the bush was not consumed. More than that, "the angel of the LORD appeared unto him in a flame of fire out of the midst of the bush." Since we have no reason to suppose that Moses had ever seen an angel before, this must have been an extraordinary visitation to him. Further, his curiosity was aroused. Then it was that God Himself spoke to Moses out of the bush.

Moses was profoundly moved. Having told him to remove his shoes because he was standing on holy ground, God identified Himself as the God of Abraham, Isaac and Jacob. At this Moses was awestruck and hid his face, fearing to look at God. God then disclosed to Moses His plan to release the Israelites from their captivity in Egypt, using Moses as their leader. When asked by Moses whom he should say had told him this when he approached the Israelites, God responded, "Say I AM hath sent me unto you."

Moses was not at all enthusiastic about what God told him to do. He began to offer what he thought were compelling reasons to be excused from that service. First, he said that the people of Israel would never believe him and therefore would not accept his leadership. In answer, God asked him what he had in his hand. Moses said, "a rod." "Cast it on the ground," God said, and suddenly it became a serpent. But when Moses picked it up, it again became a rod. Then at God's command he put his hand in his robe and, withdrawing it, found it leprous. But putting it back a second time and withdrawing it, he found it free of all disease. By such signs, God said, would He show the people Moses' divine commission.

Then Moses made another excuse: he said he couldn't talk, professing to be slow of speech. Perhaps this was the result of forty years in virtual silence on the backside of the desert, but God even refused this excuse, saying He would send Aaron to be his voice. And so Moses went from the desert to Egypt to begin the work of deliverance. But the incident is important in our study because it is tied closely to the angel of the Lord in the burning bush. This again shows that God used angels (or appeared as an angel) to make His will known and communicate His decisions to men.

The presence of angels became part of "the Exodus experience." Thus, in Numbers 20:16 the Bible says, "When we cried unto the LORD, he heard our voice, and sent an angel, and hath brought us forth out of Egypt." Isaiah says that "in all their affliction he was afflicted, and the angel of his presence saved them: in his love and in his pity he redeemed them; and he bare them, and carried them all the days of old" (63:9). It may well be that some of these instances involved angelic forms taken by Jesus Christ, the second person of the Trinity. We can only speculate. In that event, it makes alive the thrilling testimony of Paul who declared that "Jesus Christ [is] the same yesterday, and today, and forever" (Hebrews 13:8).

THE MYSTERY OF ANGELS

Therefore, just as Jesus is with us now through the Holy Spirit, revealing Himself and His will, so was He with His people in ages past, and so shall He be for all time to come, the angel of God's presence who leads us. To His "faithful" of past ages, God the Father revealed His presence through angels; through the angel of the Lord, God the Son, Jesus Christ, He revealed Himself and redeemed us by the Son's crucifixion, death, and resurrection. Here is mystery too deep for any of us to fathom fully.

Jewish scholars called the angel of the Lord by the name "Metatron, the angel of countenance," because He witnesses the countenance of God continuously and, therefore, works to extend the program of God for each of us.

God has given us the fullest revelation—Jesus Christ in the flesh—so He no longer needs to manifest Himself in the form of "the angel of the Lord" in this age of grace. Consequently, the angels who appear in the New Testament or even today are always "created spirits" and not God in that special angel form He used now and then in the Old Testament. The appearance of God the Son in physical form (a theophany) in the Old Testament is no longer necessary. Consider the presence of angels in the New Testament subsequent to the thrilling account of the birth of God the Son in the flesh through His incarnation at Bethlehem. The angels then were to minister the message of God and to establish the message of the gospel of Christ but never to supplant it or to detract from it.

ANGELS ARE MINISTERING SPIRITS

God uses both men and angels to declare His message to those who have been saved by grace. "Are they [angels] not all ministering spirits, sent forth to minister for them who shall be heirs of salvation?" (Hebrews 1:14). What a glorious honor it will be for angels to know us by name because of our faithful witness to others. Angels will share our rejoicing over those who repent (Luke 15:10), even though they cannot preach the gospel themselves.

In this regard, consider Philip the deacon, whom God was

using as a minister of revival in Samaria. An angel appeared with instructions for him to go to the desert (Acts 8:26), and by God's appointment he met the Ethiopian to whom he became the voice for God in preaching the word of truth.

Angels visited John too. As he looked out upon the lonely seas from the Isle of Patmos and wondered why he was isolated from all but heaven, the angel of the apocalypse came to announce the message that formed the book of Revelation with its prophecies of the end time (Revelation 1:1–3).

An angel ministered in a somewhat similar way in an incident in Daniel's life. Chapter 5 describes a great feast ordered by Belshazzar in Babylon. It had been prepared ostensibly to show the glory of the kingdom, but in reality Belshazzar meant it to parade his own personal greatness. It was a feast for the thousands of his kingdom's greatest nobles. But on this occasion they desecrated the sacred vessels taken from the temple at Jerusalem by using them for an ignoble purpose: they ate, drank and offered homage to idols of wood and stone, silver and gold. The god of materialism was in power. Suddenly the fingers of a man's hand appeared and traced on the wall a record of God's judgment on Babylon. "Mene, Mene, Tekel, Upharsin," the hand wrote—"You have been weighed in the balances and been found wanting. Your kingdom is finished" (verses 25–27). It was one of God's angels sent to announce the impending judgment. Not only were the days of King Belshazzar numbered, but God was finished with him.

Later Daniel prayed for the people, "And he [Gabriel] informed me, and talked with me, and said, O Daniel, I am now come forth to give thee skill and understanding. . . . therefore, understand the matter, and consider the vision" (Daniel 9:22–23). In answer to Daniel's prayer, God gave him a panoramic view of the future "history" of the human race. It is my belief that the world is now possibly reaching the climax of those great visions that God gave Daniel.

The scene in the time of Belshazzar seems almost contemporary, those times and conditions resembling so closely what we see and hear today. It may even be that God is writing another story of impending judgment through the crises of the hour. He is telling men everywhere that unless they repent of their sins, their days like Belshazzar's are numbered and they are finished.

Let us conclude this study of the personal ministry of angels by noting some further incidents when God used angels to declare His plan to men.

THE ANGEL GABRIEL

At the beginning of the New Testament, Zacharias the priest saw the angel of the Lord, receiving from him the message that proclaimed the birth of John, who was to prepare the way for the promised Messiah. The angel (Gabriel in this instance, a special angelic minister of promise) encouraged Zacharias to believe the miracle surrounding the birth of John.

Later Gabriel appeared to the Virgin Mary, announcing to her the divinely conceived plan of the incarnation by which God's Son, Jesus Christ, should be conceived miraculously in her womb by the power of the Holy Spirit. Whatever Mary's questions may have been, they were answered by the angel's witness, "The Holy

Ghost shall come upon thee, and the power of the Highest shall overshadow thee: therefore also that holy thing which shall be born of thee shall be called the Son of God" (Luke 1:35). Not only did Gabriel, the special angel of ministry and revelation, bring this message to Mary, but either he or another angel also confirmed to Joseph that he should take Mary as his wife, "For that which is conceived in her is of the Holy Ghost" (Matthew 1:20). He also told Joseph the plan of God that Jesus should "save his people from their sins" (Matthew 1:21).

The special angels of proclamation have faithfully bridged the centuries, carrying the message of God's will in times of oppression, discouragement, and waning endurance. God's restoring servants, His heavenly messengers, have encouraged, sustained, and lifted the spirits of many flagging saints; and they have changed many hopeless circumstances into bright prospects. Angels have ministered the message "All is well" to satisfy fully the physical, material, emotional, and spiritual needs of His people. They could testify, "The angel of the Lord came unto me."

8

Angels Protect and Deliver Us

The enemies of Christ who attack us incessantly would often be thwarted if we could grasp God's assurance that His mighty angels are always nearby, ready to help. Tragically, most Christians have failed to accept this fact so frequently expressed in the Bible. I have noticed, though, that in my travels the closer I get to the frontiers of the Christian faith the more faith in angels I find among believers. Hundreds of stories document extraordinary divine intervention every year: God is using His angels as ministering spirits.

ANGELS ARE DIVINE PROTECTORS

God's angels often protect His servants from potential enemies. Consider 2 Kings 6:14–17. The king of Syria had dispatched his army to Dothan, learning that Elisha the prophet was there. Upon dressing in the morning, the prophet's helper exclaimed excitedly to Elisha that the surrounding countryside bristled with armies and implements of war. Elisha assured him, "Don't be afraid! . . . our army is bigger than theirs" (verse 16 TLB). Elisha then prayed that God would open the eyes of the young man to see the hosts of protective angels. As He did so, the young man "could see horses and chariots of fire everywhere on the hills surrounding the city." This passage has been one of the great assurances and comforts to me in my ministry.

The angels minister to God's servants in time of hardship and danger. We find another outstanding illustration of this in Acts 27:23–25. Paul, on his way to Rome, faced shipwreck with more than two hundred others on board. Speaking to the fear-ridden crew, he said, "Last night an angel of the God whose I am and whom I serve, stood beside me and said, 'Do not be afraid, Paul. You must stand trial before Caesar; and God has graciously given you the lives of all who sail with you'" (verses 23–24 NIV).

Some believe strongly that each Christian may have a guardian angel assigned to watch over him or her. This guardianship possibly begins in infancy, for Jesus said, "See that you do not look down on one of these little ones. For I tell you that their angels in heaven always see the face of my Father in heaven" (Matthew 18:10).

ANGELS AT WORK FOR US

The most important characteristic of angels is not that they have power to exercise control over our lives, or that they are beautiful, but that they work on our behalf. They are motivated by an inexhaustible love for God and are jealous to see that the will of God in Jesus Christ is fulfilled in us.

David says of angels, "He who dwelleth in the secret place of the Most High shall abide under the shadow of the Almighty. . . . For he shall give his angels charge over thee, to keep thee in all thy ways. They shall bear thee up . . . lest thou dash thy foot against a stone" (Psalm 91:1, 11–12).

My wife, Ruth, tells of a strange incident in a Christian bookroom in Shanghai, China. She learned of it through her father, the late Dr. L. Nelson Bell, who served in the hospital in Tsingkiangpu, Kiangsu province. It was at this store that Dr. Bell bought his gospel portions and tracts to distribute among his patients.

The incident occurred in 1942, after the Japanese had won control of certain areas of China. One morning around nine o'clock, a Japanese truck stopped outside the bookroom. It was carrying five marines and was half-filled with books. The Christian Chinese shop assistant, who was alone at the time, realized with dismay that they had come to seize the stock. By nature timid, he felt this was more than he could endure.

Jumping from the truck, the marines made for the shop door, but before they could enter, a neatly dressed Chinese gentleman entered the shop ahead of them. Though the shop assistant knew practically all the Chinese customers who traded there, this man was a complete stranger. For some unknown reason, the soldiers seemed unable to follow him, and loitered about, looking in at the four large windows, but not entering. For two hours they stood around, until after eleven, but never set foot inside the door. The stranger asked what the men wanted, and the Chinese shop assistant explained that the Japanese were seizing stocks from many of the book shops in the city, and now this store's turn had come. The two prayed together, the stranger encouraging him, and so the two hours passed. At last the soldiers climbed into their truck and drove away. The stranger also left, without making a single purchase or even inquiring about any items in the shop.

Later that day the shop owner, Mr. Christopher Willis (whose Chinese name was Lee), returned. The shop assistant said to him, "Mr. Lee, do you believe in angels?"

"I do," said Mr. Willis.

"So do I, Mr. Lee." Could the stranger have been one of God's protecting angels? Dr. Bell always thought so.

Corrie ten Boom wrote of a remarkable experience at the terrible Nazi Ravensbruck prison camp:

> Together we entered the terrifying building. At a table were women who took away all our possessions. Everyone had to undress completely and then go to a room where her hair was checked.
>
> I asked a woman who was busy checking the possessions of the new arrivals if I might use the toilet. She pointed to a door, and I discovered that the convenience was nothing more than a hole in the shower room floor. Betsie stayed close beside me all the time. Suddenly I had an inspiration, "Quick, take off your woolen underwear," I whispered to her. I rolled it up with mine and laid the bundle in a corner with my little Bible. The spot was alive with cockroaches, but I didn't worry about that. I felt wonderfully relieved and happy. "The Lord is busy answering our prayers,

Betsie," I whispered. "We shall not have to make the sacrifice of all our clothes."

We hurried back to the row of women waiting to be undressed. A little later, after we had had our showers and put on our shirts and shabby dresses, I hid the roll of underwear and my Bible under my dress. It did bulge out obviously through my dress; but I prayed, "Lord, cause now Thine angels to surround me; and let them not be transparent today, for the guards must not see me." I felt perfectly at ease. Calmly I passed the guards. Everyone was checked, from the front, the sides, the back. Not a bulge escaped the eyes of the guard. The woman just in front of me had hidden a woolen vest under her dress; it was taken from her. They let me pass, for they did not see me. Betsie, right behind me, was searched.

But outside awaited another danger. On each side of the door were women who looked everyone over for a second time. They felt over the body of each one who passed. I knew they would not see me, for the angels were still surrounding me. I was not even surprised when they passed me by; but within me rose the jubilant cry, "O Lord, if Thou dost so answer prayer, I can face even Ravensbruck unafraid."

DIVINE SURVEILLANCE

Every true believer in Christ should be encouraged and strengthened! Angels are watching; they mark our path. They superintend the events of our lives and protect the interests of the Lord God, always working to promote His plans and to bring about His highest will for us. Angels are interested spectators and mark all we do, "for we are made a spectacle unto the world, and to angels, and to men" (1 Corinthians 4:9). God assigns angelic powers to watch over us.

Hagar, Sarah's maid, had fled from the tents of Abraham. It is ironic that Abraham, after having scaled such glorious heights of faith, should have capitulated to his wife's conniving and scolding, and to the custom of that day, to father a child by Hagar. And it is ironic that Sarah his wife should have been so jealous that when their own son, Isaac, was born years later, she wanted to get rid of both Hagar and the earlier child, Ishmael. So Abraham's self-indulgence led to sorrow, and he thrust Hagar out of his home.

Nonetheless, God sent His angel to minister to Hagar. "And the angel of the LORD found her by a fountain of water in the wilderness, by the fountain in the way to Shur" (Genesis 16:7). The angel spoke as an oracle of God, turning her mind away from the injury of the past with a promise of what she might expect if she placed her faith in God. This God is the God not only of Israel but the God of the Arabs as well (for the Arabs come from the stock of Ishmael). The very name of her son, Ishmael, meaning "God hears," was a sustaining one. God promised that the seed of Ishmael would multiply, and that his destiny would be great on the earth as he now undertook the restless pilgrimage that was to characterize his descendants. The angel of the Lord revealed himself as the protector of Hagar and Ishmael. Hagar in awe exclaimed, "Thou God seest me" (Genesis 16:13), or as it may be better translated, "I have seen Thou who seest all and who sees me."

Psalm 34:7 underscores the teaching that angels protect and deliver us, "The angel of the LORD encampeth round about those who fear him, and delivereth them." We also find this idea reflected in one of Charles Wesley's songs:

Angels, where ere we go,
Attend our steps whate'er betide.
With watchful care their charge attend,
And evil turn aside.

MIRACULOUS DELIVERIES

The great majority of Christians can recall some incident in which their lives, in times of critical danger, have been miraculously preserved—an almost plane crash, a near car wreck, a fierce temptation. Though they may have seen no angels, their presence could explain why tragedy was averted. We should always be grateful for the goodness of God, who uses these wonderful friends called angels to protect us. Evidence from Scripture as well as personal experience confirms to us that individual guardian, guiding angels attend at least some of our ways and hover protectively over our lives.

The Scriptures are full of dramatic evidences of the protective care of angels in their earthly service to the people of God. Paul admonished Christians to put on all the armor of God that they may stand firmly in the face of evil (Ephesians 6:10–12). Our struggle is not against flesh and blood (physical powers alone), but against the spiritual (superhuman) forces of wickedness in heavenly spheres. Satan, the prince of the power of the air, promotes a "religion" but not true faith; he promotes false prophets. So the powers of light and darkness are locked in intense conflict. Thank

God for the angelic forces that fight off the works of darkness. Angels never minister selfishly; they serve so that all glory may be given to God as believers are strengthened. A classic example of the protective agency of angels is found in Acts 12:5–11.

As the scene opened, Peter lay bound in prison awaiting execution. James, the brother of John, had already been killed, and there was little reason to suppose that Peter would escape the executioner's ax either. The magistrates intended to put him to death as a favor to those who opposed the gospel and the works of God. Surely the believers had prayed for James, but God had chosen to deliver him through death. Now the church was praying for Peter.

As Peter lay sleeping, an angel appeared, not deterred by such things as doors or iron bars. The angel came into the prison cell, shook Peter awake, and told him to prepare to escape. As a light shone in the prison, Peter's chains fell off, and having dressed, he followed the angel out. Doors supernaturally opened because Peter could not pass through locked doors as the angel had. What a mighty deliverance God achieved through His angel!

ANGELIC INTERVENTION

Many experiences in both Old and New Testaments grew out of the imprisonment of God's saints, calling either for God to deliver directly, or to intervene through angels acting in His name. Many today who are captive in the chains of depression can take courage to believe in the prospect of deliverance. God has no favorites and declares that angels will minister to all the heirs of faith.

If we, the sons of God, would only realize how close His ministering angels are, what calm assurance we could have in facing the cataclysms of life. While we do not place our faith directly in angels, we should place it in the God who rules the angels; then we can have peace.

Hebrews 11 contains a long list of men and women of faith. For most of them, God performed miracles, delivering them from disease, calamity, accidents, and even death. Someone has called this chapter "God's Hall of Fame." Angels helped these great men and women to subdue kingdoms, obtain promises, stop the mouths of lions, quench the violence of fire, escape the edge of the sword, and when they were weak, stand with the help of angels to defeat entire armies.

But the tempo changes in verse 35, with the opening words, "And others were tortured, not accepting deliverance." Those now mentioned were of equal faith and courage: they had to endure the trial of cruel mockings and scourgings. They suffered bonds and imprisonment. They were stoned, they were sawn asunder, they were slain with the sword. They wandered about in goatskins, being destitute, afflicted, and tormented. Time after time they must have called on God to send His mighty angels to help. No delivering angel came. They suffered and endured almost as though there were no God.

GOD'S WINNERS

Why? We find a clue when our Lord faced Calvary as He prayed, "If it be possible let this cup pass from me" (Matthew 26:39); but then He added, "nevertheless not my will, but thine, be done"

(Luke 22:42). In the sufferings and death of these great saints not physically delivered, God had a mysterious plan and was performing His will. Knowing this, they suffered and died *by faith.* This latter part of Hebrews 11 indicates that those who received no visible help in answer to prayer will have a far greater heavenly reward because they endured by "faith" alone. But having died, they did enjoy the ministry of angels who then escorted their immortal souls to the throne of God. If the first part of Hebrews 11 is called "God's Hall of Fame," the second should be called "God's Winners of the Medal of Honor."

Once when I was going through a dark period I prayed and prayed, but the heavens seemed to be brass. I felt as though God had disappeared and that I was all alone with my trial and burden. It was a dark night for my soul. I wrote my mother about the experience and will never forget her reply: "Son, there are many times when God withdraws to test your faith. He wants you to trust Him in the darkness. Now, Son, reach up by faith in the fog and you will find that His hand will be there." In tears I knelt by my bed and experienced an overwhelming sense of God's presence. Whether or not we sense and feel the presence of the Holy Spirit or one of the holy angels, by faith we are certain God will never leave us nor forsake us.

9

Angels—God's Agents in Judgment

The Bible says that throughout history angels have worked to carry out God's judgments, directing the destinies of nations disobedient to God. For example, God used angels in scattering the people of Israel because of their sins. He also used angels in bringing judgment on Sodom and Gomorrah, and eventually on Babylon and Nineveh. Further, at "the end of the age" angels will execute judgment on those who have rejected God's love.

The writer of Hebrews speaks of angelic forces as executors of God's judgments: "Who maketh his angels spirits, and his ministers a flame of fire" (Hebrews 1:7). The flaming fire suggests how awful are the judgments of God and how burning is the power of the angels who carry out God's decisions. Angels administer judgment in accord with God's principles of righteousness.

Unknown to men, they have undoubtedly in the past helped destroy evil systems like Nazism, because those governments came to the place where God could no longer withhold His hand. These same angels will carry out fearful judgments in the future, some of which the book of Revelation vividly describes.

We often get false notions about angels from plays given by Sunday school children at Christmas. It is true that angels are ministering spirits sent to help the heirs of salvation. But just as they fulfill God's will in salvation for believers in Jesus Christ, so they are also "avengers" who use their great power to fulfill God's will in judgment. God has empowered them to separate the sheep from the goats, the wheat from the chaff, and one of them will blow the trumpet that announces impending judgment when God summons the nations to stand before Him in the last great judgment.

ANGELS WARN OF JUDGMENT

In the case of Sodom and Gomorrah, there was no way judgment could be averted. Their wickedness had become too great. God had judged them; they had to be destroyed. But before God sends judgment, He warns. In this case, He used angels to point out to Abraham the approaching doom of Sodom and Gomorrah for their wickedness (Genesis 18). Abraham, whose nephew Lot and his family lived among these wicked people, began to plead with God to spare the two cities. Abraham asked God if He would avert judgment if fifty righteous people lived in Sodom. God told Abraham He would not destroy the city if there were fifty such people. Then Abraham asked for a stay of execution if there were only forty-five righteous people. God agreed. Then Abraham asked for deliverance if there were thirty righteous people. God agreed. Abraham then asked for twenty; then for ten. God agreed to withhold judgment if as many as ten righteous people could be found in Sodom. But not even ten such people lived there. Notice that God answered Abraham every time he asked. And He did not leave off answering until Abraham left off asking.

After this, God ordered the angelic ministers of judgment to rain destruction on these two wicked cities and all their inhabitants. Prior to the destruction of the cities, however, two unidentified heavenly messengers visited Sodom to warn Lot and his family to flee from the wrath about to come. So evil were the inhabitants of Sodom that they wanted to molest the angels physically. The angels blinded them and prevented them from carrying out their iniquitous conduct. In his book *All About Angels*, C. Leslie Miller states, "It is significant that although Lot, Abraham's nephew, had drifted far from the holy standards of his uncle and had sought the companionship and material benefits of an unholy alliance, yet the angels of the Lord were there to spare his life and assist him in avoiding the consequences of his own poor judgment."

Thus, we see something of the mercy, grace, and love of God toward even those who profess His name and try sincerely to live a God-honoring life in the midst of the most difficult circumstances.

THE ANGEL WHO DESTROYED THE ASSYRIAN ARMY

In 2 Kings 19, Scripture dramatically underscores God's use of angels to execute His judgments. King Hezekiah had received a letter from the commander of the Assyrian forces and immediately sought God's counsel. God gave Isaiah the answer, saying that not one Assyrian arrow would be fired into the city. He promised to defend Jerusalem on that occasion for David's sake. Dramatically, that night, just one angel struck the Assyrian encampment and 185,000 soldiers were found dead on the field of battle the next morning (verse 35).

THE ANGEL WHO SMOTE HEROD AGRIPPA

We have already referred to the case of Herod. Dressed in his royal apparel, he appeared before the people to make a speech. When he finished the people shouted, "It is the voice of a god, and not of a man" (Acts 12:22). Instead of disclaiming any such thing, Herod delighted in the impact he had made. God's response to this idolatrous act was prompt and, for Herod, disastrous. "Because he gave not God the glory," he "was eaten of worms, and gave up the ghost" (verse 23). "The angel of the Lord smote him."

THE ANGEL WHO ALMOST DESTROYED JERUSALEM

Nowhere in the Old Testament is there a more significant use of angelic power in judgment against God's own people than when David defied God's command by numbering Israel. God sent a pestilence among the Israelites and 70,000 died. He also sent a single angel to destroy the city of Jerusalem. David "saw the angel of the LORD stand between the earth and the heaven, having a drawn sword in his hand stretched out over Jerusalem" (1 Chronicles 21:16).

When David pleaded for mercy, the angel told him to set up an altar on the threshing floor of Araunah the Jebusite. God then accepted David's sacrifice there and said to the destroying angel, "It is enough: stay now thine hand" (2 Samuel 24:16). The Scripture significantly says that the same angel had already slain the 70,000 men (verse 17). Indeed, angels are God's agents in judgment.

New Testament history also records incidents where avenging angels judged the unrighteous acts of men and nations.

THE ANGEL WHO DESTROYED THE EGYPTIAN FIRSTBORN

One fateful night in Egypt just before the Exodus, the destroying angel was about to sweep over the land with a visitation of death (Exodus 12:18–30). How deeply must anxiety have etched itself upon the hearts of the Israelites. Believing Jews had offered sacrifices and generously sprinkled the blood over the doorposts and lintels of their homes. Then in accord with God's time schedule, judgment fell on Egypt as the dark and awesome moment of midnight arrived. The destroying angel (1 Corinthians 10:10; Hebrews 11:28) was God's minister of judgment, leaving death in his wake. The firstborn of every unbelieving Egyptian or Israeli household died under the judgment of a holy God who, however, had respect for the blood.

Down through the centuries this heartrending account has been the theme of Jews and Christians alike: "When I see the blood, I will pass over you." It has been the text of thousands of sermons by rabbis and Christian clergymen. It was not the quality of life of the people in the blood-sprinkled houses that counted. It was their faith, apart from works, that they showed by sprinkling the blood.

God had respect for only one thing: the blood sprinkled by faith.

How fearful it is to have these mighty angels carry out the judgments of an all-powerful God.

THE ANGEL WHO STOPPED ABRAHAM

In Genesis 22, God, wanting to test the reality of Abraham's faith, told him to sacrifice his beloved "son of promise," Isaac. God said, "Abraham . . . take now thy son, thine only son Isaac, whom thou lovest, and get thee into the land of Moriah; and offer him there for a burnt offering upon one of the mountains which I will tell thee of" (verses 1–2). What great suffering must have haunted and hurt the heart of Abraham through the long night as he considered what this supreme sacrifice entailed. Nevertheless, with nothing to go on but God's Word, Abraham by sheer, naked faith took fire, wood, and his son, and set off to do God's bidding. The Bible records no greater act of faith.

Having prepared the altar, Abraham placed Isaac, bound hand and foot, on the altar; then, unsheathing his knife, he raised his face toward heaven in submission to the Father's will. As Abraham lifted the knife in the air to plunge it into the heart of Isaac, "the angel of the LORD called unto him out of heaven, and said, Abraham, Abraham. . . . Lay not thine hand upon the lad, neither do thou any thing unto him; for now I know that thou fearest God, seeing thou hast not withheld thy son, thine only son from me" (Genesis 22:11–12).

The double use of the name always implies the importance of the message about to be given. When he heard his name called, faithful Abraham responded immediately, and God rewarded him for his unqualified obedience. "Abraham lifted up his eyes, and looked, and, behold, behind him a ram caught in a thicket by his horns: and Abraham went and took the ram, and offered him up for a burnt offering in the stead of his son" (Genesis 22:13).

Many scholars believe, as I do, that the angel here is a "theophany," an appearance of the Lord Jesus Christ Himself. He assumed the role of an angel, and God showed the principle of substitutionary atonement: God had demanded of Abraham the death of his son. The demand for the burnt offering had to be met, and it was met. But in the place of Isaac, God, through an angel, accepted the animal substitute. That same principle applies to us. True judgment demands that we die. And the judgment must be executed. But Jesus Christ Himself was the substitute offering. He died so that we do not have to die. He took our place so that the words used here, "in the stead of," can be wonderfully applied to every person who trusts in Christ. He died "in the stead of" all who believe on Him.

How could God have asked for a human sacrifice? How could He have asked Abraham to slay Isaac when He had forbidden the killing of people (Genesis 9:6)? Is not this inconsistent with the nature of God? He gives us the answer to these questions about judgment by death in the Epistle to the Romans. "He that spared not his own Son, but delivered him up for us all, how shall he not with him also freely give us all things?" (Romans 8:32). God could ask Abraham to slay Isaac because He Himself was willing to let His own Son die. He was not asking Abraham to do anything more than He was willing to do with His only begotten Son.

Neither Abraham nor Isaac had to drink the cup God presented.

Isaac did not die and Abraham did not slay him. But when we come to another cup in the Garden of Gethsemane, the picture is startlingly different. Jesus has now come; as the guiltless one for the guilty, as the sinless one for sinners, He was willing to accept the condemnation of God for the world's guilt, identifying Himself with it through His own death on Calvary.

Neither man nor angel could ever understand what was implied in the "cup" Jesus took in the Garden of Gethsemane that was to lead to His awful suffering, condemnation, and death (Mark 14:36; Luke 22:42). In the Garden as He wrestled over the cup He was to drink, no ministering angel could spare Him from it or alleviate His suffering. It was His and His alone. It settled down on the Savior as a cup of judgment He accepted and took upon Himself as the righteous one bearing the guilt of the wicked. The angels would have helped Him in that hour, but Christ did not call for their help. This one who said no to angel help said, in effect, "I will die for the sins of men because I love them so much." And in dying He was forsaken by men, by angels, and by the Father who is of purer eyes than to look upon sin and who in His Son's atoning agony turned His face from Him. That is why Jesus cried from the cross, "My God, my God, why hast thou forsaken me?" (Matthew 27:46). He died alone. Angels were ready to rescue Him, but He refused.

ANGELS AND THOSE WHO REJECT JESUS

It is clear in Scripture that angels will be God's emissaries to carry out His judgment against those who deliberately reject Jesus Christ and the salvation God offers through Him. While all men are sinners by nature, choice, and practice, yet it is their deliberate rejection of Jesus Christ as Savior and Lord that causes the judgment of eternal separation from God.

God has assigned angels at the end of the age to separate the sheep from the goats, the wheat from the tares, the saved from the lost. We are not called upon to obey the voice of angels. But we are to heed and obey the Word of God and the voice of God that calls upon us to be reconciled to Him by faith in Jesus Christ. If not, we will have to pay the penalty of unforgiven sin. The angels will administer that penalty. They "shall cast them into the furnace of fire" (Matthew 13:50). I am constantly astounded that God's decrees and warnings are considered so lightly in our modern world—even among Christians.

ANGELS AND ETERNAL LIFE

Every son of Adam's race is confronted with two ways of life: one, to eternal life; the other, to eternal death. We have seen how angels execute God's judgment on those who reject Jesus; the angels cast them into the furnace of fire. But there is a totally different judgment: the good and wonderful judgment unto everlasting life. God gives the angels a place in this too. He commissions them to escort believers to heaven and to give them a royal welcome as they enter the eternal presence of God. Each of us who trusts Christ will witness the rejoicing of angelic hosts around the throne of God.

In the story of the rich man and Lazarus (Luke 16), Jesus told of a beggar who died in the faith. He had never owned many of this world's goods, but he was rich in faith that counts for eternity.

When he died he was "carried by the angels into Abraham's bosom." Here were angelic pallbearers who took his immortal spirit to the place of glory where he was to be eternally with God—the place the Bible calls "heaven."

Another beautiful account of this kind comes from the life of the martyr Stephen (Acts 6:8–7:60). The "council, looking steadfastly on him, saw his face as it had been the face of an angel." Then Stephen in a powerful sermon declared that even unbelievers "received the law by the disposition of angels, and have not kept it" (Acts 7:53). When he had finished his discourse, Stephen saw the glory of God and Jesus at the Father's right hand. Immediately his enemies stoned him to death and he was received into heaven. Even as the angels escorted Lazarus when he died, so we can assume that they escorted Stephen; and so they will escort us when by death we are summoned into the presence of Christ. We can well imagine what Stephen's abundant entrance to heaven was like as the anthems of the heavenly host were sung in rejoicing that the first Christian martyr had come home to receive a glorious welcome and to gain the crown of a martyr.

Do you fear the judgment of God? Or do you know that Christ has taken your judgment upon Himself by His death on the cross? When you know Christ, you need not fear God's judgment, for He has fully purchased your salvation. Don't delay your decision for Christ, but open your heart to Him and you too will know the joy of sharing in His fellowship throughout all eternity in heaven.

10

Angels and the Gospel

While God has delegated angels to make special pronouncements for Him, He has not given them the privilege of proclaiming the gospel message. Why this is so, Scripture does not say. Perhaps spirit-beings who have never experienced the effects of separation from fellowship with God because of sin would be unable to preach with understanding.

But notice what the writer says in "Holy, Holy Is What the Angels Sing:

Holy, Holy is what the angels sing,
And I expect to help them make the
courts of heaven ring.
And when I sing redemption's story,

They will fold their wings,
For angels never felt the joy that our
salvation brings.

Down through the ages man's heart has remained unchanged. Whatever the color of his skin, whatever his cultural or ethnic background, he needs the gospel of Christ. But who has God ordained to bring that gospel to fallen men? Fallen angels cannot do it; they cannot even be saved from their own sins. Yet unfallen angels cannot preach the gospel either. Presumably they do not hear the gospel the way we do; in their purity they have escaped the effects of sin and are unable to comprehend what it means to be lost.

Rather, God has commanded the church to preach. This great task is reserved for believers. God has no other means. Only man can speak salvation's experience to man.

God has, however, assigned angels to assist those who preach. Their assistance includes the use of miraculous and corroborating signs. Missionaries of the eighteenth and nineteenth centuries have reported many wonderful incidents where angels seemed to help them proclaim the gospel. My wife, whose parents were missionaries to China, can remember many instances in her life where angels must have intervened in the ministry of her father and his fellow missionaries.

At any rate, you and I have the privilege of conveying a message to men from God in heaven, a message that angels cannot speak. Think of that! The story is told of a question asked of God: "In the event that men fail to preach the gospel as You have commanded, what other plan have You in mind?" "I have no other plan," He said.

No angel can be an evangelist. No angel can pastor a church, although angels watch over particular churches. No angel can do counseling. No angel can enjoy sonship in Jesus or be partaker of the divine nature or become a joint heir with Jesus in His kingdom. You and I are a unique and royal priesthood in the universe, and we have privileges that even angels cannot experience.

THE ANGEL AND ZACHARIAS

The birth of John the Baptist was dynamically connected with the "evangel" (a term meaning the gospel, the good news of God's salvation in Jesus Christ). His parents, Zacharias and Elizabeth, were both old, Elizabeth being beyond the age to bear children. She and her husband were descendants of Aaron and thus connected with the priesthood. Both walked blameless before the Lord and kept His commandments. They illustrate how God works through godly parents; not infrequently we find that some of His greatest servants have enjoyed the benefits of a godly home. John and Charles Wesley, founders of the Methodist Church, came from a godly home and were profoundly influenced by their mother. Adoniram Judson, the great missionary to Burma, came from a minister's home. Jonathan Edwards, pastor, evangelist, and educator in early America, was from a line of godly forebears.

When the angel appeared to Zacharias to announce the good news that Elizabeth would, despite her age, give birth to a son, his words were immersed in the evangel. He predicted John's ministry:

"Many of the children of Israel shall he turn to the Lord their God" (Luke 1:16). Thus, we learn that no one should presume that any person is saved, not even one born to a believing home, who has believing forebears, and grows up in a believing church. Moreover, John was "to make ready a people prepared for the Lord" (verse 17).

How great the message of the angel was and how seriously Zacharias regarded it can be seen from events some months later. Zacharias lost his ability to speak following the angel's visit; he did not regain it until the birth of John. But at that time his tongue was loosed and he was filled with the Holy Spirit. His thinking—during the long months while Elizabeth awaited the birth of the baby—now burst out in his first words, which reflect the angel's visit and concern for the evangel. Zacharias said, "Blessed be the Lord God of Israel; for he hath visited and redeemed his people, and hath raised up an horn of salvation for us in the house of his servant David." A moment later he added, "And thou, child [that is, John], shalt . . . give knowledge of salvation unto his people by the remission of their sins, through the tender mercy of our God; whereby the dayspring from on high hath visited us, to give light to them that sit in darkness and in the shadow of death, to guide our feet into the way of peace" (Luke 1:76–79).

Now that was really a message! And all of it rises from the visit of the angel, who told Zacharias about God's intention for John. But notice especially that the angel came, not simply to announce the birth of John, but to make it clear that John was to live his life as the forerunner of the Messiah and as one who would bring the knowledge of salvation and the remission of sins to his fellow Israelites.

THE ANGEL AND THE EVANGEL IN THE BIRTH OF JESUS

The announcement to Mary that she was to be the mother of Jesus was made by no ordinary angel. It was Gabriel, one of three angels whose names have been given us in Scripture, who made the announcement. And it was connected with the evangel. This was true both of the words Gabriel spoke and the words Mary spoke while she was pregnant and looking toward the birth of her son. The angel told Mary that Jesus would be the Son of the Highest, that He would inherit the throne of His father David, would reign over the house of Jacob forever, and would be an everlasting kingdom. This was something far different from anything promised anyone else in Scripture. It was not promised to Abraham, or David, or Solomon. Only Jesus' name is connected with these promises, and all of them are inextricably connected with both personal and national salvation.

After Mary became pregnant, she visited Elizabeth and sang one of the sweetest songs known to literature. In it she makes evident that she has grasped what the angel told her. And what he told her she describes as salvation and the remission of sins: "My spirit hath rejoiced in God my Saviour" (Luke 1:47). Here was the news that Mary herself needed a Savior and had found Him. The very baby who was encased in her womb would one day offer Himself as a propitiation for her and for all people. And that baby in her womb was God Almighty who had humbled Himself to dwell among us in the flesh.

Indeed, she cries out that God's "mercy is on them that fear him from generation to generation." What is this but the glorious evangel, gospel, that God was in Christ reconciling the world to Himself? And this was the message Gabriel brought to Mary. He could not preach it himself, but he could bear witness to the gospel that was to be preached by Jesus Christ and His followers through all ages.

THE ANGEL, THE EVANGEL, AND JOSEPH

Joseph, the husband of Mary, was caught up in a seemingly abysmal situation. He was legally engaged to a girl who was pregnant. He knew he was not the father because they had not yet consummated their forthcoming marriage. Yet Mary was apparently guilty of adultery under Jewish law, unless Joseph was willing to believe her story that the Holy Spirit had come upon her, and that she had never engaged in sexual relations with a man. As the innocent party, Joseph was thinking seriously of putting Mary away according to the custom of that day. The Scripture says that "while he thought on these things" (Matthew 1:20), an angel appeared to him in a dream and told him the true story of the incarnation and the role of Mary. Responding, Joseph believed the angel. But the announcement contained more than the simple fact that Mary was innocent of any transgression and that Joseph was the chosen vessel of God in affording her protection in this extraordinary event.

The angel also told Joseph something that was to witness to the gospel. Though the angel could not preach to Joseph, he struck at the root of the matter when he proclaimed, "He shall save his people from their sins" (Matthew 1:21). Here was the gospel in all of its beauty, simplicity, and purity. According to the witness of the angel, sins can be forgiven. There is someone who can forgive sins. This is Jesus the Christ. The Savior has a people about whom He is concerned and guarantees that their sins will be forgiven. In the midst of the wonder of the incarnation, we should not overlook the fact that the angel was here bearing witness to the "evangel," the gospel. Jesus was not coming simply as God. He was coming as Redeemer and Savior to make men right with His Father and to assure them of the gift of everlasting life.

GABRIEL, THE EVANGEL, AND DANIEL

Long before the days of Zacharias, Elizabeth, Mary, Joseph, and John the Baptist, the angel Gabriel had borne witness of the evangel to the prophet Daniel. He had done this in connection with the prophecy of the seventy weeks. Daniel was deep in prayer, confessing both his sin and that of his people. While he was praying, Gabriel appeared to him. Notice again that Gabriel did not preach the word of salvation, but he bore eloquent testimony to it. He said that the seventy weeks were designed "to finish the transgression, to make an end of sins, and to make reconciliation for iniquity" (Daniel 9:24). Then he foretold the cutting off of the Messiah, an event that Isaiah 53 had prophesied and depicted so dramatically.

The Jews had had difficulty understanding the notion of a suffering Messiah, rather picturing Him as one who would come in power and glory to overthrow their enemies and to reign triumphantly over them. But Gabriel told Daniel that sin is a reality and must be paid for. The Messiah will do this by being cut off;

that is, He will die for the sins of men. Then the power of sin to separate us from God will end, and men will be reconciled to Him. We see that though Gabriel could not preach, he could prophesy! And how beautifully the prophecies of the Old Testament are linked together with the fulfillment in the New Testament. How gracious God was to use His angels as agents to make it plain to all they visited in all ages that their business was to witness to the evangel.

THE ANGEL, THE EVANGEL, AND THE SHEPHERDS

Does it not seem mysterious that God brought the first message of the birth of Jesus to ordinary people rather than to princes and kings? In this instance, God spoke through His holy angel to the shepherds who were keeping sheep in the fields. This was a lowly occupation, so shepherds were not well educated. But Mary in her song, the Magnificat, tells us the true story: "He hath put down the mighty from their seats, and exalted them of low degree. He hath filled the hungry with good things, and the rich he hath sent empty away" (Luke 1:52–53). What a word for our generation!

What was the message of the angel to the shepherds? First, he told them not to be afraid. Over and over again the presence of angels was frightening to those to whom they came. But unless they came in judgment, the angels spoke a word of reassurance. They calmed the people to whom they came. This tells us that the appearance of angels is awe-inspiring, something about them awakening fear in the human heart. They represent a presence that has greatness and sends a chill down the spine. But when the angel had quieted the fears of the shepherds, he brought this message, one forever to be connected with the evangel:

> For behold I bring you good tidings of great joy, which shall be to all people. For unto you is born this day in the city of David a Saviour, which is Christ the Lord.
>
> (Luke 2:10–11)

I could preach a dozen sermons on those two verses, for they contain many important theological themes. But note once more that the angel does not preach the gospel. Rather, he witnesses to it and demonstrates again the overwhelming concern angels have for it.

What did the angel say? First, he brought good tidings, not bad ones. The shepherds already knew the bad news—the human race had sinned and was lost. But the angel had come to tell them that God was doing something about their lostness. And he pointed out that the good news was not simply for the people of one nation, but for the whole world. Isaiah said, "The God of the whole earth shall he be called" (Isaiah 54:5). Jonah learned the same truth when he was sent to preach repentance to the people of Nineveh. The angel told the shepherds that the good tidings were for all people.

The good tidings were that the Savior had come. They needed somebody who could bring them back into fellowship with God, because the blood of bulls and goats could not do this in any permanent way. But the blood of the Savior could. The angel message was that God had come, redemption was possible, the Lord had visited His people with salvation. What a testimony to the evangel this was. And it was further validated when the angel who was accompanied by "a multitude of the heavenly host" began to chant or sing, "Glory to God in the highest, and on earth peace, good will toward men." Where could there be sweeter music? What hymn writer could match those words?

ANGELS AND THE EVANGEL IN THE BOOK OF ACTS

We might call two wonderful instances "case studies" of how angels see to it that unbelievers hear the gospel, respond to it, and become saved. It shows again the concern of angels for the evangel and the steps they take to implement it.

The first case is that of the Ethiopian nobleman, a man of great authority. While reading the Old Testament Scriptures, he came to Isaiah and, unable to understand what the prophet meant, needed someone to interpret the Scripture to him. An angel knew of this situation. But the angel did not and could not do what the Ethiopian needed. He could not preach the gospel. But he could assist the Ethiopian eunuch by sending someone to him who could.

So the Scripture tells us that the angel spoke to Philip and specifically instructed him to go "toward the south unto the way that goeth down from Jerusalem unto Gaza, which is desert" (Acts 8:26). Philip obeyed the angel and approached the chariot. Then he interpreted the Scripture for the Ethiopian. Later the angel led him up and took him away. And the Ethiopian went on his way rejoicing. If the angel had been unconcerned about the evangel, he would not have sent Philip to preach the gospel to this interested inquirer.

The second instance has to do with Peter and the conversion of Cornelius. In this case, the situation is reversed. The angel had told Philip what to do so the Ethiopian could be saved. Here, he did not tell Peter what to do, but rather ordered Cornelius to send for Peter, who would then tell him the story of the gospel so he could be saved. Would it not have been much easier for the angel to have preached the gospel to Cornelius than to have had him send for Peter? After all, Peter was not a willing witness. He had the notion that it was wrong to preach the gospel for the salvation of Gentiles. Cornelius, however, followed the word of the angel and sent for Peter. Then God had to appear in a dream and convince Peter that it was all right for him to witness to a Gentile. Peter finally went, and Cornelius was wonderfully saved. But it was done through the auspices of the angel who was deeply concerned with the evangel, and for the salvation of this Roman soldier.

One other story in the Acts of the Apostles is somewhat different, though no less worthy of consideration. It has to do with Paul on his way to Rome. He was shipwrecked en route. But while it appeared that the ship would sink with all hands lost, an angel of the Lord appeared to Paul at night. The angel told those aboard the ship that they would all be saved. Then he said something that illuminates the concern of angels for the salvation of men and the witness of Christians to the unsaved. "Fear not, Paul; thou must be brought before Caesar" (Acts 27:24). Here we see that same principle. The angel could not witness to Caesar, but

Paul could. And God in His providence was sending him to Rome for precisely this purpose. If Paul had not fully known the will of God before, it was clear at this moment. God intended that Caesar should hear the gospel. And the angel, by bringing the message, revealed his own interest in the evangel.

THE SOUND OF ANGEL VOICES

The keynote of evangelism is couched in the heavenly proclamation I have mentioned, "Unto you is born this day . . . a Saviour which is Christ the Lord." And the task of world evangelization will be completed by men and women whom the Holy Spirit uses. But wherever and whenever we see the gospel working in its power to transform, there is a possibility that in some ways angels may be involved. This is a mystery that we will never quite understand until we get to heaven.

It is not unreasonable to ask, "What did the angel voices sound like?" And "What did they say when they spoke?" Angels seemed to communicate terse commands. Often the angel messengers urged haste, and this is understandable since they were communicating a directive from God. Dr. Miller points out that the contemporary expression "Hurry up" would fit most angel commands. The words "Get up" were sometimes literally used. The angel said to Peter, "Rise quickly." The angel said to Gideon, "Arise and go in this thy might." The angel said to Joseph, "Go quickly," and to Philip, "Arise and go."

In the same way, any evangelistic ministry sounds the note of urgency concerning the gospel. We have no time to waste because we can never reclaim this moment. We may never have a second chance to witness if we neglect the first.

We can illustrate this from the sinking of the *Titanic*. The greatest ship of its day, weighing 46,000 tons, it was considered unsinkable. But on the night of April 14, 1912, while moving through the ocean at 22 knots, it struck an iceberg. Because it carried only half as many life jackets as passengers, when it sank, 1,513 people drowned. Even though this event occurred more than seventy years ago, there is still a great fascination about it. The discovery of the hulk of the *Titanic* has revived our interest in the whole tragic story.

Out of tragedy, however, God can still bring triumph.

One passenger, John Harper, was on his way to preach at Moody Church in Chicago. Trying to stay afloat in the ocean he drifted toward a young man holding on to a plank. Harper asked, "Young man, are you saved?" The man said, "No." A wave separated them. After a few minutes they drifted within speaking distance of each other, and again Harper called to him, "Have you made your peace with God?" The young man said, "Not yet." A wave overwhelmed John Harper and he was seen no more, but the words, "Are you saved?" kept ringing in the young man's ears.

Two weeks later a youth stood up in a Christian Endeavor meeting in New York, told his story, and said, "I am John Harper's last convert."

11

Angel Ministries in the Life of Jesus

It would take an entire book to spell out in detail how the life of Jesus was intertwined with the attending ministry of angels. Before He was here, they followed His orders. And since He ascended into heaven, they have worshiped Him before the throne of God as the Lamb slain for our salvation.

To prepare for the coming of Jesus, an angel appeared to Zacharias to inform him that his wife would be the mother of John the Baptist (Luke 1:13). Gabriel, one of the mighty angels of God, announced to Mary that she would give birth to the Messiah. An angel and a multitude of the heavenly host spread the good news of Jesus' coming to the shepherds in the field (Luke 2:9). These angelic incidents preceded and accompanied His birth, but when Jesus began His public ministry, angels were intimately involved in His life as well.

Perhaps the most difficult period in the life of Jesus before His crucifixion was His temptation by the devil in the wilderness. After He had fasted forty days and nights, Satan tried to break Him down. In Christ's weakened human condition, Satan began his attack, seeing this as his greatest opportunity to defeat the program of God in the world since his victory in the Garden of Eden. He was out to shipwreck the hope of the human race. Wishing to prevent the salvation of sinners, he struck at the moment when Christ's physical weakness made Him most susceptible to temptation. Satan always directs his sharpest attack at his victim's weakest point. He knows where the Achilles heel may be, and he does not fail to strike at the opportune time.

Three times Satan attempted to defeat Jesus. Three times Jesus quoted Scripture, and three times Satan went down to defeat. Then the Bible declares that "he [Satan] departed from him [Jesus] for a season" (Luke 4:13). It was at this point that angels came to His assistance—not to help Him resist Satan as they help us, for He did that by Himself, but to help Him after the battle was won. The angels "ministered" to Jesus. The Greek word *diakoneo* says it well, for they served Him as a deacon would serve. "Behold, angels came and ministered unto him" (Matthew 4:11). Angelic ambassadors supported, strengthened, and sustained Him in that trying hour. From that moment on, our Lord Jesus Christ, "who has been tempted in every way, just as we are—yet was without sin" (Hebrews 4:15 NIV), could sympathize and help Christian believers for the ages to come and lead them to victory in their hour of temptation.

THE ANGEL WITH JESUS IN THE GARDEN OF GETHSEMANE

The night before His crucifixion, Jesus was in the Garden of Gethsemane. Only a short time later He was to be seized by the soldiers, betrayed by Judas Iscariot, set before the rulers, beaten, and at last crucified. Before He was hung on the cross, He went through the terrible agony in the garden made Him sweat, as it were, drops of blood. It was in this situation that the Son of Man needed inner strength to face what no other being in heaven, hell, or earth had ever known. In fact, He was to face what no created being could have faced and gone through in victory. He was about to take upon Himself the sins of men. He was to become sin for us.

Jesus had taken Peter, James, and John with Him to the Garden. They could have provided Him with reinforcement and encouragement, but instead they fell asleep. The Son of Man was all alone. He prayed, "Father, if thou be willing, remove this cup from me: nevertheless not my will, but thine, be done" (Luke 22:42). Then it was at that crucial moment that the angel came to assist Him, "strengthening Him." The Greek word for strengthening is *eniskuo*, which means to make strong inwardly. Whereas the disciples of the Lord Jesus had failed to share His agony, as they slept, the angel came to help.

ANGELS WAITING AT THE CROSS

The tragedy of sin reached its crescendo when God in Christ became sin. At this point, He was offering Himself as the sacrifice required by the justice of God if man was to be redeemed. At this moment Satan was ready to try his master stroke. If he could get Christ to come down from the cross, and if Christ allowed the mockery of the crowd to shame or anger Him, then the plan of salvation would be jeopardized. Again and again they shouted, "If thou be the Son of God, come down from the cross" (Matthew 27:40). He knew He could come down if He chose; He knew He could get help from more than twelve legions of angels who hovered about with drawn swords.

Yet for our salvation, He stayed there. The angels would have come to the cross to rescue the King of kings, but because of His love for the human race and because He knew it was only through His death that they could be saved, He refused to call for help. The angels were under orders not to intervene at this terrible, holy moment. Even the angels could not minister to the Son of God at Calvary. He died alone to take the full death penalty you and I deserved.

We can never plumb the depths of sin, or sense how terrible human sin is, until we go to the cross and see that it was "sin" that caused the Son of God to be crucified. The ravages of war, the tragedy of suicide, the agony of the poverty-stricken, the suffering and irony of the rejected of our society, the blood of the accident victim, the terror of rape and mugging victims of our generation—these all speak as with a single voice of the degradation that besets the human race at this hour. But no sin has been committed in the world today that can compare with the full cup of the universe's sin that brought Jesus to the cross. The question hurled toward heaven throughout the ages has been, "Who is He and why does He die?"

The answer comes back, "This is My only begotten Son, dying not only for your sins but for the sins of the whole world." To you sin may be a small thing; to God it is a great and awful thing. It is the second largest thing in the world; only the love of God is greater.

When we comprehend the great price God was willing to pay for the redemption of man, we only then begin to see that something is horribly wrong with the human race. It must have a Savior, or it is doomed! Sin cost God His very best. Is it any wonder that the angels veiled their faces, that they were silent in their consternation as they witnessed the outworking of God's plan? How inconceivable it must have seemed to them, when they considered the fearful depravity of sin, that Jesus should shoulder it all. But they were soon to unveil their faces and offer their praises again. A light was kindled that day at Calvary. The cross blazed with the glory of God as the most terrible darkness was shattered by the light of salvation. Satan's depraved legions were defeated and they could no longer keep all men in darkness and defeat.

THE ANGELS AT THE RESURRECTION

The Bible says that on the third day after Jesus' death, "there was a great earthquake; for the angel of the Lord descended from heaven, and came and rolled back the stone from the door, and sat upon it. His countenance was like lightning, and his raiment white as snow: And for fear of him the keepers did shake, and became as dead men" (Matthew 28:2–4).

Though some Bible students have tried to estimate how much this stone weighed, we need not speculate, because Jesus could have come out of that tomb whether the stone was there or not. The Bible mentions it so that generations to come can know something of the tremendous miracle of resurrection that took place. I have often wondered what those guards must have thought when, against the brightness of the rising sun, they saw the angel rolling away the gigantic boulder with possibly the lightest touch of his finger! The guards, though heavily armed, were paralyzed with fear.

As Mary looked into the tomb, she saw "two angels in white sitting, the one at the head, and the other at the feet, where the body of Jesus had lain" (John 20:11–12). Then one of the angels who was sitting outside the tomb proclaimed the greatest message the world has ever heard: "He is not here, but is risen" (Luke 24:6). Those few words changed the history of the universe. Darkness and despair died; hope and anticipation were born in the hearts of men.

ANGELS AND THE ASCENSION OF JESUS

We find the story of the ascension of Jesus in Acts 1. Verse 9 says, "And when he had spoken these things, while they beheld, he was taken up; and a cloud received him out of their sight." Jesus had been accompanied to earth by an angelic host. I believe that the word "cloud" suggests that angels had come to escort Him back to the right hand of God the Father.

The watching disciples were sad and despondent. Tears filled their eyes. But again two angels, looking like men and dressed in white raiment, appeared and said, "Ye men of Galilee, why stand ye gazing up into heaven? This same Jesus, which is taken up from you into heaven, shall so come in like manner as ye have seen him go into heaven" (Acts 1:11).

Thus, the angels escorted the resurrected Lord of glory back to be seated at the Father's right hand; then even the morning stars ascribed honor, glory, and praise to Him as the Son of the living God. On the other hand, some angels remained behind to assure those early disciples that they would always be near, ready to help God's people throughout the ages to come—until Christ returns in person with the angelic host.

12

Angels in Prophecy

Angels have an important role in future events! Human history began at Eden where God planted a garden and made man for His eternal fellowship. Angels were there. They have never failed to attend the human scene. And they will continue on the scene throughout the succeeding ages till time runs into eternity.

Just as millions of angels participated in the dazzling show when the morning stars sang together at creation, so will the innumerable hosts of heaven help bring to pass God's prophetic declarations throughout time and into eternity.

When God decrees it, Satan (Lucifer) will be removed from the world of disorder so God can establish righteousness everywhere and a true theocracy. Not until that event takes place will the human race know perfect peace on earth. Paul tells us in

Romans 8 that the whole creation groans and travails as it awaits the day of Christ's victory.

The prophets spoke of a wonderful day when God would lift the curse, when lion and lamb would lie down together, and when nations would learn war no more (Isaiah 2:4; 11:6). Angel hosts will fulfill His royal decrees and oversee God's purpose in the universe. Christ is coming in great power, and all His holy angels will be with Him. In Acts 1:10–11 angels gave counsel to the disciples after Jesus had ascended to heaven. As we have already seen, when He had left the Mount of Olives, angels appeared, saying, "Ye men of Galilee, why stand ye gazing up into heaven? This same Jesus . . . shall so come in like manner as ye have seen him go into heaven" (Acts 1:11). Angels encouraged those downcast believers who had seen Jesus Christ disappear from their view into a cloud. After this, angels figure prominently in the prophetic plan of God that continued on into the future events of Bible prophecy.

In every age, the true believers have asked, "Will this conflict of the ages ever end?" Each period of history seemingly has its own trials and convulsions. Each generation seems to have to "fight it out." Behind it all is the unseen struggle of the ages. We thought that modern technology would solve many of the great problems of the human race. In some ways it has, by eliminating the fear of diseases like polio and smallpox. But it has also given us Frankenstein weapons of destruction. Poverty, hunger, greed, injustice, prejudice, terrorism, lust, war, and death are still with us. This is the same war that began mysteriously in the heart of Lucifer. It seems that our world is on a suicidal course; but God has other plans. Light shines at the end of the tunnel. Someday

Satan and his demons will go down in defeat. The Bible declares that righteousness will eventually triumph, Utopia will come to earth, the kingdom of God will ultimately prevail. In bringing all this about, angels will have a prominent part.

A little girl heard a clock strike thirteen times. Breathlessly she ran to her mother and said, "Mother, it's later than it's ever been before." Almost everyone throughout the world will agree. It's later than it's ever been before. The human race is rushing madly toward some sort of climax, and the Bible accurately predicts what the climax is! A new world is coming. Through modern technology and scientific achievement we are catching glimpses of what that new world is. If it were not for depraved human nature, man could achieve it himself. But man's rebellion against God has always been his stumbling block. The penalty for man's rebellion is death. The best leaders and the best brains have many times been stopped by death. The Bible teaches that "it is appointed unto men once to die" (Hebrews 9:27). Today the world longs for a leader such as Abraham Lincoln, but death took him from us.

God will use the angels to merge time into eternity, creating a new kind of life for every creature. Even today's intellectual world speaks of a point when time will be no more. Most scientists agree that the clock of time is running out. Ecologically, medically, scientifically, morally, time seems to be running out. In almost every direction we look, man's time on earth seems to be running out. Self-destruction is overtaking us as a human race.

Will man destroy himself? No! God has another plan! Since the beginning of time, man has been interested in what lies beyond the short span of life. Modern man is turning to the occult, Eastern mysticism, palm readers, and every other kind of help available to tell him about the future. Strangely, only a minority turn to the Bible, the only book that accurately foretells the future. The Bible teaches that Jesus Christ is coming back again with His holy angels. It refers to His coming as like "a thief in the night" (2 Peter 3:10), a day of wrath (Romans 2:5), and the judgment of the great day (Jude 6), with many other references both direct and indirect. The age of utopia will be preceded by unparalleled events of suffering for the human race—totalitarianism, poverty, disease, earthquakes, moral collapse, war—until men's hearts will fail them for fear (Luke 21:26).

Luke 21 says there will be "wars and commotions. . . . Nation shall rise against nation, and kingdom against kingdom: And great earthquakes shall be in divers places, and famines, and pestilences; and fearful sights and great signs shall there be from heaven" (verses 9–11).

Believing Christians and believing Jews alike will be persecuted. Men will deliver "you up to the synagogues, and into prisons, being brought before kings and rulers for my name's sake. . . . And ye shall be betrayed both by parents, and brethren, and kinsfolk, and friends; and some of you shall they cause to be put to death. And ye shall be hated of all men for my name's sake. . . . And when ye shall see Jerusalem compassed with armies, then know that the desolation thereof is nigh. . . . And there shall be signs in the sun, and in the moon, and in the stars; and upon the earth distress of nations, with perplexity; the sea and the waves roaring; men's hearts failing them for fear, and for looking after those things which are coming on the earth: for the powers of heaven shall be shaken" (Luke 21:12–26).

Jesus continued in verse 27, "And then shall they see the Son of man coming in a cloud with power and great glory."

Even as in the beginning of time angelic forces waged war in heaven (Revelation 12:7–9), so in the very last days angels will wage still another war; Satan will make his last stand. As the time draws near, he intensifies his activities.

But it will be a victorious day for the universe, and especially planet Earth, when the devil and his angels are thrown into the lake of fire, never again to tempt and destroy man. God has assigned this task to the angels , and Scripture assures us that they will be victorious (Matthew 13:41–42).

ANGELS WILL GATHER GOD'S ELECT

Linked to this idea Jesus says that "when the Son of man shall come in his glory, and all the holy angels with him, then shall he sit upon the throne of his glory" (Matthew 25:31). In other words, when Jesus returns, He will be accompanied by the hosts of heaven. The holy angels will be with Him! As He says in Matthew 13:41–42, "The Son of man shall send forth his angels, and they shall gather out of his kingdom all things that offend, and them which do iniquity; and shall cast them into a furnace of fire: there shall be wailing and gnashing of teeth."

Earlier in this same chapter, Jesus has related a significant little story commonly called the parable of the tares and wheat (Matthew 13:24–30, 36–43). Both had been allowed to grow together until the harvest, but then the reapers were to gather them up in bundles. The tares were to be burned; the wheat gathered. We often wonder why God permits so much sin in the world, why He withholds His right arm of judgment. Why doesn't God put an end to sin now? We can give an answer from this text where Jesus said, "Let both grow together," the evil with the good (verse 30). If we were to try to wipe all evil from the face of the earth, who could count on justice? Pure justice does not exist here, because everyone is guilty, including the judges who sit in judgment. We are all guilty of sin.

Man must do his best in meting out justice, but his best is not complete justice. To angels will be delegated the ministry of separating the good from the bad, discerning even attitudes. God's judgment will be so pure that even those who are condemned will bow their knee and confess, "Thou art just." As someone has said, "When I die I do not want justice—I want mercy!" That mercy has been provided by the Lord Jesus Christ.

So angels will not only accompany Christ when He returns, but will be assigned the responsibility of gathering out of His kingdom all things that offend and work iniquity, that they might be judged (Matthew 13:47–50).

It boggles the mind to try to imagine the kind of earth this is going to be when God eliminates the devil and sin. Our minds are staggered at the thought of "Christ on the throne." The great southward moving Sahara Desert of Africa will bloom and blossom. Mankind will be able to grow new foods; land that today is useless will grow twelve crops a year. The urge in man's heart toward immorality will have vanished. In that day the great drive in man will be a thirst for righteousness.

It takes a great deal of faith in these days of despondency to believe this, but it is the clear teaching of the Bible. Without this hope of the future I do not know what modern man does, except turn to drugs and alcohol.

Today we have the choice of whether or not to receive the ministry of angels. In choosing to follow Jesus Christ, we also choose the protective watch and care of the angels of heaven. In the time of the Second Coming, we will no longer be afforded the privilege of choice. If we delay now, it will be too late, and we forfeit forever the gracious ministry of angels and the promise of salvation to eternal life.

ANGELS IN OUR FUTURE

Dr. Miller asks the question, "What does the future hold for this weary old world? . . . for the physical earth? The answers to such questions are not to be found in astrology or necromancy but in the divinely inspired Word of God. And we may be certain that, as the passing of time fulfills the prophetic Scriptures, the holy angels will be deeply involved in the fulfillment." God will renovate the earth, order the New Jerusalem to descend from heaven, and give redeemed man a position above the angels—what a future!

Elijah was one of the greatest prophets, suddenly appearing on the scene in one of Israel's darkest hours (1 Kings 17). He was a strong, suntanned son of the desert. At times he could be bold as a lion, and at times crushed with frustration. On one occasion he challenged the prophets of the heathen god Baal to a duel to see who was the true God (1 Kings 18:19). When the prophets of

Baal could get no answer from their false god, and Elijah's God answered by fire, Queen Jezebel, unable to accept the prophet's verdict, determined to take his life and pursued him with her chariot for many miles. Elijah, weary from his flight and desperately hungry, lay down under a juniper tree to rest. Feeling extremely sorry for himself, he went to sleep, to be wakened by an angel's touch. Then food was set before him to eat, and the angel said, "Arise, eat."

"And he looked, and, behold, there was a cake baken on the coals, and a [jar] of water at his head. And he did eat and drink, and laid him down again. And the angel of the Lord came again the second time, and touched him, and said, Arise and eat; because the journey is too great for thee. And he arose, and did eat and drink, and went in the strength of that meat forty days and forty nights unto Horeb the mount of God" (1 Kings 19:6–8).

God did not let his faithful prophet down. He provided just what he needed physically, psychologically, and spiritually. Many of us despair of coping with the pressures of our lives, but if we are living Spirit-filled and Spirit-directed lives, we can claim God's promises. The prophetic Scriptures give us "hope." Without Scripture's plan of God for the future and the hope it brings, I do not know what the average thinking person does. Certainly a person will not find the answer by wringing his hands, or by committing suicide, or by turning to the occult. We find the answer to the future in Holy Scripture. It is summed up in the person of Jesus Christ. God has centered all our hopes and dreams on Him. He is the Commander-in-Chief of these angelic armies that will accompany Him on His return.

ANGEL AUTHORITY

New Testament writers have reaffirmed the badge of authority given to angels to fulfill the prophetic dictates of God. The apostle Peter emphasized this truth when speaking of Christ, who was at the right hand of God, having gone into heaven after "angels and authorities and powers [had been] made subject unto him" (1 Peter 3:22). The time is coming when the twenty-four elders of His angelic creation will fall down before the Lamb and sing their new song (Revelation 5:9–10). Thereafter, the holy angels will gather round the throne and join in a great testimony to the Lamb, expressing praise with such words as, "Worthy is the Lamb that was slain to receive power and riches and wisdom and might and honor and glory and blessing" (Revelation 5:12 NASB). While angels have tremendous authority, it is limited to doing only the will of God. They never deviate from God's message, never dilute His message, never change God's plan. Throughout the ages they have glorified only Him, never themselves.

The Bible teaches that the demons are dedicated to controlling this planet for their master, Satan. Even Jesus called him "the prince of this world" (John 12:31). He is the master-organizer and strategist. Many times throughout biblical history, and possibly even today, angels and demons engage in warfare. Many of the events of our times may very well be involved in this unseen struggle.

We are not left in doubt about who will ultimately triumph. Time after time Jesus has assured us that He and the angels would be victorious. "When the Son of man shall come in his glory, and all the holy angels with him, then shall he sit upon the throne of his glory" (Matthew 25:31). The apostle Paul wrote, "The Lord Jesus shall be revealed from heaven with his mighty angels in flaming fire" (2 Thessalonians 1:7,–8).

Jesus also taught that "Whosoever shall confess me before men, him shall the Son of man also confess before the angels of God" (Luke 12:8). It is impossible to comprehend one's suffering of eternal loss when he learns that angels do not acknowledge him because he has been false in his claims to know Christ. But what a moment it is going to be for believers throughout all the ages, from every tribe, nation, and tongue, when they are presented in the court of heaven. Scripture calls it "the marriage supper of the Lamb" (Revelation 19:9). This is the great event when Jesus Christ is crowned King of kings and Lord of lords. Both believers of all ages and all the angelic hosts will join in bowing their knees and confessing that He is Lord.

The book of Revelation, from chapter 4 to 19, gives us a picture of judgments to befall the earth such as the world has never known. Angels will be involved in all of these judgments. But after these terrifying events, Christ will come with His holy angels to set up His kingdom.

Whether the battle between the forces of Satan and the forces of God involve other planets and galaxies we do not know. But we do know that the earth is the scene of the conflict; however, it is a struggle that affects the entire universe. It is mind-boggling that you and I, with such a short period of time on this planet, play a part in this battle of the ages. It is incredible to us that supernatural beings from outer space are engaged in a struggle for this planet.

It all started in the Garden of Eden, a place located somewhere between the Tigris and the Euphrates rivers in the Middle East. It is significant that the nations prominent in early history are once again becoming prominent: Israel, Egypt, Syria, Iran, and so on. In that garden God gave a great promise, "And I will put enmity between thee and the woman, and between thy seed and her seed; it shall bruise thy head, and thou shalt bruise his heel" (Genesis 3:15). As we approach the end of the age, the head of Satan is being battered and bruised as the forces of God gain momentum. Under the command of God, Michael the archangel is now organizing his forces for the last battle—Armageddon. The last picture in the Bible is one of heaven.

Many years ago I was visiting the dining room of the United States Senate. As I was speaking to various people, one of the senators called me to his table. He said, "Billy, we're having a discussion about pessimism and optimism. Are you a pessimist or an optimist?" I smiled and said, "I'm an optimist." He asked, "Why?"

I said, "I've read the last page of the Bible."

The Bible speaks about a city whose builder and maker is God, where those who have been redeemed will be superior to angels. It speaks of "a pure river of water of life, clear as crystal proceeding out of the throne of God and of the Lamb" (Revelation 22:1). It says, "And they shall see his face; and his name shall be in their foreheads. And there shall be no night there; and they need no candle, neither light of the sun; for the Lord God giveth them light: and they shall reign for ever and ever" (verses 4–5).

The next verse has a thrilling last word to say about angels: "These sayings are faithful and true: and the Lord God of the holy prophets sent his angel to shew unto his servants the things which must shortly be done."

Christian and non-Christian alike should meditate on the seventh verse, where God says, "Behold I come quickly: blessed is he that keepeth the sayings of the prophecy of this book."

13

The Angels and Death

The angel who came to the garden where Jesus' body lay rolled away the stone and permitted fresh air and morning light to fill His tomb. The sepulcher was no longer an empty vault or dreary dormitory; rather, it was a life-affirming place that radiated the glory of the living God. No longer was it a dark prison but a transformed reminder of the celestial light that sweeps aside the shadows of death. Jesus' resurrection changed it.

An unknown poet has said of the tomb, "'Tis now a cell where angels used to come and go with heavenly news." No words of men or angels can adequately describe the height and depth, the length and breadth of the glory to which the world awakened when Jesus came forth to life from the pall of death. As Charles Wesley says in his hymn:

'Tis mystery all! Th' Immortal dies!
Who can explore His strange design?
In vain the first-born seraph tries
To sound the depths of love Divine!
'Tis mercy all! Let earth adore!
Let angel minds inquire no more.

In contrast to Jesus, we all still have to die. Yet just as an angel was involved in Christ's resurrection, so will angels help us in death. Only one thin veil separates our natural world from the spiritual world. That thin veil we call death. However, Christ both vanquished death and overcame the dark threats of the evil fallen angels. So now God surrounds death with the assurance of angelic help to bring pulsing life out of the darkness of that experience for believers. We inherit the kingdom of God.

CHRISTIANS AT DEATH

Death for the Christian cuts the cord that holds us captive in this present evil world so that angels may transport believers to their heavenly inheritance. Death is the fiery chariot, the gentle voice of the King, the invitation to nonstop passage into the banquet house of the world of glory.

In another connection I have already mentioned Lazarus, whom angels escorted to Abraham in heaven. This story has always been a tremendous comfort to me as I think about death. I will actually be taken by angels into the presence of God. These ministering spirits who have helped me here so often will be with me in my last great battle on earth. Death is a battle, a profound crisis event. Paul calls it "the last enemy" (1 Corinthians 15:26). While the sting of death has been removed by the work of Christ on the cross, and by His resurrection, yet the crossing of this valley still stimulates fear and mystery. However, angels will be there to help us. Could not the "rod and staff," which help us in the valley of the shadow of death (Psalm 23:4), be these holy angels?

We who have made our peace with God should be like the evangelist D. L. Moody. When he was aware that death was at hand, he said, "Earth recedes, heaven opens before me." It appeared as though he was dreaming. Then he said, "No, this is no dream . . . it is beautiful, it is like a trance. If this is death, it is sweet. There is no valley here. God is calling me, and I must go."

After having been given up for dead, Moody revived to indicate that God had permitted him to see beyond that thin veil separating the seen from the unseen world. He had been "within the gates, and beyond the portals," and had caught a glimpse of familiar faces whom he had "loved long since and lost awhile." Then he could remember when he had proclaimed so vociferously earlier in his ministry, "Some day you will read in the papers that D. L. Moody of East Northfield is dead. Don't you believe a word of it. At that moment I shall be more alive than I am now. I shall have gone up higher, that is all—out of this old clay tenement into a house that is immortal; a body that death cannot touch, that sin cannot taint, a body fashioned like unto His glorious body. . . . That which is born of the flesh may die. That which is born of the Spirit will live forever" (*The Life of Dwight L. Moody* by W. R. Moody). If Moody were to witness to us now, he would surely tell us of the glowing experience that became his as the angelic hosts ushered him into the presence of the Lord.

Phillips Brooks, the writer of "O Little Town of Bethlehem," was one of the greatest pulpit orators and best-loved preachers of the nineteenth century. No greater tribute could be paid him than the words of a five-year-old Boston girl, who exclaimed after her mother had told her that the beloved Mr. Brooks had died, "Mother, how happy the angels will be!"

Death is not natural, for man was created to live and not to die. It is the result of God's judgment because of man's sin and rebellion. Without God's grace through Christ, it is a gruesome spectacle. I have stood at the bedside of people dying without Christ; it was a terrible experience. I have stood at the bedside of those who were dying in Christ; it was a glorious experience. Charles Spurgeon said of the glory that attends the death of the redeemed, "If I may die as I have seen some die, I court the grand occasion. I would not wish to escape death by some by-road if I may sing as they sang. If I may have such hosannas and alleluias beaming in my eyes as I have seen as well as heard from them, it were a blessed thing to die."

Death is robbed of much of its terror for the true believer, but we still need God's protection as we take that last journey. At the moment of death the spirit departs from the body and moves through the atmosphere. But the Scripture teaches us that the devil lurks then. He is "the prince of the power of the air" (Ephesians 2:2). If the eyes of our understanding were opened, we would probably see the air filled with demons, the enemies of Christ. If Satan could hinder the angel of Daniel 10 for three weeks on his mission to earth, we can imagine the opposition a Christian may encounter at death.

But Christ on Calvary cleared a road through Satan's kingdom. When Christ came to earth, He had to pass through the devil's territory and open up a beachhead here. That is one reason He was accompanied by a host of angels when He came (Luke 2:8–14). And this is why holy angels will accompany Him when He comes again (Matthew 16:27). Till then, the moment of death is Satan's final opportunity to attack the true believer; but God has sent His angels to guard us at that time.

In telling the story in Luke 16, Jesus says that the beggar was "carried by the angels." He was not only escorted; he was carried. What an experience that must have been for Lazarus! He had lain begging at the gate of the rich man until his death, but then suddenly he found himself carried by the mighty angels of God!

Once I stood in London to watch Queen Elizabeth return from an overseas trip. I saw the parade of dignitaries, the marching bands, the crack troops, the waving flags. I saw all the splendor that accompanies the homecoming of a queen. However, that was nothing compared to the homecoming of a true believer who has said good-bye here to all of the suffering of this life and been immediately surrounded by angels who carry him upward to the glorious welcome awaiting the redeemed in heaven.

The Christian should never consider death a tragedy. Rather he should see it as angels do: They realize that joy should mark the journey from time to eternity. The way to life is by the valley of death, but the road is marked with victory all the way. Angels revel in the power of the resurrection of Jesus, which assures us of our resurrection and guarantees us a safe passage to heaven.

Hundreds of accounts record the heavenly escort of angels at death. When my maternal grandmother died, for instance, the room seemed to fill with a heavenly light. She sat up in bed and almost laughingly said, "I see Jesus. He has His arms outstretched toward me. I see Ben [her husband who had died some years earlier] and I see the angels." She slumped over, absent from the body but present with the Lord.

When I was a student in a Bible school a godly young missionary volunteer was suddenly taken ill. The physician said she had only a few hours to live. Her young husband and one or two faculty members were in the room when she suddenly exclaimed, "I see Jesus. I can hear the singing of the angels."

The Reverend A. A. Talbot, missionary to China, was at the bedside of a dying Chinese Christian. Suddenly the room was filled with heavenly music. The Chinese Christian looked up with a radiant smile exclaiming, "I see Jesus standing at the right hand of God, and Margaret Gay is with Him." (Margaret Gay was the Talbots' little daughter who had died months before.)

Susanna Wesley said, "When I am gone, sing a song of praise to God."

Dying patients are given so many drugs today that we do not hear as many of these stories now. But to those who face death in Christ, it is a glorious experience. The Bible guarantees every believer an escorted journey into the presence of Christ by the holy angels.

The angelic emissaries of the Lord are often sent not only to catch away the redeemed of the Lord at death, but also to give hope and joy to those who remain, and to sustain them in their loss. He has promised to give "the oil of joy for mourning, the garment expressive of praise instead of a heavy, burdened and failing spirit."

Today man has been overtaken by an increasing sense of gloom about life. In his Responding to Suicidal Crisis, Doman Lum quotes Minna Field on the inadequacy of the counsel and treatment given by those who merely "attempt to escape what is to them an unbearable prospect by a pat on the back and by telling the patient that he is talking nonsense." Death seminars are now being held in major medical centers, and teams of psychiatrists, psychologists, and therapists are constantly encouraged to become involved. Robert J. Lifton, in studying the cessation of life, points out in the same book some interesting views held by survivors of the atomic destruction of Hiroshima. He says that "there was a lasting sense of an overwhelming and permanent encounter with death. As a result, there was a breakdown of faith or trust in any human structure, a psychological closure in which people literally numbed themselves to any emotional feelings regarding death, and an overwhelming sense of guilt and self-condemnation as if they were responsible for the tragedy. . . . We are obsessed with the fear of sudden death . . . and recognize the unpredictable nature of life."

In popular thinking you and I have heard people speaking of death as "crossing the Jordan." It is found in spirituals and in some hymns of the Christian faith. It comes, of course, from the victorious march of the Israelites who crossed the Jordan to enter the Promised Land. They passed over Jordan on dry ground. By analogy we can consider that the ministering angels will see us safely across the Jordan River of death as we enter the promised land of heaven. So the Christian does not sorrow as those who have no hope (1 Thessalonians 4:13).

When the apostle Paul spoke of his own approaching death, he said, "We are confident, I say, and willing rather to be absent from the body, and to be present with the Lord" (2 Corinthians 5:8). When that glorious physical and spiritual separation takes place, the angels will be there to escort us into the presence of our Savior with abounding joy, and it will mean "life everlasting."

THE WONDERFUL WELCOME TO COME

I believe that death can be beautiful. I have come to look forward to it, to anticipate it with joy and expectation. I have stood at the side of many people who died with expressions of triumph on their faces. No wonder the Bible says, "Precious in the sight of the Lord is the death of his saints" (Psalm 116:15). No wonder David said, "Even though I walk through the valley of the shadow of death, I will fear no evil, for you are with me" (Psalm 23:4 NIV).

You may be filled with dread at the thought of death. Just remember that at one moment you may be suffering, but in another moment, you will be instantly transformed into the glorious likeness of our Savior. The wonders, beauties, splendor, and grandeur of heaven will be yours. You will be surrounded by these heavenly messengers sent by God to bring you home where you may rest from your labors, though the honor of your works will follow you (Revelation 14:13).

No wonder the apostle Paul said, "Therefore, my dear brothers, stand firm. Let nothing move you. Always give yourselves fully to the work of the Lord, because you know that your labor in the Lord is not in vain" (1 Corinthians 15:58 NIV).

Are you ready to face life? Are you ready to face death? No one is truly ready to die who has not learned to live for the glory of God. You can put your confidence in Jesus because He died for you, and in that last moment—the greatest crisis of all—He will have His angels gather you in their arms to carry you gloriously, wonderfully into heaven.

14

Angel Spectators

How would you live if you knew that you were being watched all the time, not only by your parents, wife, husband, or children, but by the heavenly host? The Bible teaches in 1 Corinthians 4:9 that angels are watching us.

Paul says we are a "spectacle" to them. A. S. Joppie points out that the word referred to the arenas where first-century crowds went to see animals killed for sport, men battle to the death and, later, Christians torn apart by lions. In using the word spectacle, Paul is picturing this world as one vast arena. All true Christians participate in this great drama as they seek to obey Christ since this throws them into severe conflict with the forces of evil, who are bent on humiliating them. Yet Scripture says, "They did not love their lives so much as to shrink from death" (Revelation 12:11 NIV).

During this conflict, which was not limited to the arena, the angels were watching them, longing to hasten to their rescue to set free those men and women who often went joyfully to their death. Yet God forbade the angels to rush in as armies of deliverance. Nor had He allowed them to rescue Jesus at the cross when He tasted the death of separation from God the Father. The angel spectators were poised and ready to intervene; the attack order never came. Why? Because God's moment of final victory over the vicious forces of evil had not yet come.

As I mentioned earlier we face many perplexing questions today, such as, Why does God permit evil? Why doesn't God intervene and punish sin? Why does God allow disease? Why does God permit catastrophe? Yet God's timing is precise! Angel hosts who witness everything that transpires in our world are not free to bear up the righteous and deliver the oppressed until God gives the signal. One day He will. Christ has reminded us that the wheat and the tares, the righteous and the unrighteous, are to grow in the field together until the harvest time when the holy angels gather God's elect and bring them into His kingdom.

ANGELS AT ATTENTION

As God's angels have watched the drama of this age unfolding, they have seen the Christian church established and expand around the world. They miss nothing as they watch the movements of time, "to the intent that now unto the principalities and powers in heavenly places might be known by the church the manifold wisdom of God" (Ephesians 3:10). Dr. Joppie reminds us that the word "now" actually covers the vast expanse of this church age. Angel hosts have witnessed the formation of the church of Christ Jesus and have watched the walk of each believer as the Lord worked His grace, love, and power into each life. The angels are observing first-hand the building of the body of the true church in all places of His dominion this very hour.

But what are they thinking as we live in the world's arena? Do they observe us as we stand fast in the faith and walk in righteousness? Or may they be wondering at our lack of commitment? These two possibilities seem evident from Ephesians 3:10: "(The purpose is) that through the church the complicated, many-sided wisdom of God in all its infinite variety and innumerable aspects might now be made known to the angelic rulers and authorities (principalities and powers) in the heavenly sphere" (AMP).

Our certainty that angels right now witness how we are walking through life should mightily influence the decisions we make. God is watching, and His angels are interested spectators too. The Amplified Bible expresses 1 Corinthians 4:9 this way: "God has made an exhibit of us . . . a show in the world's amphitheater—with both men and angels (as spectators)." We know they are watching, but in the heat of the battle, I have thought how wonderful it would be if we could hear them cheering.

INCENTIVES FOR RIGHTEOUSNESS

The charge to live righteously in this present world sobers us when we realize that the walk and warfare of Christians is the primary concern of heaven and its angelic hosts. Paul said, "I solemnly charge you in the presence of God and of Christ Jesus and of the chosen angels, that you guard and keep (these rules)" (1 Timothy 5:21 AMP). Paul was stirring up Timothy to remember that the elect angels were constantly watching how he served the Savior and lived the Christian life. What fact could provide a greater motivation to righteous living than that? I must say to myself, "Careful, angels are watching!"

It must give the angels great satisfaction to watch the church of Jesus Christ minister the unsearchable riches of Christ to lost men everywhere. If the angels rejoice over one sinner who repents (Luke 15:10), then the angel hosts are numbered among the spectators in the heavenly grandstands. They are included among those who are referred to as "so great a cloud of witness" (Hebrews 12:1); and they never miss any of the details of our earthly pilgrimage. Yet they do not jeer as did the Greek crowds of Paul's day. Rather, as we declare the gospel and see our friends saved, they rejoice with us.

In his book *Though I Walk Through the Valley*, Dr. Vance Havner tells of an old preacher who worked into the night on a sermon for his small congregation. His wife inquired why he spent so much time on a message that he would give to so few. To this the minister replied, "You forget, my dear, how large my audience will be!" Dr. Havner adds, "Nothing is trivial here if heaven looks on. We shall play a better game if, 'seeing we are encompassed,' we remember who is in the grandstand!"

Our valleys may be filled with foes and tears; but we can lift our eyes to the hills to see God and the angels, heaven's spectators, who support us according to God's infinite wisdom as they prepare our welcome home.

15

Angels in Our Lives Today

In the early days of World War II, Britain's air force saved it from invasion and defeat. In her book *Tell No Man*, Adela Rogers St. John describes a strange aspect of that weeks-long air war. Her information comes from a celebration held some months after the war, honoring air chief marshal Lord Hugh Dowding. The king, the prime minister, and scores of dignitaries were there. In his remarks, the air chief marshal recounted the story of his legendary conflict where his pitifully small complement of men rarely slept, and their planes never stopped flying. He told about airmen on a mission who, having been hit, were either incapacitated or dead. Yet their planes kept flying and fighting; in fact, on occasion pilots in other planes would see a figure still operating the controls. What was the explanation? The air chief marshal said he believed angels had actually flown some of the planes whose pilots sat dead in their cockpits.

That angels piloted planes for dead men in the battle for Britain we cannot finally prove. But we have already seen from Scripture some of the things angels have certainly done, can do, and are yet going to do as history approaches its climax. The important question for each of us is how angels can assist us in our lives here and now: How do they help us attain victory over the forces of evil? What is our continuing relationship to them?

We know that God has given His angels charge over us so that without their help we could never get the victory over Satan. The apostle Paul said, "For we wrestle not against flesh and blood, but against principalities, against powers, against the rulers of the darkness of this world, against spiritual wickedness in high places" (Ephesians 6:12). Let's consider how we can gain help from God through angels.

THE GOD OF THIS AGE

Lucifer, our archenemy, controls one of the most powerful and well-oiled war machines in the universe. He controls principalities, powers, and dominions. Every nation, city, village, and individual has felt the hot breath of his evil power. He is already gathering the nations of the world for the last great battle in the war against Christ—Armageddon. Yet Jesus assures us that Satan is already a defeated foe (John 12:31; 16:11). In 2 Timothy 1:10, Paul says that Jesus Christ has abolished death and brought life and immortality to light through the gospel. Peter declares that Jesus "has gone into heaven and is at God's right hand—with angels, authorities and powers in submission to him" (1 Peter 3:22 NIV).

THE DEFEAT OF SATAN

While Satan is a defeated foe in principle, obviously God has not yet eliminated him from the world scene. The Bible teaches, however, that God will use angels to judge and totally eliminate him from the universe. In Revelation 12, we read of Satan's earlier defeat: "Michael and his angels fought against the dragon; and the dragon fought and his angels, and prevailed not; neither was their place found any more in heaven. and the great dragon was cast out, that old serpent, called the Devil, and Satan, which deceiveth the whole world: he was cast out into the earth" (verses 7–9).

In chapter 20 John describes how Satan's present earthly rule will be temporarily restricted: "And I saw an angel come down from heaven, having the key of the bottomless pit and a great chain in his hand. And he laid hold on the dragon, that old serpent, which is the Devil, and Satan, and bound him a thousand years, and cast him into the bottomless pit, and shut him up, and set a seal upon him, that he should deceive the nations no more. . . ." John then tells us that after a temporary release followed by the last great battle, God will cast Satan into the lake of fire and brimstone, there to be tormented forever (Revelation 20:10).

Some will say, "It is well and good to talk about the final defeat of the devil, but until that happens it doesn't help me because I have to contend with him every day." But this is not the whole story. We have been given specific instructions in Scripture about how to get victory over the devil.

We are told, for example, "Do not give the devil a foothold" (Ephesians 4:27 NIV). In other words, don't leave any vacant places in your heart for him. The apostle Peter taught, "Be sober, be vigilant; because your adversary the devil, as a roaring lion, walketh about, seeking whom he may devour" (1 Peter 5:8). Thus, we cannot be too careful. This includes the injunction to join God's resistance movement: "Whom resist stedfast in the faith" (1 Peter 5:9). And James says, "Resist the devil, and he will flee from you" (James 4:7).

But these admonitions to be vigilant and to resist tell only part of the story. We are not in the battle alone, nor must we rely on our strength alone. Instead, we are to rely on the Holy Spirit, who dwells within us and is willing and able to help us in every situation if we will turn to Him. In addition we can count on the powerful presence of angels many times more numerous and powerful than Satan and his demons. As Increase Mather wrote centuries ago in *Angelographia*, "Angels both good and bad have a greater influence on this world than men are generally aware of. We ought to admire the grace of God toward us sinful creatures in that He hath appointed His holy angels to guard us against the mischiefs of wicked spirits who are always intending our hurt both to our bodies and to our souls."

We have already considered Elisha at Dothan, ringed by apparently overwhelming enemy forces.

Yet if we, like his servant, had open spiritual eyes, we would see not only a world filled with evil spirits and powers—but also powerful angels with drawn swords, set for our defense.

At Dothan thousands of soldiers surrounded the city and intended to do Elisha harm. Yet he had peace. His servant, however, did not, and needed his eyes opened. We, who are troubled, confused, fearful, frustrated Christians need God to open our eyes this very moment. As Vance Havner says, "Our primary problem is not light, but sight. Light is of no value to a blind man. Reading books galore on the subject will not reveal the angels unless our eyes are touched by faith."

We must not get so busy counting demons that we forget the holy angels. Certainly we are up against a gigantic war machine. But we are encompassed by a heavenly host so powerful that we need not fear the warfare—the battle is the Lord's. We can boldly face Satan and his legions with all the confidence of the old captain who, when told that his outfit was completely surrounded, shouted, "Good, don't let any of them escape." If your valley is full of foes, raise your sights to the hills and see the holy angels of God arrayed for battle on your behalf.

When Abraham sent his eldest servant back to his blood relations to look for a bride for Isaac, he urged him to go confidently because of God's angel: "he shall send his angel before thee, . . . and prosper thy way" (Genesis 24:7, 40). Isaiah the prophet said, "In all their affliction he [the Lord] was afflicted, and the angel of his presence saved them" (63:9). God promised Moses in the midst of all his exasperations, "Mine angel shall go before thee" (Exodus 23:23). The Bible also says we may see the angels God has sent but fail to recognize them: "Be not forgetful to entertain strangers: for thereby some have entertained angels unawares" (Hebrews 13:2). Angels, whether noticed by men or not, are active in our twentieth-century world too. Are we aware of them?

It was a tragic night in a Chinese city. Bandits had surrounded the mission compound sheltering hundreds of women and children. On the previous night the missionary, Miss Monsen, had been put to bed with a bad attack of malaria, and now the tempter harassed her with questions: "What will you do when the looters come here? When firing begins on this compound, what about those promises you have been trusting?" In his book *1,000 New Illustrations*, Al Bryant records the result. Miss Monsen prayed, "Lord, I have been teaching these young people all these years that Thy promises are true, and if they fail now, my mouth shall be forever closed; I must go home."

Throughout the next night she was up, ministering to frightened refugees, encouraging them to pray and to trust God to deliver them. Though fearful things happened all around, the bandits left the mission compound untouched.

In the morning, people from three different neighborhood families asked Miss Monsen, "Who were those four people, three sitting and one standing, quietly watching from the top of your house all night long?" When she told them that no one had been on the housetop, they refused to believe her, saying, "We saw them with our own eyes!" She then told them that God still sent angels to guard His children in their hour of danger.

We have also noted the provision of angels. On occasion they have even given food, as we know from the life of Elijah, following his triumph over the priests of Baal. Fearful, tired and discouraged, "as he lay and slept under a juniper tree, behold, then an angel touched him, and said . . . Arise and eat" (1 Kings 19:5–7). God has promised, "Are they not all ministering spirits, sent forth to minister for them who shall be heirs of salvation?" (Hebrews 1:14). Need we think this provisioning by angels ceased thousands of years ago?

When I was visiting the American troops during the Korean War, I was told of a small group of American marines in the First Division who had been trapped up north. With the thermometer at twenty degrees below zero, they were close to freezing to death. And they had had nothing to eat for six days. Surrender to the enemy seemed their only hope of survival. But one of the men, a Christian, pointed out certain verses of Scripture and taught his comrades to sing a song of praise to God. Following this they heard a crashing noise and turned to see a wild boar rushing toward them. As they tried to jump out of his way, he suddenly stopped in his tracks. One of the soldiers raised his rifle to shoot, but before he could fire, the boar inexplicably toppled over. They rushed up to kill him only to find that he was already dead. That night they feasted on meat and began to regain their strength.

The next morning just as the sun was rising, they heard another noise. Their fear that an enemy patrol had discovered them suddenly vanished as they found themselves face to face with a South Korean who could speak English. He said, "I will show you out." He led them through the forest and mountains to safety behind their own lines. When they looked up to thank him, they found he had disappeared.

ANGELS IN JUDGMENT

As we continue to study how to gain the help of angels in our lives today, we need to look soberly once again at the relation of angels to judgment.

Just before fire and brimstone fell on Sodom because of its sins, the angel said, "For we will destroy this place . . . the LORD hath sent us to destroy it" (Genesis 19:13).

In Daniel 7:10 the Word of God says, "A fiery stream issued and came forth from before him . . . the judgment was set, and the books were opened." In scores of places in the Bible God tells us that He will use angels to execute His judgments on all those who have refused to obey His will by failing to receive Christ as Savior and Lord. As Jesus said, "The Son of man shall send forth his angels, and they shall gather out of his kingdom all things that offend, and them which do iniquity; and shall cast them into a furnace of fire: there shall be wailing and gnashing of teeth" (Matthew 13:41–42). Jesus also said, "It shall be more tolerable for Tyre and Sidon at the day of judgment, than for you" (Matthew 11:22). And again, "every idle word that men shall speak, they shall give account thereof in the day of judgment" (Matthew 12:36). "For there is nothing covered, that shall not be revealed; neither hid, that shall not be known" (Luke 12:2).

God is recording not only the words and actions but all the thoughts and intents of our hearts. Someday you and I will have to give an account, and our final destiny will be determined by whether we have received or rejected Jesus. Paul said that God would give "to you who are troubled rest with us, when the Lord Jesus shall be revealed from heaven with his mighty angels, in flaming fire taking vengeance on them that know not God and that obey not the gospel of our Lord Jesus Christ" (2 Thessalonians 1:7–8).

Justice demands that the books of life be balanced, but without a final judgment this would be impossible. Laws too are meaningless unless accompanied by a penalty for those who break them. Reason alone should tell us that there must come a time when God will call upon the Hitlers and the Idi Amins of the world for an accounting. Otherwise there is no justice in the universe.

Thousands of wicked men have lived evil lives and perpetrated their evil designs upon others without seeming to pay any penalty for their misdeeds in this life. However, the Bible says that a time will come when the crooked places will be made straight (Isaiah 45:2). In the great day of God's judgment men will call on Him for mercy, but it will be too late. In that day if men were to seek God, they would not be able to find Him. It would be too late. They could cry out for angels to deliver them, but it would be of no avail.

ANGELS REJOICE IN THE SALVATION OF SINNERS

While angels will play an important role in executing the judgment of God on those who refuse Jesus Christ as Savior and Lord, yet at the same time the Bible informs us that they also rejoice in the salvation of sinners. Jesus tells several striking stories in Luke 15. In the first, a man had a hundred sheep. When one was lost, he left the ninety-nine in the wilderness to seek it. When he found the sheep he slung it over his own shoulders and brought it back to the fold. At home he summoned all his friends, saying, "Rejoice with me: for I have found my sheep which was lost" (verse 6). Jesus said, "I say unto you, that likewise joy shall be in heaven over one sinner that repenteth, more than over ninety and nine just persons, which need no repentance" (verse 7).

His second story is that of a woman who lost a valuable silver coin. She looked everywhere. She swept her house carefully. At last when she recovered the coin she called all her friends and neighbors, saying, "Rejoice with me; for I have found the piece which I had lost" (verse 9). "Likewise, I say unto you, there is joy in the presence of the angels of God over one sinner that repenteth" (Luke 15:10).

In these two parables is not Jesus telling us that the angels of heaven have their eyes on every person? They know the spiritual condition of everybody on the face of the earth. Not only does God love you, but the angels love you too. They are eager for you to repent and turn to Christ for salvation before it is too late. They know the terrible dangers of hell that lie ahead. They want you to turn toward heaven, but they know that this is a decision that you and you alone will have to make.

A rich young ruler came running to kneel before Christ one day and asked, "Good Master, what shall I do that I may inherit eternal life?" (Mark 10:17). When Peter had preached his great sermon at Pentecost, Luke says the people were "pricked in their heart, and said unto Peter, . . . what shall we do?" (Acts 2:37). The African nobleman riding in the chariot across the desert talked with Philip the evangelist. Suddenly the nobleman stopped his chariot and said, "What doth hinder me to be baptized?" (Acts 8:36). At midnight the Philippian jailer asked Paul and Silas, "Sirs, what must I do to be saved?" (Acts 16:30). Modern man forever asks this same question. It is old but always new. It is just as relevant today as it was in the past.

Just what must you do to cause the angels to rejoice? How do you become reconciled to God? How do you repent of your sin? A simple question demands a simple answer. Jesus made everything so simple, and we have made it so complicated. He spoke to people in short sentences, using everyday words, illustrating His message with never-to-be-forgotten stories. He presented the message of God in such simplicity that many were amazed at what they heard. They could hardly believe their ears because the message was so simple.

In the Acts of the Apostles, the Philippian jailer asked the apostle Paul, "What must I do to be saved?" Paul gave him a very simple answer, "Believe on the Lord Jesus Christ, and thou shalt be saved" (Acts 16:30–31). This is so simple that millions stumble over it. The one and only way you can be converted is to believe on the Lord Jesus Christ as your own personal Lord and Savior. You don't have to straighten out your life first. You don't have to try to give up some habit that is keeping you from God. You have tried all that and failed many times. You can come "just as you are." The blind man came just as he was. The leper came just as he was. The thief on the cross came just as he was. You can come to Christ right now wherever you are and just as you are—and the angels of heaven will rejoice!

Some of the greatest and most precious words recorded in all of Scripture were spoken by Satan himself (not that he intended it to be so). In his discussion with God about Job, he said, "Hast not thou made an hedge about him, and about his house, and about all that he hath on every side? thou hast blessed the work of his hands, and his substance is increased in the land" (Job 1:10).

As I look back over my life, I remember the moment I came to

Jesus Christ as Savior and Lord. The angels rejoiced! Since then I have been in thousands of battles with Satan and his demons. As I yielded my will and committed myself totally to Christ—as I prayed and believed—I am convinced that God "put a hedge about me," a hedge of angels to protect me.

The Scripture says there is a time to be born and a time to die. And when my time to die comes an angel will be there to comfort me. He will give me peace and joy even at that most critical hour, and usher me into the presence of God, and I will dwell with the Lord forever. Thank God for the ministry of His blessed angels!

PEACE WITH GOD

CONTENTS

PART TWO: ADVANCING THE SOLUTION

PART THREE: APPLYING THE ANTIDOTE

Publisher's Note

Since its first publication almost fifty years ago, Dr. Billy Graham's *Peace with God* has blessed us with the voice of spiritual calm through decades of war, turmoil, and world change. While some of the statistics and world situations have changed since the book's most recent revision, the need for a clear message of calmness and peace in our lives has not. Thomas Nelson Publishers is honored and pleased, therefore, to join Dr. Graham in reaffirming his timeless biblical message by republishing this devotional classic, as revised in 1984, so that it may continue to bring you "peace with God through our Lord Jesus Christ."

Part One

Assessing the Situation

1

The Great Quest

And ye shall seek me, and find me, when ye shall search for me with all your heart.
Jeremiah 29:13

You started on the Great Quest the moment you were born. It was many years perhaps before you realized it, before it became apparent that you were constantly searching—searching for something you never had—searching for something that was more important than anything in life. Sometimes you have tried to forget about it. Sometimes you have attempted to lose yourself in other things so there could be time and thought for nothing but the business at hand. Sometimes you may even have felt that you were freed from the need to go on seeking this nameless thing. At moments you have almost been able to dismiss the quest completely. But always you have been caught up in it again—always you have had to come back to your search.

At the loneliest moments in your life you have looked at other men and women and wondered if they too were seeking something they couldn't describe but knew they wanted and needed. Some of them seemed to have found fulfillment in marriage and family living. Others went off to achieve fame and fortune in other parts of the world. Still others stayed at home and prospered, and looking at them you may have thought: *These people are not on the Great Quest. These people have found their way. They knew what they wanted and have been able to grasp it.*

It is only I who travel this path that leads to nowhere. It is only I who goes asking, seeking, stumbling along this dark and despairing road that has no guideposts.

THE CRY OF MANKIND

But you are not alone. All mankind is traveling with you, for all mankind is on this same quest. All humanity is seeking the answer to the confusion, the moral sickness, the spiritual emptiness that oppresses the world. All mankind is crying out for guidance, for comfort, for peace.

We are told that we live in the "age of anxiety." Historians point out that there have been few times in all history when man has been subject to so much fear and uncertainty. All the familiar props seem to have been swept away. We talk of peace but are confronted by war at every turn. We devise elaborate schemes for security but have not found it. We grasp at every passing straw and, even as we clutch, it disappears.

For generations we have been running like frightened children, first up one blind alley and then another. Each time we have told ourselves: "This path is the right one; this one will take us where we want to go." But each time we have been wrong.

The Path of Political Freedom

One of the first paths we chose was labeled "political freedom." Give everyone political freedom, we said, and the world will become a happy place. Let us select our own government leaders and we shall have the kind of government that will make life worth living. So we achieved political freedom, but we did not achieve our better world. Our daily newspapers give us reports of corruption in high places, of favoritism, of exploitation, of hypocrisy equal to and sometimes surpassing the despotism of ancient kings. Political freedom is a precious and important thing, but it alone cannot give us the kind of world we long for.

There was another very hopeful path marked "education," and many put their whole faith in it. Political freedom coupled with education will do the trick, they said, and we all rushed madly along the educational path. It seemed a bright, well-lighted, sensible path for a long time, and we traveled it with eager, expectant feet, but where has it led us? You know the answer. We are the most informed people in the history of civilization—and yet the most confused. Our high-school students know more about the physical laws of the universe than the greatest scientist in the days of Aristotle. But, though our heads are crammed with knowledge, our hearts are empty.

The brightest, most inviting path of all was the one marked "higher standards of living." Almost everyone felt he could trust this one to carry him automatically into that better and more joyful world. This was felt to be the sure route. This was the "press the button and you're there" route! This was the path that led through the beautiful full-color magazine advertisements, past all the shining new cars, past the gleaming rows of electric refrigerators and automatic washing machines, past all the fat chickens cooking in brand-new copper-bottomed pots. We knew we'd hit the jackpot this time! The other paths might have been false leads, but this time we had it!

All right, look around you right this minute. At this very moment in history you see in America a country that has political freedom to an extent undreamed of in many parts of the civilized world. You see the greatest and most far-reaching public education system that man has ever created, and we are eulogized at home and abroad for our high standard of living. "The American way of life" is what we like to call this fully electrified, fully automatic, chrome-plated economy of ours—but has it made us happy? Has it brought us the joy and satisfaction and the reason for living that we were seeking?

No. As we stand here feeling smug and proud that we have accomplished so much that generations before us only dreamed about; as we span our oceans in hours instead of months; as we produce miracle drugs that wipe out some of man's most dreaded diseases; as we erect buildings that make the Tower of Babel seem like an anthill; as we learn more and more of the mysterious secrets that lie in the depths of the sea and probe further and further into outer space, do we lose one iota of that empty feeling within us? Do all these modern wonders bring us a sense of fulfillment? Do they help to explain why we are here? Do they point out what we are supposed to learn?

Or does that awful hollow feeling persist? Does every further discovery of the magnitude of the universe comfort us or make us feel more alone and helpless than ever? Does the antidote for human fear and hatred and corruption lie in some laboratory test tube or in an astronomer's telescope?

THE SEDUCTION OF SCIENCE

We cannot deny that science has given man many things he thought he wanted. But this same science has now presented us the most dreaded gift ever bestowed upon humanity. The life and future of every living being on this planet is affected by this gift of science. It stands like a somber shadow behind our waking thoughts. It stalks like a specter of horror through our children's dreams. We pretend it isn't there. We try to pretend that we haven't received this gift, that it's all a joke, and that some morning we'll wake up and find that we haven't conquered outer space and that nuclear weaponry has never been perfected—but our morning newspaper tells us a different story.

There are other paths, of course, and many are traveling them this very moment. There are the paths of fame and fortune, of pleasure and power. None of them leads anywhere but deeper into the mire. We are ensnared in the web of our own thinking, trapped so cleverly and so completely that we can no longer see either the cause or the cure of the disease that is inflicting such deadly pain.

If it is true that "for every illness there is a cure," then we must make haste to find it. The sand in civilization's hourglass is rapidly falling away, and if there is a path that leads to the light, if there is a way back to spiritual health, we must not lose an hour!

THE SEARCH FOR SOLUTIONS

Many are floundering in this time of crisis and finding that their efforts are leading them not up but only further down into the pit.

The suicide rate has skyrocketed in the '80s. For children ages ten to fourteen the suicide rate has tripled in the last ten years. *Leadership* magazine estimates that half a million people attempt suicide annually—and fifty thousand succeed. In 1981 more people died by suicide than by homicide.

Last year thousands of Americans, many of them teenagers, who couldn't find even the wrong answers took their own lives in preference to wandering any further in this man-made jungle we call civilization.

Over the past couple of decades our divorce rates have soared, even within the church, with one out of two marriages ending in divorce. The divorce rate has increased 100 percent since 1900!

We spend a fortune to "adopt" cute Cabbage Patch dolls, while our children are caught up in child abuse or subjected to the horrible atrocities of "kiddy-porn." We hear about abortion on demand, surrogate motherhood, sperm banks, and so on. Our families are riddled with all kinds of abuses and aberrations.

So "Where are we?" you ask. "Where are we now and where are we going?" Let me tell you where we are and what we are. We are a nation of empty people. Our heads are crammed full of knowledge, but within our souls is a spiritual vacuum.

We complained in the past that the youth of this country had lost its drive, its push, its willingness to work and to get ahead. Every day I heard parents say that they didn't understand why their children didn't want to work but just wanted everything handed to them. Parents didn't seem to realize that their well-educated, carefully brought-up children were actually empty inside. They weren't filled with the spirit that makes work a joy. They weren't filled with the determination that makes pushing ahead a pleasure. And why were they so empty? Because they didn't know where they had come from, why they were here, or where they were going!

Today our young people are asking for direction and perspective. They are looking for models to follow, for patterns of purpose. They are like rows of beautiful new automobiles, perfect in every detail but with no gasoline in the tanks. The exteriors are fine, but there's nothing inside to give them power. And so they just sit and rust—with boredom.

THE BREADTH OF BOREDOM

America is said to have the highest per capita boredom of any spot on earth! We know that because we have the greatest variety and greatest number of artificial amusements of any country. People have become so empty that they can't even entertain themselves. They have to pay other people to amuse them, to make them laugh, to try to make them feel warm and happy and comfortable for a few minutes, to try to lose that awful, frightening, hollow feeling—that terrible, dreaded feeling of being lost and alone.

You may think that boredom is a minor matter. Everyone gets bored sometimes; it's only natural. But let me tell you something about boredom and this dangerous apathy that is creeping over the land and over the minds and hearts of the people. Man is the only one of God's creatures who is capable of being bored, although I've seen animals in a zoo that look very bored! No other living thing except man can ever be bored with itself or its surroundings. This is very significant, for the Creator never does anything without a purpose, and if He gave man the capacity for boredom, He did it for a purpose.

Boredom is one of the sure ways to measure your own inner emptiness! It's as accurate as a thermometer for telling just how hollow your inner spirit really is. The person who is thoroughly bored is living and working in a vacuum. His inner self is a vacuum, and there is nothing that nature resents more than a vacuum. It is one of the unfailing rules of this universe that all vacuums must be filled, and filled immediately.

A Nation of Empty People

We do not have to go back to ancient times to see what happens to a nation of empty people. We need look no further than the recent history of Germany or Italy to see with what deadly speed nature fills up the vacuums that occur within us. Nazism in Germany and fascism in Italy could find no place in the heart and soul of a person who was filled with the Spirit of God, but false ideologies flood with the greatest ease into the minds and hearts of those who are empty and waiting. Nature abhors a vacuum, but it is up to us as individuals to determine with what our inner vacuums shall be filled.

So that is where we stand today—nations of empty people. We have tried to fill ourselves with science and education, with better living and pleasure, with the many other things we thought we wanted. We have increasingly decadent capitalism at one extreme, and godless communism at the other. But we are still empty. Why are we empty? Because the Creator made us for Himself; and we shall never find completeness and fullness apart from fellowship with Him.

In a recent interview in the *Presbyterian Journal* (2 November 1983) the eminent Catholic columnist Michael Novak says of our situation, "Socialism is a system for saints, . . . democratic capitalism . . . is a system for sinners." That's why he feels socialism won't work in this world.

Jesus told us long ago that "Man shall not live by bread alone" (Luke 4:4), but we have paid no heed. We have tried to do just that.

We cannot stand the terrible emptiness of ourselves; we cannot look at the lonely, desolate road that lies ahead. We are desperately weary of the hatred and greed and lust that we know are within us, but we are helpless to be rid of them and be filled with something better.

"Time and tide wait for no man," said Sir Walter Scott. The tools of total annihilation have been placed within our reach. We cannot scurry up any more false paths, we cannot explore any more unknown roads, we cannot afford to be trapped in any more blind alleys. We don't have that much time! Our generation has accomplished what other generations only tried to do—or dreamed of doing in their most insane moments of power and ruthlessness! We have achieved the weapons of total destruction. We are witnessing the climax of man's madness—the impending nuclear holocaust.

How the demons must have laughed as some of the most brilliant men on earth worked furiously for years to achieve this horror! The atom cleaved! Divide and conquer! Split apart, destroy, shatter, crush, crumble! The great deceiver has done his work, and men have been eager to aid him. We see before us Satan's masterpiece, his clever counterfeit of the cloven tongues of divine fire. For this satanic fire and the pentecostal flames both fall from above, both are cloven, both illuminate, both instantly transform everything they touch—but with such a difference. The difference of heaven and hell!

A Topsy-Turvy World

We are living in a topsy-turvy world, where all is confusion. But you may be sure that it is confusion with a plan—Satan's plan! The Bible tells us that Satan is the great deceiver and he has devoted himself to the cause of our great self-deception and to the deceptions that lie between nations all over this world. He has led us to believe that things were getting better, when they are really getting worse.

We all recognize that the world has changed radically since the beginning of this century. We are aware of its increased tempo, of the spirit of revolution that is sweeping away the established landmarks and traditions, of the speed with which language, fashions, customs, housing, and our ways of living and thinking are being altered and changed.

Only a few years ago children were delighted at the prospect of a trip to the train station to watch the trains come in. Today they are blasé about the space shuttle. How many know when the next shuttle flight takes off, or who will be aboard? We who once marveled at the telegraph now take the far greater miracle of television for granted. Not so long ago many of man's physical diseases were termed hopeless and incurable. Today, we have drugs so effective that many age-old diseases are disappearing. We have accomplished much, of that there is no doubt.

But with all this progress, man has not solved the basic problem of the human race. We can build the highest buildings, the fastest planes, the longest bridges. We have successfully probed the far reaches of space and conquered the unknown. But we still can't govern ourselves or live together in equality and peace!

We may create great new schools of art and music, we may discover newer and better vitamins, but there is nothing new about our troubles. They are the same old ones that man has always had, only they seem magnified and more abundant. They may come upon us in new ways; they may seem to give sharper pain and deeper anguish; but fundamentally we are facing the same temptations, the same trials, the same testings that have always confronted mankind.

Since that tragic moment in the Garden of Eden, when man gave up God's will for his own will, man has been plagued by the same problems. Their cause is stated in the third chapter of Genesis. The terrible conditions that produced them are related in the first chapter of Romans. And the gospel of Jesus Christ gives us their remedy.

It is man's depraved and sinful nature that fills him with hate, envy, greed, and jealousy. The curse of sin is upon his body, and he is forever haunted by the fear of death. His inventive genius has enabled him to change everything but himself. For man, in spite of the loudly acclaimed "progress" of our times, remains just as he was in the beginning.

SIN IS STILL THE SAME

Sin, too, has remained unchanged, although man has done his best to alter it. We've tried to dress it up with other names. We've put new labels on the same old bottle of poison. We've tried to white-wash the rotting building and pretend it is sound (or new).

We've tried calling sin "errors" or "mistakes" or "poor judgment," but sin itself has stayed the same. No matter how we try to salve our conscience, we've known all along that men are still sinners; and the results of sin are still disease, disappointment, disillusionment, despair, and death.

Sorrow hasn't changed, either. It began when Adam and Eve looked with broken hearts upon the lifeless body of their murdered son Abel and knew the crushing weight of grief. It has gone on, until today sorrow is the universal language of man. No one escapes it; everyone experiences it. It even seemed to one of Job's comforters that it was the aim of life, for he said, "Yet man is born unto trouble, as the sparks fly upward" (Job 5:7).

Death is also still the same. Men have tried to change its appearance. We have changed the word "undertaker" to "mortician." We place bodies in "caskets" now instead of "coffins." We have "funeral homes" instead of "undertaking parlors" and "memorial parks" instead of "graveyards." We try to soften the starkness of the last rites, but regardless of what we call it—or how lifelike we make the corpse through makeup—the cold, hard, cruel reality of death has not changed throughout all of man's history. A friend, struggling with terminal cancer, recently wrote: "It has dawned on me that cancer is not terminal—life is!"

Three facts constitute the true story of man: his past is filled with sin; his present is overflowing with sorrow; and the certainty of death faces him in the future.

The Bible says, "It is appointed unto men once to die" (Hebrews 9:27), and to the average person this seems a stark and hopeless situation. Hundreds of philosophies and scores of religions have been invented by men in their efforts to circumvent the Word of God. Modern philosophers and psychologists are still trying to make it appear that there is some way out other than the path of Jesus. But man has tried them all and none of them leads anywhere but down.

Christ came to give us the answers to the three enduring problems of sin, sorrow, and death. It is Jesus Christ, and He alone, who is also enduring and unchanging, "the same yesterday, and today and forever" (Hebrews 13:8). As the hymn writer Henry F. Lyte wrote: "Change and decay in all around I see; O Thou who changest not, abide with me."

All other things may change, but Christ remains unchangeable. In the restless sea of human passions, Christ stands steadfast and calm, ready to welcome all who will turn to Him and accept the blessings of safety and peace. For we are living in an age of grace, in which God promises that whosoever will may come and receive His Son. But this period of grace will not go on indefinitely. We are even now living on borrowed time.

2

The Indestructible Bible

Heaven and earth shall pass away,
but my words shall not pass away.
Matthew 24:35

Time is running out. The seconds are ticking away toward midnight. The human race is about to take the fatal plunge. Have we just been placed here by some unknown creator or force without any clue as to where we came from, why we are here, and where we are going? Which way shall we turn? Is there any authority left? Is there a path we can follow? Is there any light penetrating the inky darkness? Can we find a code book that will give us the key to our dilemmas? Is there any source of authority to which we can turn?

The answer to the first question is no. The answer to all the rest is yes. We do have a code book. We do have a key. We do have authoritative source material. It is found in the ancient and historic Book we call the Bible. This Book has come down to us through the ages. It has passed through so many hands, appeared in so many forms—and survived attack of every kind. Neither barbaric vandalism nor civilized scholarship has touched it. Neither the burning of fire nor the laughter of skepticism has accomplished its annihilation. Through the many dark ages of man, its glorious promises have survived unchanged. It is interesting to note that when Bible reading was outlawed in our public schools, it was required reading in the Catholic schools of Communist Poland.

The British and Foreign Bible Society was on Jerusalem Street, one of the main streets of Old Warsaw in World War II. When the Germans began bombing the city, the wife of the director went to the storeroom and carried some two thousand Bibles down to the basement. She was trapped by the bombing and later captured by the Germans and put in a prison camp. She managed to escape and after the war was over was able to get to those two thousand Bibles and distribute them to people in need. Warsaw was flattened, but on Jerusalem Street one wall of the old British and Foreign Bible Society remained standing. On it were these words, painted in large letters: "heaven and earth shall pass away, but my words shall not pass away."

Now, as we approach what appears to be another decisive hour in world history, let us reexamine this indestructible Book of wisdom and prophecy; let us find out why this particular volume has endured and been man's unfailing source of faith and spiritual strength.

The Bible Is More Than Just Great Literature

There are those who regard the Bible principally as the history of Israel. Others admit that it sets forth the soundest ethics ever enunciated. But these things, important as they are, are only incidental to the real theme of the Bible, which is the story of God's redemption as it exists in Jesus Christ. In an editorial which appeared June 30, 1983, the *International Herald Tribune* recommended that the Bible should be read as literature because it is "the English language at its best." Those who read the Scriptures as magnificent literature, breathtaking poetry, or history and overlook the story of salvation miss the Bible's real meaning and message.

God caused the Bible to be written for the express purpose of revealing to man God's plan for his redemption. God caused this Book to be written that He might make His everlasting laws clear to His children and that they might have His great wisdom to guide them and His great love to comfort them as they make their way through life. For without the Bible, this world would indeed be a dark and frightening place, without signpost or beacon.

The Bible easily qualifies as the only Book in which is God's revelation. There are many bibles of different religions; there is the Muslim Koran, the Buddhist Canon of Sacred Scripture, the Zoroastrian Zend-Avesta, and the Brahman Vedas. All of these have been made accessible to us by reliable translations. Anyone can read them, comparing them with the Bible, and judge for themselves. It is soon discovered that all these non-Christian bibles have parts of truth in them, but they are all developments ultimately in the wrong direction. They all begin with some flashes of true light and end in utter darkness. Even the most casual observer soon discovers that the Bible is radically different. It is the only Book that offers man a redemption and points the way out of his dilemmas. It is our one sure guide in an unsure world.

Sixteen hundred years were needed to complete the writing of the Bible. It is the work of more than thirty authors, each of whom acted as a scribe of God. Those men, many of whom lived generations apart, did not set down merely what they thought or hoped. They acted as channels for God's revelation; they wrote as He directed them; under His divine inspiration they were able to see the great and enduring truths and to record them that other men might see and know them too.

During these sixteen hundred years, the sixty-six books of the Bible were written by men of different languages—living in different times—and in different countries, but the message they wrote was one. God spoke to each man in his own language—in his own time, but His message basically in each case was the same. When the great scholars gathered together the many ancient manuscripts written in Hebrew, Aramaic, and Greek and translated them into a single modern tongue, they found that God's promises remained unchanged; His great message to man had not varied. As we read these ageless words today, we find that the rules of conduct set forth by the ancient scribes are as fresh and meaningful to this generation as they were to the people of Jesus' time. John Ruskin said: "The Bible is the one Book to which any thoughtful man may go with any honest question of life or destiny and find the answer of God by honest searching."

THE WORLD'S BESTSELLER!

It is small wonder, then, that the Bible has always been the world's bestseller! No other book can touch its profound wisdom, its poetic beauty, or the accuracy of its history and prophecy.

Its critics, who claimed it to be filled with forgery, fiction, and unfulfilled promises, are finding that the difficulties lie with themselves and not the Bible. Greater and more careful scholarship has shown that apparent contradictions were caused by incorrect translations rather than divine inconsistencies. It was man and not the Bible who needed correcting. Someone has said, "The Bible does not have to be rewritten, but reread."

And yet in many homes and among so-called educated people it has become fashionable to joke about the Bible and to regard it more as a dust catcher than as the living Word of God. When asked by her minister if she knew what was in the Bible, one little girl proudly replied that she knew everything that was in it and proceeded to list the picture of her sister's boyfriend, the coupon for Mother's favorite hand lotion, a lock of baby brother's hair, and the ticket for Pa's watch! That was all she knew about the family Bible. Too many families have used the Bible as a safe storage place for old letters and pressed flowers and have overlooked entirely the help and assurance that God intended this Book to give them.

This attitude is changing now, and changing fast! Life is being stripped of its artificialities, its meaningless trimmings. The false promises that man has made to man are standing forth now as the glaring errors they are. As we cast our frightened eyes around for something that is real and true and enduring, we are turning once more to this ancient Book that has given consolation, comfort, and salvation to millions in the centuries past. My wife, Ruth, once said, "If our children have the background of a godly, happy home and this unshakeable faith that the Bible is indeed the

Word of God, they will have a foundation that the forces of hell cannot shake." I thank God for her godly influence in the lives of our children.

Yes, people are "discovering" the Bible again! They are dusting off their old copies or buying new ones. They are finding that the familiar but almost forgotten phrases ring with a current meaning that makes them seem to have been written only yesterday. This is because the Bible embodies all the knowledge man needs to fill the longing of his soul and solve all his problems. It is the blueprint of the Master Architect, and only by following its directions can we build the life we are seeking.

Here in America we have another great document that we value and respect. It was written some two hundred years ago by a number of men who labored long and debated even longer over its many provisions and finally sent it to the thirteen federated states for ratification. The men who framed our Constitution knew they were writing the basic document for a government of free men; they recognized that men could live as free and independent beings only if each one knew and understood the law. They were to know their rights, their privileges, and their limitations. They were to stand as equals before the court of law and few judges could be unfair, for the judge, too, was bound by the same law and required to try each case accordingly.

THE TRUTH SHALL SET US FREE!

While the rest of the world watched this great human experiment, men found that if they knew the law and lived according to it, they could, in truth, be free! A man could know just where he stood. He had his constitutional rights, and he also had his constitutional responsibilities. If he neglected one, the other would suffer—as so many negligent voters who came later were to discover when they found themselves saddled with governmental restrictions they didn't like!

Just as America has grown and prospered within the framework of our Constitution, so Christianity has flourished and spread according to the laws set forth in the Bible. Just as the Constitution was intended to apply equally to all men living under it, without special favor or interpretation, so the Bible stands as the supreme Constitution for all mankind, its laws applying equally to all who live under its domain, without exception or special interpretation.

As the Constitution is the highest law of the land, so the Bible is the highest law of God. It is in the Bible that God sets forth His spiritual laws. It is in the Bible that God makes His enduring promises. It is in the Bible that God reveals the plan of redemption for the human race.

In the wonders of nature we see God's laws in operation. Who has not looked up at the stars on a cloudless night and marveled in silent awe at the glory of God's handiwork? Even our astronauts have lauded the Lord as Creator of the vastness of space and the intricacies of our universe that we are just now beginning to explore. If we could not depend on His laws, we could not make these excursions into space. Who has not felt his heart lifted in the spring of the year, as he sees all creation bursting with new life and vigor? In the beauty and abundance around us we see the magnitude of God's power and the infinite detail of His planning, but nature tells us nothing of God's love or God's grace. We do not find the promise of our personal salvation in nature.

Conscience tells us in our innermost being of the presence of God and of the moral difference between good and evil, but this is a fragmentary message, in no way as distinct and comprehensive as the lessons of the Bible. It is only in its pages that we find the clear and unmistakable message upon which all true Christianity is based.

The laws of our land find their genesis in the Ten Commandments. Sir William Blackstone, the great English jurist, wrote: "The Bible has always been regarded as part of the Common Law of England."

Christianity finds all its doctrines stated in the Bible, and Christianity denies no part, nor attempts to add anything to the Word of God. While the Constitution of the United States may be amended from time to time, no amendment is ever necessary for the Bible. We truly believe that the men who wrote the Bible were guided by the Holy Spirit, both in the thoughts they expressed and in their choice of words. As Peter said, "For the prophecy came not in old time by the will of man: but holy men of God spake as they were moved by the Holy Ghost" (2 Peter 1:21).

Paul tells us that "All scripture is given by inspiration of God, and is profitable for doctrine, for reproof, for correction, for instruction in righteousness: That the man of God may be perfect, thoroughly furnished unto all good works" (2 Timothy 3:16–17).

In setting down their forthright messages, biblical scribes have never attempted to gloss over the realities of life. The sins of the great and small are freely admitted, the weaknesses of human nature are acknowledged, and life in biblical times is recorded as it was lived. The startling thing is that the lives and motivations of these people who lived so long ago have such a modern flavor! As we read, the pages seem like mirrors held up before our own minds and hearts, reflecting our own prides and prejudices, our own failures and humiliations, our own sins and sorrows.

Truth is timeless. Truth does not differ from one age to another, from one people to another, from one geographical location to another. Men's ideas may differ, men's customs may change, men's moral codes may vary, but the great all-prevailing Truth stands for time and eternity.

The message of Jesus Christ, our Savior, is the story of the Bible—it is the story of salvation. Profound students of the Bible have traced the story of Jesus Christ from the beginning of the Old Testament, for He is the true theme of the Old as well as the New Testament.

The fact of Jesus Christ is the eternal message of the Bible. It is the story of life, peace, eternity, and heaven. The Bible has no hidden purpose. It has no need for special interpretation. It has a single, clear, bold message for every living being—the message of Christ and His offer of peace with God.

One day upon a mountain near Capernaum Jesus sat with His disciples. They gathered before Him—perhaps Peter on one side and John on the other. Jesus may have looked quietly and tenderly at each of these devoted disciples, looked at them the way a loving parent looks at the members of his family—loving each child separately, loving each one for a special reason, loving them in such a way that each child feels singled out and individually embraced. That is how Jesus must have loved His disciples.

The little group must have become very reverent under His serene and loving gaze. They must have become very still within themselves with the feeling that something momentous was about to be said, something they must remember, something they must be able to transmit to others all over the world who were not privileged, as they were, to hear these words from the Master's own lips.

For there, on the mountain, standing perhaps under the silvery gray-green leaves of an olive tree, Jesus preached the greatest sermon that human ears have ever heard. He explained the essence of Christian living. When He was through and a holy hush had settled on His wide-eyed listeners, they "were astonished at his doctrine: for he taught them as one having authority, and not as the scribes" (Matthew 7:28, 29).

Indeed He did teach with authority, the authority of God Himself; and the rules He set forth were God's own rules, the ones that every Christian with the hope of salvation in his heart must follow.

YOU AND THE BIBLE

If you do not have a Bible in your home, go out and get one now—get the one that suits you best, get the size that is most comfortable for you to handle, get the kind of type that is most pleasant for you to read, and then settle down and find out for yourself why this one Book has endured. Don't be afraid to invest in the best Bible you can afford, for that is what you are making: an investment. We spend our money for expensive clothing that perishes but hesitate to buy the best in Bibles, which is an investment in eternity. Find out for yourself why it answers every human need, why it supplies the faith and strength that keeps humanity marching forward.

If you and the Bible have had a long absence from each other, it might be good for you to renew your acquaintance by reading again the Gospel of John. While this is considered one of the most profound books in the Bible, it is also the clearest and most readily understood. It was written for the very purpose of showing the how and the why of man's salvation, so that the questions of the mind as well as the gropings of the heart might be satisfied.

After reading the Book of John, you might acquaint yourself with the gospel as taught by Mark, Luke, and Matthew, noting how these men of widely different personalities and writing styles set forth the eternal story of redemption through Jesus. You will become aware of the powerful, universal truth that underlies all gospel teaching and be impressed anew with what the biblical writer meant when he said, "Jesus Christ is the same yesterday, and today, and forever" (Hebrews 13:8).

When you have read each of the Gospels individually, start at the beginning of the New Testament and read straight through all the books in order. When you have done that, you will have developed such a taste for Bible reading, you will have found it such a fountain of inspiration, such a practical counselor and guide, such a treasure chest of sound advice, that you will make Bible reading a part of your daily life.

A knowledge of the Bible is essential to a rich and meaningful life. The words of this Book have a way of filling in the missing pieces, of bridging the gaps, of turning the tarnished colors of our life to jewel-like brilliance. Learn to take your every problem to the Bible. Within its pages you will find the correct answer.

Most of all, the Bible is a revelation of the nature of God. The philosophers of the centuries have struggled with the problem of a Supreme Being. Who is He? What is He? Where is He? If there is such a Person, is He interested in me? If so, how can I know Him? These and a thousand other questions about God are revealed in this Holy Book we call the Bible.

A Christian once asked, "Do you know a book that you are willing to put under your head for a pillow when you are dying? Very well," Joseph Cook went on, "that is the Book you want to study when you are living. There is only one such Book in the world!"

3

What Is God Like?

Canst thou by searching find out God?
Job 11:7

Who is God? What is He like? How can we be sure He exists? When did He begin? Can we know Him?

Everyone has asked these questions either aloud or to himself, for we cannot look at the world around us and not wonder about its creation. We are daily faced with the miracle of life and the mystery of death, of the glory of flowering trees, the magnificence of the star-filled sky, the magnitude of mountains and of sea. Who made all this? Who conceived the law of gravity by which everything is held in its proper place? Who ordered the day and the night and the regular procession of the seasons? What about the infinity of the universe? Can we honestly believe (as someone has written), "This is all there is or was or ever will be"?

The only possible answer is that all these things and many more are the work of a Supreme Creator. As a watch must have a designer, so our precise universe has a Great Designer. We call Him God. His is a name with whom the whole human race is familiar. From earliest childhood we have breathed His name. The Bible declares that the God we talk about, the God we sing about, the God "from whom all blessings flow!" is the God who created this world and placed us in it. Our exploration of space would be impossible in a universe ungoverned by the laws of God.

No less a wise man than Benjamin Franklin said, "I have lived a long time and the longer I live the more convincing proofs I see that God governs in the affairs of men." Another wise man, Blaise Pascal, wrote: "If a man is not made for God, why is he happy only in God? If man is made for God, why is he opposed to God?" This is our dilemma.

But who is He? you ask. Where is He? We know that He exists. We call upon Him in our hours of greatest difficulty and trial. Some try to let the thought of Him fill every waking moment. Others say they don't believe in Him, that He doesn't exist. And still others say, "Explain Him to me and maybe I'll accept God."

For those who, at this crucial point in world history, are wondering what God is like,? it has been simply stated: God is like Jesus Christ. Just as Jesus came to make God visible to mankind and to become our Redeemer, even so, on His return to Heaven, He sent the Holy Spirit to indwell believers and enable them to live so as to make Christ visible to an unbelieving world.

If that is how you feel—if all your life you have been hearing about God and talking about God but waiting for someone to explain God to you before you could put your faith in Him and

Him alone—let us see just how concrete a description the Bible can give us.

What Is God Like?

At this crucial point in world history, everyone should be seeking an answer to the question, what is God like?

Everyone should ask it, and everyone should make very sure of the answer. Everyone should know beyond a shadow of a doubt exactly who God is and what He is capable of accomplishing. The Bible says, "Because that which may be known of God is manifest in them; for God hath shewed it unto them" (Romans 1:19).

It is the absence of the knowledge of God and man's refusal to obey Him that lie at the root of every problem that besets us. It is man's confusion about God's plan that has the world in chaos. It is man's unwillingness to learn and to obey God's laws that has laid such a heavy burden on our souls. So let us learn all that we can about Him.

Where shall we go for this knowledge? Who among us can tell us the truth? Are we not all finite creatures here together? Has God designated any one person here on earth to speak with final authority about Him? No—the one Man who could do that lived two thousand years ago, and we crucified Him! How then, are we to find out?

We can ask the learned scholars, and they may tell us that God is the expression of everything in nature and life, that all living beings are one with God, that life itself is an expression of His Divine Being. They will tell you that you can see God in the tiniest drop of water and in the great arch of the sky above.

Ask a philosopher, and he will tell you that God is the original and immutable force behind all creation, that He is the Master Dynamo who keeps all the worlds in motion—that He is the Power without beginning or end. The philosopher will say that every bit of life and beauty we see is a manifestation of this power that flows in an unending current out from the Dynamo and back again.

Ask still further and you may be told that God is absolute, that He is All in All, and that no one can possibly know any more about Him. There are many differing definitions for God. Dr. Akbar Haqq says that originally all people were monotheistic in their concept of God. Every country, every race of people, every family, every individual has tried to explain the Great Being behind the universe. Men of all ages have tried to discover the Creator whose work they saw, but whom they did not know. Which of these varied explanations is right? Which of these many theories are we to accept? By which of these self-appointed authorities are we to be guided?

As we have already seen in our previous chapter, God has revealed Himself in the Book called the Bible. In the Bible we have a revelation of God—and based on it our minds can be satisfied and our hearts filled. We can rest assured that we have the correct answer, that we are on our way to knowing and understanding the true nature of God.

God reveals Himself in hundreds of ways in the Bible, and if we read the Bible as carefully and as regularly as we read the daily papers, we would be as familiar with and as well informed about

God as we are about our favorite player's batting average during baseball season!

As a diamond has many facets, so there are innumerable aspects of God's revelation of Himself which would take volumes to fill. Suffice it to say, with our limited space we can cover four aspects of God's revelation of Himself that seem to be the most significant and which we should carry with us always.

God as Spirit

First, the Bible declares God to be *Spirit*. Jesus talking to the woman at the Well of Sychar made this straightforward statement about God: "God is Spirit" (John 4:24).

What do you think of when you hear the word *spirit*? What mental image does it bring to your mind? Do you think of a wisp of vapor drifting across the sky? Does *spirit* mean the sort of thing that frightens children on Halloween? Is *spirit* just a formless nothingness to you? Do you think that was what Jesus meant when He said, "God is Spirit"?

To discover what "spirit" really is, and what Jesus meant when He used that particular word, we must turn again in the Bible to the scene where Christ after His resurrection says: "Handle me, and see; for a spirit hath not flesh and bones, as ye see me have" (Luke 24:39). Therefore we can be sure that spirit is *without* body. It is the *opposite* of body. Yet it has being and power. This is difficult for us to understand because we are trying to understand it with our limited, finite minds.

As human beings deprived of the unlimited vision that God

originally intended His creatures to have, we cannot comprehend the glory and the magnitude of the Spirit that lies so far outside ourselves. When we hear the word *spirit*, we immediately try to reduce it to our puny size, to make it fit within the scope of our small minds. It is like trying to explain the sweep and majesty and awe-inspiring grandeur of the ocean to a person who has never seen a body of water larger than a mud puddle! How can such a person envision the boundless sea? How can such a person, looking into a shallow, murky pool, fathom the bottomless depths, the mysterious life, the surging power, the ceaseless roll, the terrible ruthlessness of ocean storm or the all-surpassing beauty of ocean calm? How could anyone who had looked only into a mud puddle know what you were talking about? What words could you use to describe the mighty sea convincingly? How could you make a person believe that such a wonder really exists?

How infinitely more difficult it is for us to grasp what Jesus meant when He said, "God is Spirit." Jesus knew! His mind was not limited as our minds are limited. His eyes were not focused on the mud puddle of life. He knew full well the borderless reaches of the Spirit, and He came to try to give us some understanding of its wonders, its comfort, and its peace.

We do know that the spirit is not something bound in a body. Spirit is not wearable as a body. Spirit is not changeable as a body. The Bible declares that God is a Spirit—that He is not limited to body; He is not limited to shape; He is not limited to boundaries or bonds; He is absolutely immeasurable and undiscernible by eyes that can see only physical things. The Bible tells us that because He has no such limitations, He can be everywhere at once—that He can hear all, see all, and know all.

We can't do any of that, and so we try to limit God as we are limited. We try to deny God the power to do things we can't do. We try to say that because we can't be everywhere at once, God can't be, either! We are rather like the person who, having heard about the ocean, finally makes his way to the beach one day and, going down to the edge of the water, scoops up a few drops and holds them in his hands.

"Ah," he exclaims, "at last I have made the ocean mine! I hold the ocean in my hands. I possess it!" True, he does have a part of the ocean, but at the same moment other people on a thousand other shores may be reaching down and claiming a few drops of the ocean for themselves. The world's millions could come down to the beach and reach out their hands to be filled with sea water. They could each take as much as they wanted, as much as they needed—and still the ocean would remain unchanged. Its mightiness and power would be the same; the life in its unfathomable depths would continue unaltered, although it had supplied the needs of every single person standing with outstretched hands along its many shores.

So it is with God. He can be everywhere at once, heeding the prayers of all who call out in the name of Christ; performing the mighty miracles that keep the stars in their places and the plants bursting up through the earth and the fish swimming in the sea. There is no limit to God. There is no limit to His wisdom. There is no limit to His power. There is no limit to His love. There is no limit to His mercy.

If you have been trying to limit God—stop it! Don't try to confine Him or His works to any single place or sphere. You wouldn't try to limit the ocean. You cannot limit the universe. You wouldn't be bold enough to try to change the course of the moon, or to stop the earth as it turns on its axis! How everlastingly more foolish it is to try to limit the God who created and controls all these wonders!

I am eternally grateful to my mother for many things, but one of the most enduring blessings she brought into my life was to teach me in the catechism at the age of ten that "God is a Spirit, infinite, eternal, and unchangeable in His being, wisdom, power, holiness, justice, goodness, and truth." That definition of God has been with me all my life, and when a man knows in his heart that God is an infinite, eternal, and unchangeable Spirit, it helps to overcome the temptation to limit Him. It helps to overcome all doubt about His ability to accomplish things that we can't do ourselves!

Some doubt that the Bible is the true Word of God because they are unwilling to ascribe to God anything they cannot themselves achieve. If you have any uncertainty about the inspiration of the Bible, go back and look at it again. Look at it in the light of a person who has been staring at a mud puddle all his life and who is confronted for the first time by a view of the ocean! Perhaps you are only now catching your first glimpse of God's unlimited power. Perhaps you are only now beginning to understand Him for what He actually is. For if God is the Spirit that Jesus declares Him to be, there is no problem of providence, there is no problem of His sovereignty in the affairs of men, there is no problem of His inspiration of the men who wrote the Bible.

Everything fits into place once you understand who and what God really is.

God Is a Person

Second, the Bible reveals Him as a *Person.* All through the Bible it says, "God loves," "God says," "God does." Everything that we attribute to a person is attributed to God. A person is one who feels, thinks, wishes, desires, and has all the expressions of personality.

Here on earth we confine personality to the body. Our finite minds cannot envision personality that is not manifested through flesh and bones. We know that our own personalities will not always be clothed in the bodies they now inhabit. We know that at the moment of death our personalities will leave our bodies and go on to the destinations that await them. We know all this—yet it is difficult for us to accept it.

What a revelation if we could all realize that personality does not have to be identified with a physical being. God is not bound by a body, yet He is a Person. He feels, He thinks, He loves, He forgives, He sympathizes with the problems and sorrows that we face.

God is Holy and Righteous

Third, the Bible states that God is not only a Spirit and a Person, but God is also a *Holy and Righteous Being.* From Genesis to Revelation, God reveals Himself as a Holy God. He is utterly perfect and absolute in every detail. He is too holy to tolerate sinful man, too holy to endure sinful living.

If we could envision the true picture of His majestic righteousness, what a difference it would make in the way we live as individuals and as nations! If we could but realize the tremendous gulf that separates unrighteous man from God's perfect righteousness! The Scripture declares Him to be the Light in whom there is no darkness at all—the one Supreme Being without flaw or blemish.

Here again is a difficult concept for imperfect man to understand. We, whose faults and weaknesses are everywhere apparent, can scarcely imagine the overwhelming holiness of God—but we must recognize it if we are to understand and benefit from the Bible.

The chasm that separates imperfect man from perfect God is emphasized all through the Scriptures. We see it in the division of the Old Testament tabernacle and the New Testament temple into the Holy and Most Holy places. It is pointed out in the prescribed offering that must be brought if a sinner would approach God. It is underscored by a special priesthood to mediate between God and the people. It is emphasized by the laws concerning impurity in the book of Leviticus. We see it in the many feasts of Israel, by the isolation of Israel in Palestine. The holiness of God regulates all other principles of God.

The Scripture declares that His throne is established on the basis of His holiness. It is because God is holy and man is unholy that so wide a rift exists between God and the unrepentant sinner. The Bible tells us that our iniquities have separated us from God—separated us so completely that His face is hidden from us and He will not hear us when we call. "If I regard iniquity in my heart," says the psalmist, "the Lord will not hear me" (Psalm 66:18). On the other hand, the psalmist says, "The eyes of the Lord are upon the righteous, and his ears are open unto their cry . . . The Lord . . . will fulfill the desire of them that fear him: he also will hear their cry, and will save them" (Psalms 34:15; 145:18, 19).

God is too pure to look with approval upon evil, which means that He is too holy to have any dealings with sin. Before sin entered into the human race, God and man had fellowship with each other. Now that fellowship is broken, and all communication between God and man is lost outside of Jesus Christ. It is only through Jesus Christ that man can ever again reestablish His fellowship with God. There are those who say that all roads lead to God. But Jesus said, "I am the way, the truth, and the life, no man cometh unto the Father but by me" (John 14:6). He also said, "I am the door: by me if any man enter in, he shall be saved, and shall go in and out, and find pasture" (John 10:9).

Man is a sinner, powerless to change his position, powerless to reach the pure ear of God unless he cries out for mercy sincerely. Man would have remained forever lost if God in His infinite mercy had not sent His Son to earth to bridge this gulf.

It is in God's holiness that we find the reason for the death of Christ. Jesus was the only one good enough, pure enough, strong enough to bear the sins of the whole world. God's holiness demanded the most exacting penalty for sin, and His love provided Jesus Christ to pay this penalty and provide man with salvation. Because the God we worship is a pure God, a holy God, a just and righteous God, He sent us His only begotten Son to make it possible for us to have access to Him. But if we ignore the help He has sent, if we fail to obey the laws He has set forth, we cannot cry out to Him for mercy when the punishment we deserve falls upon us!

God Is Love

Fourth, God is *Love*. But as with the other attributes of God, many persons who do not read their Bibles fail to recognize what is meant when the Scriptures say: "God is love" (1 John 4:8).

We aren't always sure ourselves what we mean when we use the term *love*. That word has become one of the most widely misused words in our language. We use the word *love* to describe the basest as well as the most exalted of human relationships. We say we "love" to travel; we "love" to eat chocolate cake; we "love" our new car, or the pattern in the wallpaper in our home. Why, we even say we "love" our neighbors—but most of us don't do much more than just say it and let it go at that! No wonder we don't have a very clear idea of what the Bible means when it says, "God is love."

Don't make the mistake of thinking that because God is Love everything is going to be sweet, beautiful, and happy and that no one will be punished for his sins. God's holiness demands that all sin be punished, but God's love provides the plan and way of redemption for sinful man. God's love provided the cross of Jesus, by which man can have forgiveness and cleansing. It was the love of God that sent Jesus Christ to the cross!

Never question God's great love, for it is as unchangeable a part of God as is His holiness. No matter how terrible your sins, God loves you. Were it not for the love of God, none of us would ever have a chance in the future life. But God is Love! And His love for us is everlasting! "But God commendeth his love toward us, in that while we were yet sinners, Christ died for us" (Romans 5:8).

The promises of God's love and forgiveness are as real, as sure, as positive as human words can make them. But like describing the ocean, its total beauty cannot be understood until it is actually seen. It is the same with God's love. Until you actually accept it, until you actually experience it, until you actually possess true peace with God, no one can describe its wonders to you.

It is not something that you do with your mind. Your finite mind is not capable of dealing with anything as great as the love of God. Your mind might have difficulty explaining how a black cow can eat green grass and give white milk—but you drink the milk and are nourished by it. Your mind can't reason through all the intricate processes that take place when you plant a small flat seed that produces a huge vine bearing luscious red and green watermelons—but you eat them and enjoy them! You can't understand radio, but you listen. Your mind can't explain the electricity that may be creating the light by which you are reading at this very moment—but you know that it's there and that it is making it possible for you to read!

You have to receive God by faith—by faith in His Son, the Lord Jesus Christ. When that happens, there isn't any room for doubt. You don't have to question whether or not God is in your heart; you can know it.

Whenever anyone asks me how I can be so certain about who and what God really is, I am reminded of the story of the little boy who was out flying a kite. It was a fine day for kite flying; the wind was brisk and large billowy clouds were blowing across the sky. The kite went up and up until it was entirely hidden by the clouds.

"What are you doing?" a man asked the little boy.

"I'm flying a kite," he replied.

"Flying a kite, are you?" the man said. "How can you be sure? You can't see your kite."

"No," said the boy, "I can't see it, but every little while I feel a tug, so I know for sure that it's there!"

Don't take anyone else's word for God. Find Him for yourself, and then you too will know by the wonderful, warm tug on your heartstrings that He is there for sure.

4

THE TERRIBLE FACT OF SIN

For all have sinned, and come short of the glory of God.
ROMANS 3:23

If God is a righteous and loving Being, why then is there so much wickedness, suffering, and sorrow? How did all this hatred come to be? Why have we created false idols? Why do we worship at the shrines of greed, self-interest, and war? How did the human race, which God made in His own image, sink so deep into depravity that the Ten Commandments had to be set forth with the demand that they be kept? Why did God have to send His own Son to save us? How did God's creatures become so filled with lust and evil?

To understand it, to see clearly why nation is pitted against nation, why families are divided, why every newspaper is filled with reports of violent, insane acts of brutality and hatred, we must go back to the very beginning. We must go back to the story of Adam in the Garden, back to the first chapter of Genesis.

Some people say that this familiar story of creation is only a myth. They say it is but a simple way to explain an unanswerable question to children. But this is not so. The Bible tells us exactly what happened in the beginning and why man has moved steadily along the path of his own destruction ever since.

God created this world as a perfect whole. He created the beautiful, harmonious world that man threw away—the perfect world that we are longing to find again, the world for which we are all searching.

In this perfect world God placed a perfect man. Adam was perfect because nothing that God does can ever be less than perfect, and upon this perfect man God bestowed the most precious gift of all—the gift of life eternal. He also gave him the gift of freedom. God gave to man the freedom of choice.

A friend of ours, the great preacher Dr. M. L. Scott, tells about a friend of his. The friend's son had gone away to the university for study and returned home for a visit, filled with his newly acquired knowledge.

"Dad," he said one evening with vast importance, "now that I've been to university, I'm no longer sure I can go along with your simple, childlike faith in the Bible."

The friend sat there studying his son with unblinking eyes. Finally he said, "Son, that is your freedom—your terrible freedom." That is what God gave to Adam—his freedom to choose. His terrible freedom.

The first man was no cave dweller—no gibbering, grunting, growling creature of the forest trying to subdue the perils of the jungle and the beasts of the field. Adam was created full-grown with every mental and physical faculty developed. He walked with God and had fellowship with Him. He was intended to be as a king on earth, ruling by the will of God.

This, then, was Adam's position as he stood in the Garden, the perfect man, the first man, with his priceless—if terrible gift—of freedom. Adam had total freedom—freedom to choose or to reject, freedom to obey God's commands or to go contrary to them, freedom to make himself happy or miserable. For it is not the mere possession of freedom that makes life satisfying—it is what we choose to do with our freedom that determines whether or not we shall find peace with God and with ourselves.

THE HEART OF THE PROBLEM

This is the real heart of the problem, for the moment a man is given freedom he is faced by two paths. Freedom is meaningless if there is only one possible path to follow. Freedom implies the right to choose, to select, to determine one's individual course of action.

We all know men and women who are honest, not so much from free choice, but because they have no opportunity to be dishonest. Dr. Manfred Gutzke has said, "You old people, don't think you are becoming better just because you are becoming deader." We all know people who pride themselves on being good, when it is actually their surroundings and way of life that keep them from being bad. We cannot take credit for resisting temptation if no temptation is placed before us!

God gave Adam no such handicap. He granted him freedom of choice and He gave him every opportunity to exercise it. Because God could do nothing that was less than perfect, He provided

Adam with the perfect setting in which to prove whether or not he would serve God.

As Adam stood there in the Garden he was without sin, his innocence was without blemish. The whole universe lay before him. The as yet unwritten history of the human race stretched like a great sheet of purest parchment beneath his hand, waiting for him to write the opening chapter—waiting for him to determine which road future generations would take.

God had completed His work. He had created an earthly garden, rich in everything that man might need. He had created a perfect man in His own likeness. He had endowed this man with a mind and a soul and had given him complete freedom to use his mind and to dispose of his soul as he saw fit. Then, like the wise Parent that He was, God waited to see what choice this child of His would make.

THE CHOICE MAN MADE

This was the test! This was the moment when Adam would use his free will to choose the right path or the wrong path—choose it because he wanted to, and not because there was only one path open to him!

Adam made his choice. He suffered the consequences of it, and he set the pattern that all humanity was to follow. "Therefore, as by the offense of one, judgment came upon all men to condemnation" (Romans 5:18). Paul also says, "Wherefore, as by one man sin entered into the world, and death by sin; and so death passed upon all men, for that all have sinned" (Romans 5:12).

For Adam was the fountainhead of the human race. He sprang like a crystal-clear spring from the ground. He was permitted to choose whether he would become a river running through pleasant and productive green pastures or a muddy torrent forever dashing against rocks and churning between deep, sunless cliffs—cold and miserable in itself and unable to bring joy and fruitfulness to the surrounding land.

God is not to blame for the tragic snarl in which the world has so long found itself. The fault lies squarely with Adam—Adam who was given his choice and who chose to listen to the lies of the Tempter rather than to the truth of God! The history of the human race from that day to this has been the story of man's futile effort to gain back the position that was lost by Adam's fall and, failing that, to reverse the curse.

"But this is unfair!" you may say. "Why should we suffer today because the first man sinned way back in the furthest reaches of time? Why hasn't mankind recovered during the intervening years? Why should we go on being punished every day of our lives?" There is a thought current today that it is possible to improve man by improving his environment. Isn't it strange to recognize that the first sin was committed in the perfect environment?

Let us turn again to the story of the river—the cold, dark river that runs at the bottom of the deep, dreary gorge. Why doesn't this river make its way back up to the warm, pleasant fields that lie above it? Why doesn't it leave its mournful route and become the happy, bubbling stream it was when it burst spontaneously from the earth?

It doesn't, because it can't. It has no power within itself to do other than it has always done. Once it has plunged down the steep banks into darkness, it cannot lift itself again to the bright, sunny land above. The means by which it could be lifted exists, the way is at hand, but the river does not understand how to make use of it. This reminds me of the Yangtze River in China (also called the Chang Jiang). This river spews its mud for miles out to sea, turning the blue-green waters of the ocean to a murky yellow. It is helpless to do otherwise.

A miracle stands ever ready to bring the river of humanity out of its misery and to place it once more in the warm valley of peace, but the river doesn't see or heed it. It feels that it can do nothing but continue on its tortuous way until it finally loses itself in the sea of destruction.

The story of the river is the story of man since the time of Adam, winding, twisting, plunging ever deeper into the frightening darkness. Though we lift up our voices and cry out for help, still we deliberately choose—as Adam did—the wrong way. In our despair we turn against God and blame Him for our dilemma. We question His wisdom and judgment. We find fault with His mercy and love.

We forget that Adam was the head of the human race, even as in this country our president is the head of our government. When the president acts, it is really the American people acting through him. When the president makes a decision, that decision stands as the decision of the entire people.

Adam stands as the federal head of the human race. He is also our first forefather. Just as we inherit characteristics, such as intellect, coloring, body size, temperament, etc., from our parents and grandparents, mankind inherited its fallen, corrupt nature from

Adam. When he failed, when he succumbed to temptation and fell, the generations yet unborn fell with him, for the Bible states very clearly that the results of Adam's sin shall be visited upon every one of his descendants. We know all too well the bitter truth of those passages in Genesis 3:17–19, which describe the tragedy that Adam's act brought upon us all:

> Cursed is the ground for thy sake, in sorrow shalt thou eat of it all the days of thy life; Thorns also and thistles shall it bring forth to thee; and thou shalt eat the herb of the field; In the sweat of thy face shalt thou eat bread, till thou return unto the ground; for out of it wast thou taken: for dust thou art, and unto dust shalt thou return.

To Eve, God said, "I will greatly multiply thy sorrow and thy conception; in sorrow thou shalt bring forth children; and thy desire shall be to thy husband, and he shall rule over thee" (Genesis 3:16).

In other words, because of Adam's original sin, the ground which once bore only beautiful and nourishing plants now produces both good and bad alike. Man, who once had but to walk in the Garden and reach out his hand for food, who had no need for clothing or for shelter, must now toil all the days of his life to provide these necessities for himself and his family. Woman, once the most carefree of creatures, is now burdened with sorrow and pain; and both man and woman are under penalty of spiritual and physical death. Death is a threefold circumstance: 1) immediate spiritual death; 2) the beginning of physical death (the minute we are born, we begin to die); and 3) ultimate eternal death.

SIN MAKES ITS ENTRY

Sin entered the human race through Adam, and the human race has been trying without success to get rid of it ever since. And, short of that, mankind has been seeking in vain to reverse the curse. The Bible teaches that God warned Adam before he sinned that if he ate of the tree of knowledge he would surely die. The Bible also tells us that God instructed Adam and Eve to be fruitful and to multiply and to replenish the earth. But, although they had been created in the image of God, after the Fall Adam and Eve gave birth to children after their own likeness and image. Consequently, Cain and Abel were infected with the death-dealing disease of sin, which they inherited from their parents and which has been passed on to every generation since. We are all sinners by inheritance, and try as we will, we cannot escape our birthright.

We have resorted to every means to win back the position that Adam lost. We have tried through education, through philosophy, through religion, through governments to throw off our yoke of depravity and sin. We have sought to accomplish with our sin-limited minds the things that God intended to do with the clear vision that can come only from on high. Our motives have been good and some of our attempts have been commendable, but they have all fallen far, far short of the goal. All our knowledge, all our inventions, all our developments and ambitious plans move us ahead only a very little before we drop back again to the point from which we started. For we are still making the same mistake that Adam made—we are still trying to be king in our own right, and with our own power, instead of obeying God's laws.

Before we label God as unjust or unreasonable for permitting sin to envelop the world, let us look at the situation more carefully. God in His infinite compassion sent His Son to show us the way out of our difficulties. He sent His Son to experience the same temptations that were set before Adam and to triumph over them. Satan tempted Jesus, just as he tempted Adam. Satan offered Jesus power and glory if He would forsake God, just as he offered it to Adam through Eve.

THE CHOICE CHRIST MADE

The great difference was that Jesus Christ resisted the temptation! When the devil showed Him all the kingdoms of the world and promised Him all the glory of them if He would but follow Satan instead of God, our blessed Lord said: "Get thee hence, Satan: for it is written, Thou shalt worship the Lord thy God and him only shalt thou serve" (Matthew 4:10). He completely triumphed over the Tempter to reveal to all peoples of all succeeding generations His sinless character. He is our victory!

In our weakness and because of our depraved nature, we have proved to be the true sons of Adam and have followed faithfully in his steps. We may deplore Adam's choice but we still imitate him!

There is not a single day that we do not face the same test that was set before Adam. There is not a day that we do not have a chance to choose between the devil's clever promises and God's sure Word.

We long for the day to come when disappointment, disease, and death will vanish—but there is no possibility of this dream coming true as long as we are the unregenerate sons of Adam. Something must be done about our sins. In succeeding chapters we will see that God has done something about this basic problem of the human race.

From the beginning of time until the present moment, man's ungodly quest for power, his determination to use his gift of free choice for his own selfish ends, has brought him to the brink of doom. The rubble and ruins of many civilizations lie scattered over the earth's surface—mute testimony to man's inability to build a lasting world without God. New rubble, new misery is being created daily, yet man plunges on his pernicious way.

God, meanwhile, in His infinite understanding and mercy, has looked on, waiting with a patience and compassion that passes all understanding. He waits to offer individual salvation and peace to the ones who will come to His mercy. The same two paths that God set before Adam still lie before us. We are still free to choose. We are living in a period of grace while God withholds the eternal punishment we so justly deserve.

It is the presence of sin that prevents man from being truly happy. It is because of sin that man has never been able to obtain the utopia of which he dreams. Every project, every civilization that he builds ultimately fails and falls into oblivion because man's works are all wrought in unrighteousness. The ruins around us at this moment are eloquent witness to the sin that fills the world.

Cause and Effect

Man seems to have lost sight of the ever-present law of cause and effect that operates on every level of this universe. The effects are plain enough, but the deep-seated, all-prevailing cause seems to be less distinct. Perhaps it is the blight of the modern-day philosophy of "progress" that dims man's vision. Perhaps it is because man is so enamored of this foolish, man-created theory that he clings to the belief the race is advancing slowly but surely toward ultimate perfection.

Many philosophers will even argue that the present world tragedy is but an incident in the upward march, and they point to other periods in human history when the prospect seemed as bleak and the outcome as hopeless. Philosophers would try to say that the sad conditions through which we are now living are but the birth pangs of a better day! They would say that men are still children groping and stumbling along in the kindergarten of existence, still a long, long way from the mature and sensible beings that they will become centuries hence!

But the Bible makes plain what natural science seems so unwilling to admit—that nature reveals both a Creator and a corrupter. Man blames the Creator for the work of the corrupter. Man forgets that our world is not as God made it. God made the world good. Sin corrupted it. God made man innocent, but sin entered and made him selfish. Every manifestation of evil is the result of basic sin—sin that has remained unchanged since the moment it first entered the human race. It may manifest itself in different ways, but fundamentally it is the same sin that causes an African savage to skulk along a jungle trail awaiting his victim with spear in hand, and a well-trained, educated pilot to fly a jet plane over the same jungle ready to bomb an unsuspecting village.

The two men are separated by centuries of culture. One can be said to be much further "progressed" than the other; one has all the advantages of man-made civilization, while the other is still in the "primitive" state—and yet, are they really so different? Are they not both motivated by fear and distrust of their fellow men? Are both not selfishly bent on achieving their own goals at any cost to their brothers? Is a bomb any less savage or brutal, or more civilized than a naked spear? Can we hope to find a solution to our problems so long as both the most "primitive" and the most "progressive" among us are more eager to kill than to love our neighbors?

All the sorrow, all the bitterness, all the violence, tragedy, heartache, and shame of man's history are summed up in that one little word—sin. Today, the general reaction is "so what?" In fact, there is a definite attempt to popularize and glamorize sin. Our most popular TV series are concerned with the *decadent* rich. Our magazine covers frequently feature the immoral, the perverted, the psychologically sick. Sin is "in." People don't like to be told they are sinners, even as their parents and grandparents were sinners before them! Yet, the Bible declares, "there is no difference: for all have sinned, and come short of the glory of God" (Romans 3:22–23). The Bible declares that every person on earth is a sinner in the sight of God; whenever I hear anyone take exception to so strong a statement, I am reminded of the story of the church officer who came to talk to the minister one day about sin. He said to the minister, "Doctor, we of the congregation wish you wouldn't talk quite so much or so plainly about sin. We feel that if our boys and girls hear you discuss the subject so much they will all the more easily become sinners. Why don't you call it a 'mistake' or say that our young people are often guilty of using 'poor judgment'—but please don't talk so openly about sin." The minister walked over and took down a bottle of poison from a high shelf and showed it to his visitor. The bottle was plainly marked in big red letters: Poison! Do not touch! "What would you have me do?" asked the minister. "Do you feel it would be wise for me to remove this label and put on one that reads 'Essence of Peppermint'? Don't you see that the milder you make the label, the more dangerous you make the poison?"

Sin—plain, old-fashioned sin, the selfsame sin that caused Adam's downfall—is what we are all suffering from today, and it will do us far more harm than good to try to dress it up with a fancy, more attractive label. We don't need a new word for it. What we need is to find out what the word we already have means! Because, although sin is certainly prevalent in the world today, however popularized, however glamorized, there are multitudes of people who are wholly ignorant of its real meaning. It is the misguided, shortsighted view of sin that stands in the way of conversion for many men and women. It is the lack of real understanding of sin that keeps many Christians from living the true life of Christ.

The old spiritual says, "Everybody talkin' 'bout heaven, ain't going there," and the same thing is true of sin. Everybody who talks about sin doesn't have a clear realization of what it means, and it is of supreme importance that we become familiar with how God looks at sin.

We may try to take a light view of sin and to refer to it as "human weakness." We may try to call it a trifle, but God calls it a tragedy. We would pass it off as an accident, but God declares it an abomination. Man seeks to excuse himself of sin, but God seeks to convict him of it and to save him from it. Sin is no amusing toy—it is a terror to be shunned! Learn, then, what constitutes sin in the eyes of God!

Dr. Richard Beal gives us five words for sin. First, sin is *lawlessness*, the transgression of the law of God (1 John 3:4). God established the boundary line between good and evil, and whenever we overstep that boundary, whenever we are guilty of intrusion into the forbidden area of evil, we are breaking the law. Whenever we fail to live up to the Ten Commandments, whenever we go contrary to the precepts of the Sermon on the Mount, we have transgressed the law of God and are guilty of sin.

If you look at the Ten Commandments one by one, you will note how today mankind is deliberately, it seems, not only breaking them, but glamorizing the breaking! From idolatry, which is anything we put before God, to remembering the Sabbath day to keep it holy (where would professional baseball and football be if Christians refused to watch them on Sunday?), to honoring parents (books like *Mommie Dearest* that expose the sins of parents), to covetousness, to adultery—it appears there has been a concerted effort to deliberately break each commandment. Not only that, but there seems to be a deliberate attempt to make it attractive to do so!

James made it plain that we are all guilty when he said, "But every man is tempted, when he is drawn away of his own lust, and enticed. Then when lust hath conceived, it bringeth forth sin: and sin, when it is finished, bringeth forth death" (James 1:14–15). It is because we have all broken God's laws, all transgressed His commands, that we are all classified as sinners.

Second, the Bible describes sin as *iniquity*. Iniquity is the deviation from right, whether or not the particular act has been expressly forbidden. Iniquity has to do with our inner motivations, the very things that we so often try to keep hidden from the eyes of men and God. They are the wrongs that spring from our own corrupt nature rather than the evil acts which force of circumstances sometimes cause us to commit.

Jesus described this inner corruptness when He said, "From within, out of the heart of men, proceed evil thoughts, adulteries, fornications, murders, thefts, covetousness, wickedness, deceit, lasciviousness, an evil eye, blasphemy, pride, foolishness: All these evil things come from within, and defile the man" (Mark 7:21–23).

Third, the Bible defines sin as *missing the mark*, falling short of the goal that has been set. God's goal is Christ. The object and end purpose of all of life is to live up to the life of Christ. He came to show us what it is possible for man to achieve here on earth; when we fail to follow His example, we miss the mark and fall short of the divine standard.

Fourth, sin is a form of *trespass*. It is the intrusion of self-will into the sphere of divine authority. Sin is not merely a negative thing; it is not just the absence of love for God. Sin is the making of a positive choice, the preference for self instead of God. It is the centering of affection in one's own being instead of reaching out with all one's heart to embrace God. Egoism and selfishness are the marks of sin as surely as are theft and murder. Perhaps this is the most subtle and destructive form of sin, for in this form it is so easy to overlook the label on the bottle of poison.

Those who cling to themselves, those who center their entire attention on their own beings, those who regard only their own interests and fight to protect only their own rights—these are sinners as much as the drunkard or harlot.

Jesus said, "What shall it profit a man, if he shall gain the whole world, and lose his own soul?" (Mark 8:36). Translated into modern terms, could we not say, "What shall it profit a man to build a vast industrial empire if he is eaten away by ulcers and can enjoy nothing of life? What shall it profit a dictator, though he conquer a hemisphere, if he must live in constant fear of an avenger's bullet or an assassin's knife? What shall it profit a parent to bring up children with harsh domination if he is rejected by them later and left to a lonely old age?" Without question, the sin of self is a deadly sin.

Fifth, sin is *unbelief*. Unbelief is a sin because it is an insult to the truthfulness of God. "He that believeth on the Son of God hath the witness in himself. He that believeth not God hath made him a liar because he believeth not the record that God gave of his Son" (1 John 5:10).

It is unbelief that shuts the door to heaven and opens it to hell. It is unbelief that rejects the Word of God and refuses Christ as Savior. It is unbelief that causes men to turn a deaf ear to the gospel and to deny the miracles of Christ.

Sin incurs the penalty of death, and no man has the ability in himself to save himself from sin's penalty or to cleanse his own heart of its corruption. Angels and men cannot atone for sin. It is only in Christ that the remedy for sin can be found. It is only Christ who can save the sinner from the fate that surely awaits him: "For the wages of sin is death" (Romans 6:23); "The soul that sinneth, it shall die" (Ezekiel 18:4); "None of them can by any means redeem his brother, nor give to God a ransom for him" (Psalm 49:7); "Neither their silver nor their gold shall be able to deliver them in the day of the Lord's wrath" (Zephaniah 1:18).

THE ONLY REMEDY

Man's only salvation from sin stands on a lonely, barren, skull-shaped hill; a thief hangs on one cross, a murderer on another, and between them, a Man with a crown of thorns. Blood flows from His hands and feet, it pours from His side, it drops down His face—while those who stand looking on sneer and mock Him.

And who is this tortured figure, who is this Man whom other men seek to humiliate and kill? He is the Son of God, the Prince of Peace, heaven's own appointed Messenger to the sin-ridden earth. This is He, before whom angels fall down and veil their faces. And yet He hangs bleeding and forsaken upon the cross.

What brought Him to this place of horrors? Who inflicted this hideous torture upon the Man who came to teach us love? You did and I did, for it was for your sin and my sin that Jesus was nailed to the cross. In this immortal moment the human race experienced the darkest reaches of sin, it sank to its lowest depths, it touched its foulest limits. No wonder that the sun could not endure and veiled its face!

As Charles Wesley writes:

And can it be that I should gain
An interest in the Savior's blood?
Died He for me, who caused His pain? . . .
Amazing love! how can it be
That Thou, my God, shouldst die for me?

But sin overreached itself on the cross. Man's hideous injustice that crucified Christ became the means that opened the way for man to become free. Sin's masterpiece of shame and hate became God's masterpiece of mercy and forgiveness. Through the death of Christ upon the cross, sin itself was crucified for those who believe in Him. Sin was conquered on the cross. His death is the foundation of our hope, the promise of our triumph! Christ bore in His own body on the tree the sins that shackle us. He died for us and rose again. He proved the truth of all God's promises to man, and if you will accept Christ by faith today, you, too, can be forgiven for your sins. You can stand secure and free in the knowledge that through the love of Christ your soul is cleansed of sin and saved from damnation.

5

Dealing with the Devil

For we wrestle not against flesh and blood, but against principalities, against powers, against rulers of the darkness of this world, against spiritual wickedness in high places.
Ephesians 6:12

There is a satanic principle involved in all that is happening today. The Bible describes "that old serpent, called the Devil and Satan, which deceiveth the whole world" (Revelation 12:9), and we know him to be at work confusing all peoples and all nations. His handiwork is to be seen at every turn.

While we would like to take hope that universal peace is drawing closer, it appears instead that we are standing on the brink of Armageddon. We are told that there were hundreds of "little" wars between 1945 and 1979 which caused between twelve and thirteen million deaths. For Satan is determined that the dark, joyless river of humanity shall continue on its tormented way until the end of time. He won over Adam in the Garden, and he is convinced that he can claim the souls of Adam's descendants for himself.

There is not a thinking person in the world today who has not wondered many times about the existence of the devil. That he does exist, there is no doubt. We see his power and influence everywhere. The question is not is there a devil, but how and why did the devil come to be?

We know from the story of Adam and Eve that the devil was already present on earth before God made the first man. Evil already existed, else God would not have made a tree whose fruit gave the awareness of good and bad. There would have been no necessity for such a tree, no possibility of it, if evil had not already been present and man been in need of protection from it.

DID GOD CREATE EVIL?

Here we face the greatest of all mysteries, the most significant of all secrets, the most unanswerable of all questions. How could God—who is all-powerful, all-holy, and all-loving—have created evil, or permitted the devil to create it? Why did Adam have to be tempted? Why didn't God strike the devil dead when he entered the body of the serpent to whisper evil thoughts to Eve?

The Bible gives us a few hints as to what the answer may be. But the Bible also makes it very clear that man is not supposed to know the full answer until God has allowed the devil and all his designs to help work out His own great plan.

Before the fall of Adam, long before Adam even existed, it would appear that God's universe was divided into spheres of influence, each of which was under the supervision and control of an angel or heavenly prince, all of whom were responsible directly to God. Paul tells us of "thrones, governments, princedoms, and authorities" in both the visible and the invisible world (Colossians 1:16; Ephesians 1:21). The Bible makes frequent mention of angels and archangels, showing that there was established order among them, some being more powerful than others.

The devil must have been just such a powerful, heavenly prince, having the earth assigned to him, perhaps, as his special province. Known as Lucifer, the "lightbearer," he must have stood very close to God—so close, in fact, that ambition entered his heart and he determined not to be God's beloved prince, but to place himself on an equal footing with God Himself! Lucifer was not the counterpart of God, but the counterpart of Michael or Gabriel; he was not a fallen god, but a fallen angel.

It was at this moment that the breach appeared in the cosmos. It was at this moment that the universe—which had been all good and all harmonious to God's will—split, and a portion of it set itself in opposition to God. Just as there are today regimes and sects that deny the existence of God or defy His authority, the devil defied God and attempted to set up his own authority. He abandoned his own position in the government of God and descended into the lower heavens and cried out that he would be like the Most High God. He had been set by God as the prince of this world; God has not yet removed him from that position, though the righteous basis for that removal has been laid by the death of Christ. Ever since that moment, the devil has been contesting God on earth.

THE DEVIL'S KINGDOM

As a mighty prince, with hosts of angels at his command, he has set up his kingdom on earth. His power and position here are the very reasons that the Scriptures came to be written. Had Satan not defied God and attempted to rival His power and authority, the story of Adam in the Garden would have been very different. Had Satan not set himself in opposition to God, there would have been no need to give mankind the Ten Commandments; there would have been no need for God to send His Son to the cross.

Jesus and His apostles were well aware of the devil. Matthew records an actual conversation between Jesus and the devil (Matthew 4:1–10). The devil was very real to the Pharisees—so real, in fact, that they accused Jesus of being the devil himself (Matthew 12:24)! There was no doubt in Jesus' mind of the existence of the devil, nor of the power that he wields here on earth.

The devil's strength is clearly demonstrated in the passage from Jude 9 which relates: "Yet Michael the archangel, when contending with the devil he disputed about the body of Moses, durst not bring against him a railing accusation, but said, The Lord rebuke thee."

Modern confusion about the personality of the devil has resulted in large measure from the caricatures of him that became popular during the Middle Ages. To allay their fear of the devil, people tried to laugh at him and pictured him as a foolish, grotesque creature with horns and a long tail. They put a pitchfork in his hand and a feeble-minded leer on his face, and then said to themselves, "Who's afraid of a ridiculous figure like this?"

The truth is that the devil is a creature of vastly superior intelligence, a mighty and gifted spirit of infinite resourcefulness. We forget that the devil was perhaps the greatest and most exalted of all God's angels. He was a sublime figure who decided to use his divine endowments for his own aims instead of God's. His reasoning is brilliant, his plans ingenious, his logic well nigh irrefutable. God's mighty adversary is no bungling creature with horns and tail—he is a prince of lofty stature, of unlimited craft and cunning, able to take advantage of every opportunity that presents itself, able to turn every situation to his own advantage. He is unrelenting and cruel. He is not, however, all-powerful, omniscient, or omnipresent.

The devil is quite capable of bringing forth the false prophet of which the Bible warns. Upon the wreckage of disbelief and faltering faith the devil will set his masterpiece, the counterfeit king. He will create a religion without a Redeemer. He will build a church without a Christ. He will call for worship without the Word of God.

The apostle Paul predicted this when he said:

> But I fear, lest by any means, as the serpent beguiled Eve through his subtlety, so your minds should be corrupted from the simplicity that is Christ. For if he that cometh preacheth another Jesus, whom we have not preached, or if ye receive another spirit, which ye have not received, or another gospel, which ye have not accepted, ye might well bear with him . . . For such are false apostles, deceitful workers, transforming themselves into the apostles of Christ (2 Corinthians 11:3, 4, 13).

THE DEVIL AND THE ANTICHRIST

We know that the Antichrist will appear and try to ensnare the minds and hearts of men. The time draws close, the stage is set—confusion, panic, and fear are abroad. The signs of the false prophet are everywhere at hand, and many may be the living witnesses of the awesome moment when the final act of this age-old drama begins. It may well come in our time, for the tempo is speeding up, events move more swiftly, and on every side we see men and women consciously or unconsciously choosing up sides—aligning themselves with the devil or with God.

It will be a battle to the death, in the truest meaning of that word—a battle that will give no quarter, that will make no allowances or exceptions. The human phase of this battle started in the Garden of Eden when the devil seduced mankind from God, making it possible for there to be billions of warring wills, every man turning to his own way: "All we like sheep have gone astray; we have turned every one to his own way; and the Lord hath laid on him [Christ] the iniquity of us all" (Isaiah 53:6). It will continue until the end of time, until one or the other of these two mighty forces—the force of good or evil—triumphs and places the True King or the false king on the throne.

At this moment in history, two mighty trinities stand face to face: the Trinity of God (the Father, Son, and Holy Ghost) and the false trinity that Satan would have us worship in its place. The trinity of evil (the devil, Antichrist, and false prophet) is described in the Book of Revelation: "And I saw three unclean spirits like frogs come out of the dragon, and out of the mouth of the beast, and out of the mouth of the false prophet" (Revelation 16:13).

Never for a second of your waking or sleeping life are you without the influence of these two powerful forces, never is there a moment when you cannot deliberately choose to go with one or the other. Always the devil is standing at your side tempting, coaxing, threatening, cajoling. And always on your other side stands Jesus, the all-loving, the all-forgiving, waiting for you to turn to Him and ask His aid, waiting to give you supernatural power to resist the evil one. You belong to one or the other. There isn't a no-man's land in between where you can hide.

In moments of your greatest fear and anxiety, in moments when you feel yourself helpless in the grip of events you cannot control, when despair and disappointment overwhelm you—in these moments many times it is the devil who is trying to catch you at your weakest point and push you further along the path that Adam took.

In these perilous moments remember that Christ has not deserted you. He has not left you defenseless. As He triumphed over Satan in His hour of temptation and trial, so He has promised that you, too, can have daily victory over the Tempter. Remember, "ye are of God . . . and have overcome them: because greater is he that is in you, than he that is in the world" (1 John 4:4).

The same Book that tells us over and over again of God's love warns us constantly of the devil who would come between us and God, the devil who is ever waiting to ensnare men's souls. "Be sober, be vigilant; because your adversary the devil, as a roaring lion, walketh about, seeking whom he may devour" (1 Peter 5:8).

The Bible describes a personal devil who controls a host of demon spirits that attempt to dominate and control all human activity, "the prince of the power of the air, the spirit that now worketh in the children of disobedience" (Ephesians 2:2).

DON'T DOUBT THE DEVIL

Don't doubt for a moment the existence of the devil! He is very personal and he is very real! And he is extremely clever! Perhaps the cleverest thing that he has ever done is to convince people he does not exist. Look again at the front page of today's newspaper if you have any question about the personality of the devil. Listen to your local radio or television news commentator. Note the local theater listings, glance at the magazine stands and book racks—in short, just look around you if you feel you need concrete evidence!

Would sane, thinking men and women behave in this way if they were not in the grip of evil? Could hearts filled only with God's love and God's goodness conceive and carry out the acts of violence and malice that are reported to us every day? Could men of education, intelligence, and honest intent gather around a world conference table and fail so completely to understand each other's needs and goals if their thinking was not being deliberately clouded and corrupted?

Whenever I hear an "enlightened" person of our time take issue with the plausibility of a personal, individualized devil in command of a host of evil spirits, I am reminded of this poem by Alfred J. Hough:

Men don't believe in the Devil now, as their fathers used to do;
They've forced the door of the broadest creed to let his majesty through.
There isn't a print of his cloven foot or fiery dart from his brow
To be found on earth or air today, for the world has voted it so.
Who dogs the steps of the toiling saint and digs the pits for his feet?
Who sows the tares in the fields of time whenever God sows the wheat?
The Devil is voted not to be, and of course, the thing is true;
But who is doing the kind of work that the Devil alone can do?
We are told that he doesn't go about as a roaring lion now;
But whom shall we hold responsible for the everlasting row
To be heard in home, in church and state, to the earth's remotest bound,
If the Devil by unanimous vote is nowhere to be found?
Won't someone step to the front forthwith and make their bow and show
How the frauds and crimes of a single day spring up? We want to know!
The Devil was fairly voted out, and of course, the Devil's gone;
But simple people would like to know who carries the business on.

Who, indeed, is responsible for the infamy, terror, and agony that we see all around us? How can we account for the sufferings that we all experience if evil is not a potent force? Modern education has, in truth, impeded our minds. Because of allegedly scientific findings, some have lost their belief in the supernatural powers of Satan, while others worship him.

George Galloway summed up this dubious contribution of current education when he said, "The theory that there is in the universe a power or principle, personal or otherwise, in eternal opposition to God is generally discarded by the modern mind."

The modern mind may discard it, but that doesn't cause the evil principle itself to disappear! Once asked how he overcame the devil, Martin Luther replied, "Well, when he comes knocking upon the door of my heart and asks, 'Who lives here?' the dear Lord Jesus goes to the door and says, 'Martin Luther used to live here but he has moved out. Now I live here.' The Devil, seeing the nail-prints in His hands, and the pierced side, takes flight immediately."

THE CERTAINTY OF SIN

Sin is certainly a grim fact! It stands like a titanic force, contesting all the good that men may try to accomplish. It stands like a dark shadow, ever ready to blot out whatever light may reach us from on high. We all know this. We all see it. We all are conscious of it in every move we make. Call it what we may, we know of its very real existence: "For we wrestle not against flesh and blood, but against principalities, against powers, against the rulers of the darkness of this world, against spiritual wickedness in high places" (Ephesians 6:12).

How do those who deny the devil and his minions account for the speed with which evil spreads? How do they explain the endless stumbling blocks that are placed in the path of the righteous? How can they reason away the fact that destruction and disaster are but the work of seconds, while construction and rehabilitation are often agonizingly slow?

Breathe a lie into the air, let loose a slanderous tongue—and the words are carried as by magic to the farthest corners. Speak a truth, perform a generous and honest act—and unseen powers will be at work at once to try to hide this tiny ray of light and hope.

When this book was first written thirty years ago, no one built churches to the devil, no one constructed pulpits to preach his word. And yet today they do. His word is everywhere, and all too often his word is translated into desperate deeds. If no unseen power is at work corrupting men's hearts and distorting men's thoughts, how can you explain humanity's eagerness to listen to the base and vulgar and vile, while it turns a deaf ear to the good and clean and pure? One has only to listen to the blasphemous words of punk rock to realize that Satan is alive and well on earth.

Would one single person among us ever pass up a piece of ripe delicious fruit to select a rotten piece that was crawling with worms and reeking with decay, if we were not driven to this dreadful choice by a great and sinister power? Yet that is exactly what we all do over and over again. We constantly pass up the rich and beautiful and ennobling experiences and seek out the tawdry, the cheap, and the degrading. These are the works of the devil, and they flourish on every side!

THE STRUGGLE BETWEEN GOOD AND EVIL

What we see happening here on earth is but a reflection of the far greater struggles between good and evil in the unseen realm. We like to think that our planet is the center of the universe, and we attach too much importance to earthly events. In our foolish pride we see with human eyes. But a struggle of infinitely greater magnitude is being waged in the world we cannot see!

The wise men of old knew this. They knew that there is much that the human eye fails to discern and much to which the human ear is deaf. Modern man likes to feel that he "created" radio, television, and computers, that he made it possible to send audible sounds and visible images through space and to make and record impossible amounts of data. The truth is, of course, that these waves, unknown to man, have always existed, and that far greater wonders exist in outer space, of which man may never gain the slightest knowledge. That these wonders were there, the ancient prophets knew—but even they had but a suggestion of their magnitude, even they could catch but the faintest echoes of the mighty battle of the spheres.

One of the many prices Adam paid for listening to the devil was to lose the vision of spiritual dimensions. He lost for himself and all of humanity the capacity for seeing and hearing and understanding anything that was not basely material. Adam closed himself off from the eternal wonders and splendors of the unseen world. He lost the power of true prophecy, the ability to look ahead, and by so doing to better understand and perform the work of the present. He lost his sense of continuity. He became literally "dead in trespasses and sins." He had alienated himself from God.

G. Campbell Morgan says:

> Our distance from God is that of inability to know and apprehend the near. It is the distance of the blind man from the glory of the picture in front of him. The distance of the deaf man from the beauty of the symphony sounding round about him. It is the distance of the sensate man from all the movement of life in the midst of which he lives.

But let tragedy or sickness come to us, let us suffer the consequences of our own sins, and we immediately blame God for it! We may be somewhat patient and understanding with our television sets when they do not give us what we want, but we are quick to rail against God and His universe when we get a distorted picture of it.

Let someone get the business promotion we wanted, let someone we consider less deserving succeed where we have failed, and we cry out against God's injustice. We demand to know why God permits such inequalities! We lose sight of the fact that God, like a great master television station, is sending out a perfect image of love and righteousness all the time and that the faulty reception lies with us!

THE EVIL IN OUR EYESIGHT

It is the evil and distortion within ourselves that keeps us from seeing and experiencing God's perfect world. It is our own sin that blurs the image, that keeps us from being God's pure children instead of the children of evil. Paul spoke for all of us when he said: "For the good that I would I do not, but the evil which I would not, that I do" (Romans 7:19). Paul recognized the dreaded enemy, the powerful foe of all mankind, and cried out, "O wretched man that I am! Who shall deliver me from the body of this death? I thank God through Jesus Christ our Lord. So then with the mind I myself serve the law of God; but with the flesh the law of sin" (Romans 7:24–25).

Two overwhelming adversaries were clearly apparent to Paul

and he was acutely aware of being torn between their mighty magnetisms. The power of good was pulling his mind and heart toward God, while the power of evil was trying to drag his body down into death and destruction. Two books on demon possession and the rise of the cults might be of interest to you: *Demon Possession*, by John L. Nevivus (published by Kregel), and *Unholy Devotion: Why Cults Lure Christians*, by Harold L. Bussell (copyright 1983 by The Zondervan Corporation).

You are caught between these same two forces: life and death! Choose God's way, and there is life. Choose Satan's way, and it is death!

6

The Despair of Loneliness

I am forgotten as a dead man out of mind.
I am like a broken vessel.
Psalm 31:12

After the death of her husband, Queen Victoria said, "There is no one left to call me Victoria." Even though she was a queen, she knew what it meant to be lonely.

H. G. Wells said on his sixty-fifth birthday, "I am sixty-five, and I am lonely and have never found peace."

Isadora Duncan, the great ballet dancer who danced before the royalty of Europe and was considered one of the greatest ballet dancers of all time, said, "I have never been alone but that my heart did ache, my eyes fill with tears, and my hands tremble for a peace and a joy that I never found." She went on to say that in the midst of millions of admirers, she was actually a very lonely woman.

A few years ago, a beautiful young Hollywood star with apparently everything a girl could want ended her life. In the brief note that she left was an incredibly simple explanation—she was unbearably lonely.

The psalmist said, "I am like a pelican of the wilderness: I am like an owl of the desert. I watch, and am as a sparrow alone upon the house top" (Psalm 102:6).

Again the psalmist said, "Reproach hath broken my heart; and I am full of heaviness: and I looked for some to take pity, but there was none; and for comforters, but I found none" (Psalm 69:20).

The Loneliness of Solitude

First, there is the *loneliness of solitude*. I have felt the loneliness of the ocean where there is never a sound except the booming of the surf along rock-strewn shores. I have felt the loneliness of the prairie with only the occasional mournful howl of the coyote. I have felt the loneliness of the mountains broken only by the sighing of the wind. The sentry standing duty alone at an outpost, the thousands in mental institutions, and those in solitary confinement in prisons and concentration camps know the meaning of the loneliness of solitude. Louis Zamperini, the great Olympic track star, has told of the terrible loneliness of solitude on a life raft where he spent forty-eight days during the Second World War.

In his fascinating book, *Alone*, Admiral Richard E. Byrd told about the time he spent in bewildering and soul-shattering darkness. He lived alone in a shack that was literally buried in the great glacial icecap that covers the South Pole. He spent five months there. The days were as black as the nights. No living creature of any kind existed within a hundred miles. The cold was so intense that he could hear his breath freeze and crystallize as the wind blew it past his ears.

"At night," he says, "before blowing out the lantern, I formed the habit of planning the morrow's work." He had to, in order to preserve his sanity. "It was wonderful," he continues:

> to be able to dole out time in this way. It brought me an extraordinary sense of command over myself; and without constant activity, the days would have been without purpose; and without purpose, they would have ended—as such days always end—in disintegration.

THE LONELINESS OF SOCIETY

Probably you think that in that frozen wasteland, Richard Byrd was of all people most lonely. But the *loneliness of society* is far worse than the loneliness of solitude, for there is loneliness in great cities far worse than his.

That poor creature living in the dingy tenement who never receives a letter, who never hears one word of encouragement, who never experiences the handclasp of a friend—that wealthy society leader whose money has bought everything but love and happiness—each knows a loneliness few can understand.

There is the loneliness of the street people living in doorways or cardboard boxes, scrounging food in garbage cans—a unique loneliness.

A recent television program showed the demoralizing loneliness of some of our neglected and forgotten old people in dilapidated institutions. The aimless sitting, the vacant eyes, haunted me. They are the living dead. Yet in the background an old derelict, with one finger, was picking out on an equally derelict piano "What a Friend We Have in Jesus."

In John 5 we read about Jesus as He made His way through the narrow streets of Jerusalem. When He reached the sheep gate by the pool of Bethesda, He observed the great multitudes plagued with various infirmities, waiting to be moved into the water. Suddenly He noticed a poor creature who seemed more needy than all the rest, and tenderly He asked, "Wilt thou be made whole?"

The helpless paralytic looked up and answered, "Sir, I have no man, when the water is troubled, to put me into the pool." Think of it, thirty-eight long, weary years this bundle of pain had been buffeted by the surging human tide of Jerusalem, and after all these years, he must say to Jesus, "Sir, I have no man." He was absolutely friendless.

You can have a friend who sticks closer than a brother. Jesus Christ can make life joyful, satisfying, and glorious to you. All over the world are millions of men and women who love and serve Jesus Christ. The moment you accept Him, you are closer to them than you are to your own blood relatives.

There is not a city in the United States that does not have a warm church to which you could go and meet the most wonderful people in America. There is a giant network of true Christians in every community of America. The moment you clasp their hands, you know that you have friends.

But first, you must repent, surrender, and commit your heart and life to Christ. Let Him forgive your past sins, and He will take you into His family; He will bring you to the hearth, and you will feel the warmth of the fire. If you are lonely today, I beg you, come to Christ and know the fellowship that He brings.

THE LONELINESS OF SUFFERING

Third, there is the *loneliness of suffering.* Some years ago we received a letter from a radio listener who for five years had been crippled into a sitting position by arthritis. For five long, weary, painful years she was unable to stretch out or to lie down, yet she wrote, "I have spent many a day alone, but never a lonely day." Why? It was Christ who made the difference. With Christ as your Savior and constant Companion, you, too, although alone, need never be lonely.

You today who are lying on a hospital bed enduring the loneliness of suffering can rest assured that Christ can give you His grace and strength. While you lie there, you can be useful to Him. You can know something of the ministry of intercession, the greatest ministry on earth, as you pray for others.

THE LONELINESS OF SORROW

Fourth, there is the *loneliness of sorrow.* In the eleventh chapter of John we read of Mary and Martha. Their brother Lazarus was dead. Jesus had not yet come. They stood beside the body of their brother and wept.

For you, too, perhaps the world has become a vast cemetery containing but one grave. You have stood in the sick room and watched the one dearer than all the world to you slip beyond your reach. You crave fellowship.

You want someone to come along with a strong hand to help wipe the tears away, put the smile back on your face, and give you joy through the sorrow. Jesus can do just that. The Bible says, "Casting all your care upon him, for he careth for you" (1 Peter 5:7). God loves His children. If you are willing to trust Him and give yourself to Him, He can carry your sorrow.

THE LONELINESS OF SIN

Fifth, there is the *loneliness of sin*. In John 13 we find the story of the Last Supper. Jesus prophesied the betrayal of Judas. In amazement the innocent disciples looked at one another. John asked, "Lord, who is it?" And Jesus said, "He it is, to whom I shall give bread when I have dipped it." And when He had dipped the bread, He gave it to Judas Iscariot, the son of Simon, and then we are told that Satan entered into Judas. Immediately Jesus said, "That thou doest, do quickly." The Bible then says, "He then, having received the bread, went immediately out, and it was night." He went out—out from the presence of Christ— and it was night.

Perhaps you at one time thought you knew the joy and peace of being born into God's family. You experienced the sweet fellowship of God's people. You tasted the complete happiness and satisfaction of Christ's presence with you, but you sinned. You went out from the presence of Christ, and you have found that it is night. You have neither the fellowship of Christians nor the fellowship of sinners, and certainly you no longer have the fellowship of Christ. Perhaps there is no loneliness quite so bitter as the loneliness of a backslidden Christian.

Yet there is forgiveness for you. As you confess and forsake your sins, your fellowship with Christ will be restored. "If we confess our sins, he is faithful and just to forgive us our sins, and to cleanse us from all unrighteousness" (1 John 1:9).

Perhaps you say you are having a pretty good time sinning—and you well may. The Bible says there is a certain pleasure in sin. However, it is short-lived and fatal. Perhaps you have read Dr. Kinsey's report or some other survey and are finding a certain satisfaction in knowing how many sinners there are who are as bad as—or worse than—you. You're not alone. No. You're in the vast majority. Where then, you ask, does the loneliness of sin come in? You may be one of a crowd now, but the day is coming when each one of you must stand alone before Almighty God and be judged. That will be for you the climax of all the loneliness of earth, and but the preview of the loneliness of hell.

For all of these who travel the pathway of sin, there is an engulfing pall of night that isolates them from all good and true fellowship. Sin always has been darkness. Sin always will be darkness. Judas was lonely because of his sin. God says in Hosea 4:17, "Ephraim is joined to idols, let him alone." Because of the covetousness and idolatry of the people of Ephraim, God had said, "Have no fellowship with him, let him completely alone." "All we like sheep have gone astray; we have turned every one to his own way" (Isaiah 53:6). Here again we find the loneliness of sin.

One hour before his fatal duel with Alexander Hamilton, Aaron Burr, sitting in his library at Richmond Hill in New York, wrote to his daughter, "Some very wise man has said, 'O fools, who think it solitude to be alone.'" Already, even before the fatal shot was fired and the bloody deed was done, he felt the loneliness of his sin. In a few hours he was to be a fugitive from the sudden and deep abhorrence of his fellow citizens. His political career was gone forever, and his great ambitions were wrecked.

There are thousands of lonely people in the city and in the country who carry heavy and difficult burdens of grief, anxiety, pain, and disappointment; but the loneliest soul of all is the man whose life is steeped in sin.

I want to tell you that every sin you deliberately cling to is a mighty power in making you lonely. The older you get, the lonelier you will be. I beg you, come to the foot of the cross and confess that you are a sinner; forsake your sins.

Christ can give you power to overcome every sin and habit in your life. He can break the ropes, fetters, and chains of sin; but you must repent, confess, commit, and surrender yourself to Him first. Right now, it can be settled, and you can know the peace, joy, and fellowship of Christ.

THE LONELINESS OF THE SAVIOR

Last, there is the *loneliness of the savior*. Thousands of human beings were swarming around Him. There was great joy at the Passover season everywhere, but Jesus was:

> despised and rejected of men; a man of sorrows and acquainted with grief: and we hid as it were our faces from him; he was

> despised, and we esteemed him not. Surely he hath borne our griefs, and carried our sorrows: yet we did esteem him stricken, smitten of God, and afflicted. But he was wounded for our transgressions, he was bruised for our iniquities: the chastisement of our peace was upon him; and with his stripes we are healed. All we like sheep have gone astray; we have turned every one to his own way; and the Lord hath laid on him the iniquity of us all. (Isaiah 53:3–6)

Jesus was alone. He had come to His own, and His own received Him not. "But all this was done, that the Scriptures of the prophets might be fulfilled. Then all the disciples forsook him, and fled" (Matthew 26:56). The crowds who had so recently shouted, "Hosanna," had that very day shouted, "Crucify him. Crucify him." Now even His loyal twelve had left. And at last we hear Him cry out, "My God, my God, why hast thou forsaken me?" (Mark 15:34). Not only had He been forsaken by His human companions, but now in that desperate and lonely hour He—because He was bearing our sins in His own body on the cross—had been forsaken by God as well. Jesus was enduring the suffering and judgment of hell for you and me.

Hell, essentially, is separation from God. Hell is the loneliest place in the universe. Jesus suffered its agony for you, in your place. Now God says, Repent, believe on Christ, receive Christ, and you will never know the sorrow, the loneliness, and the agony of hell.

"Whosoever shall call upon the name of the Lord shall be saved" (Romans 10:13).

7

After Death—What?

There is but a step between me and death.
1 Samuel 20:3

It has been said that all of life is but a preparation for death. The psalmist said, "What man is he that liveth, and shall not see death?" (Psalm 89:48).

This is supposed to be a free-thinking age of radical experiment. We have sought to change the world and the laws that govern it through knowledge, science, invention, discovery, philosophy, and materialistic thinking. We have tried to enthrone the false gods of money, fame, and human intelligence; but however we try, the end is always the same: "It is appointed unto men once to die" (Hebrews 9:27).

In the midst of life, we see death on every hand. The wail of the ambulance, the illuminated mortuary signs, the graveyards we so frequently pass, and the sight of a hearse threading its way through traffic all remind us that the Grim Reaper may call for us at any moment. None of us can be sure when that exact moment will be, but we are well aware that it may come at any time.

Someone has said, "The only certain thing about life is death." Oscar Wilde said, "One can survive everything nowadays—except death!" Books on death and dying have proliferated in recent days—as have books by those who claim to have experienced death and come back to tell about it. Rather than looking for a way to make our peace with God, the world has instead come up with classes on dying and how to face death—accepting it as a normal part of living. Actually, all mankind is sitting on Death Row. How we die or when is not the main issue, but where do we go after death?

Each year hundreds of Americans step into their automobiles little realizing this is to be their last ride. In 1980, 53,200 Americans died in automobile accidents. In spite of all the increased safety measures, another 469,000 persons were killed in accidents at home, when all thought of death was far from their minds. Death stalks mankind relentlessly, and although medical science and safety engineers wage a constant war against it, in the end, death is always the victor.

Because of this long-fought scientific battle, we now have the advantage of a few years more of life, but death is still standing at the end of the road, and the life span of the average person does not far exceed the biblical threescore years and ten.

Heart diseases still cut down far too many of our citizens in the prime of life. Cancer still presses its pain into the bodies of thousands. Blood disorders take their toll, although medical research has greatly decreased their annual number. Herpes and

AIDS (acquired immune deficiency syndrome) were the illnesses of the '80s. They are on the rise around the world and have been reported on all the major continents. But however optimistic the statistical surveys, however much our life span has been increased since 1900, whatever the figures may show on murder, suicide, and other forms of violent death, the inevitable fact of death remains unchanged—it is still our ultimate experience on earth!

A Lifelong Battle

From the moment a child is born, the death process, and the fight against it, begins. The mother devotes years of attention to protecting the life of her child. She watches the food, the clothes, the environment, the medical checkups and inoculations, but in spite of her loving care, the child has already begun to die.

Before many years the tangible signs of weakness will be obvious. The dentist will check the decay of our teeth. Glasses will be needed to help improve our fading vision. Skin will wrinkle and sag as time passes, and our shoulders will droop and our step become slower and less sure. The brittleness of our bones will increase as our energy lessens. Almost without realizing it, we have begun to move closer to death.

Health insurance and hospitalization will be used to help us cushion the blow. Life insurance will be purchased to cover our final expenses and obligations, and we shall suddenly see our whole life as a great and never-ending battle with death. We shall see that we are all running a race in which the most we can hope for is a little more time and, outwit our opponent as we may, in the end we know that death will always win!

What a mysterious thing is this enemy of ours—as mysterious as life itself. For the life that we see so plentifully around us in plants and animals, as well as in human beings, cannot be reproduced by us, or even explained. Death is also without explanation, although we are as aware of its presence as we are of life. How little we like to talk about it, however, or consider its importance! When life comes, and a child is born, we rejoice. When life goes, and a man dies, we try to dismiss the thought as quickly as possible.

Today there are over six billion people living on this planet. Almost all of them will be dead in a hundred years. Their bodies will be without feeling. But what about their souls—the essential and eternal part of life? Here is the mystery. What is missing when a man dies? Where does that missing thing go?

Why Do Men Reject God?

Some years ago a newspaper columnist died in Denver, Colorado. The mourners listened to his recorded voice at the funeral when he said:

> This is my funeral. I am an atheist and have been for many years. I have the utmost contempt for theological nonsense. Clergymen are moral cowards. Miracles are the product of the imagination. If any four reporters were sent to an execution and got their facts as twisted as the apostles in the Bible report, they would be fired

forthwith. I want no religious songs. This is going to be a perfectly rational funeral.

Contrast this to the beautiful description of death pictured by Alfred Lord Tennyson in his poem "In Memoriam": "God's finger touched him, and he slept."

Every age has produced men who in their hatred of God have attempted to heap ridicule and abuse upon the church, the Scriptures, and Jesus Christ. Without presenting evidence they cry out against the voice of God. History testifies of the George Bernard Shaws, the Robert Ingersolls, the B. F. Skinners, and many other philosophers who strove, by argument, to destroy the fear of death.

Listen to the anthropologist tell of death in the jungle. There is no "theological nonsense" there, for they have not heard of Jesus Christ. What of death there? In some tribes the old are turned into the bush so that the wild animals might attack them and death need not be faced by the young. In another tribe the clothes are stripped off and the bodies of the mourners painted with white. Hour after hour the moans and screams of the women tell the world that a soul is about to leave a body. Death outside of Christian influence is filled with horror and despair—or, at best, resignation and indifference. Among the Moslems, for instance, death is looked forward to in anticipation, for Moslems believe that great pleasures await the faithful—if they die while killing infidels or fighting for their faith.

Compare this to the death of the Christian. When Christ came He gave a new approach to death. Man had always looked upon death as an enemy, but Jesus said that He had conquered death and taken the very sting out of death. Jesus Christ was the Master Realist when He urged men to prepare for death, which was certain to come. Do not worry, said the Lord Jesus, about the death of the body, but rather concern yourself with the eternal death of the soul.

I think of Helen Morken who, as she lay dying, was surrounded by her husband and children singing hymns for hours each day. Literally, she was sung into the presence of the Lord. And I think of those saints of God described by Alexander Smellie in his book, *Men of the Covenant*. He tells of the great men of faith who died during those "killing times" in Scotland when executions were anything but pleasant. There were no electric chairs, firing squads, or lethal injections to make death as painless as possible. It was a time of torture—thumb screws, the boot, of being hanged and then quartered. For this reason, each man described by Smellie had a horror of death. Yet each one, when he came to the actual point of dying, died in an ectasy of joy!

The Bible indicates that there are actually two deaths: one is physical death and the other is eternal death. Jesus warned that we are to fear the second death far more than the first death. He described the second death as hell, which is eternal separation from God. He indicated that the death of your body is nothing compared to the conscious everlasting banishment of a soul from God.

THE DEATH OF A SAINT

The last statements of dying men provide an excellent study for those who are looking for realism in the face of death.

Matthew Henry—"Sin is bitter. I bless God I have inward supports."

Martin Luther—"Our God is the God from whom cometh salvation: God is the Lord by whom we escape death."

John Knox—"Live in Christ, live in Christ, and the flesh need not fear death."

John Wesley—"The best of all is, God is with us. Farewell! Farewell!"

Richard Baxter—"I have pain; but I have peace. I have peace."

William Carey, the missionary—"When I am gone, speak less of Dr. Carey and more of Dr. Carey's Savior."

Adoniram Judson—"I am not tired of my work, neither am I tired of the world; yet when Christ calls me home, I shall go with the gladness of a boy bounding away from school."

How different is the story of the Christian who has confessed his sin and by faith received Jesus Christ as his personal Savior!

For many years Dr. Effie Jane Wheeler taught English and literature where I attended college. Dr. Wheeler was noted for her piety as well as for her knowledge of the subjects she taught. In May of 1949, on Memorial Day, Dr. Wheeler wrote the following letter to Dr. Edman, then president of the college, her colleagues, and former students:

> I greatly appreciate the moment in chapel that may be given to reading this, for before you leave for the summer I should like to have you know the truth about me as I learned it myself only last Friday. My doctor at last has given what has been his real diagnosis of my

> illness for weeks—an inoperable case of cancer. Now if he had been a Christian he wouldn't have been so dilatory or shaken, for he would have known, as you and I do, that life or death is equally welcome when we live in the will and presence of the Lord. If the Lord has chosen me to go to Him soon, I go gladly. Please do not give a moment's grief for me. I do not say a cold goodbye but rather a warm *Auf Wiedersehen* till I see you again—in the blessed land where I may be allowed to draw aside a curtain when you enter. With a heart full of love for every individual of you. (Signed) Effie Jane Wheeler.

Just two weeks after writing this letter, Dr. Wheeler entered the presence of her Savior, who had kept His promise to take the sting out of death.

While we were writing this chapter, in one mail we received four letters. One was from a ninety-four-year-old saint, eager to be with her Lord; one from a woman on Death Row who, since becoming a Christian six years ago, can now look beyond her approaching execution to the glory that lies ahead; and two letters from women whose husbands had just died after many years of marriage (one just short of their forty-ninth wedding anniversary). Each is looking beyond death to the glory that lies ahead.

The great Dwight L. Moody on his deathbed said: "This is my triumph; this is my coronation day! It is glorious!"

The Bible teaches that you are an immortal soul. Your soul is eternal and will live forever. In other words, the real you—the part of you that thinks, feels, dreams, aspires; the ego, the personality—will never die. The Bible teaches that your soul will live forever in one of two places—heaven or hell. If you are not a

Christian and you have never been born again, then the Bible teaches that your soul goes immediately to a place Jesus called Hades, where you will await the judgment of God.

AN UNPOPULAR SUBJECT

I am conscious of the fact that the subject of hell is not a very pleasant one. It is very unpopular, controversial, and misunderstood. In my crusades across the country, however, I usually devote one evening to the discussion of this subject. Following my discussion many letters to the editors of newspapers appear for days as people argue the pros and cons, for the Bible has almost as much to say about this subject as any other. In student discussions on many campuses of America I am continually asked the question, "What about hell? Is there fire in hell?" and similar questions. As a minister I must deal with it. I cannot ignore it, even though it makes people uncomfortable and anxious. I grant that it is the hardest of all teachings of Christianity to receive.

There are those who teach that everybody eventually will be saved, that God is a God of love and He will never send anyone to hell. They believe that the words eternal or everlasting do not actually mean forever. However, the same word which speaks of eternal banishment from God is also used for the eternity of heaven. Someone has said that "fairness demands that we make the joy of the righteous and the punishment of the wicked both qualify, as they are the same Greek word and of the same duration."

There are others who teach that after death those who have refused to receive God's plan of redemption are annihilated; they cease to exist. In searching the Bible from cover to cover I cannot find one shred of evidence to support this view. The Bible teaches that whether we are saved or lost, there is conscious and everlasting existence of the soul and personality.

There are others who teach that after death there is still a possibility of salvation, that God will offer a second chance. If this is true, the Bible gives no hint of it because the Bible is continually warning that "now is the accepted time; behold, now is the day of salvation" (2 Corinthians 6:2).

WHAT THE BIBLE SAYS

Scores of passages of Scripture could be quoted to support the fact that the Bible does teach there is hell for every man who willingly and knowingly rejects Christ as Lord and Savior:

> I am tormented in this flame (Luke 16:24).

> Whosoever shall say, Thou fool, shall be in danger of hell fire (Matthew 5:22).

> The Son of Man shall send forth his angels, and they shall gather out of his kingdom all things that offend, and them which do iniquity; and shall cast them into a furnace of fire: there shall be wailing and gnashing of teeth (Matthew 13:41–42).

> So shall it be at the end of the world: the angels shall come forth, and sever the wicked from among the just, and shall cast them

into the furnace of fire: there shall be wailing and gnashing of teeth (Matthew 13:49–50).

Then shall he say also unto them on the left hand, Depart from me, ye cursed, into everlasting fire, prepared for the devil and his angels (Matthew 25:41).

But he will burn up the chaff with unquenchable fire" (Matthew 3:12).

In flaming fire taking vengeance on them that know not God, and that obey not the gospel of our Lord Jesus Christ: Who shall be punished with everlasting destruction from the presence of the Lord, and from the glory of his power (1 Thessalonians 1:8–9).

The same shall drink of the wine of the wrath of God, which is poured out without mixture into the cup of his indignation; and he shall be tormented with fire and brimstone in the presence of the holy angels, and in the presence of the Lamb: and the smoke of their torment ascendeth up for ever and ever: and they have no rest day nor night (Revelation 14:10–11).

And death and hell were cast into the lake of fire. This is the second death. And whosoever was not found written in the Book of Life was cast into the lake of fire (Revelation 20:14–15).

But the fearful, and unbelieving, and the abominable, and murderers, and whoremongers, and sorcerers, and idolaters, and all liars,

> shall have their part in the lake which burneth with fire and brimstone: which is the second death (Revelation 21:8).

But I hear someone say, "I don't believe in hell. My religion is the Sermon on the Mount." Well, let's listen to a passage from the Sermon on the Mount:

> And if thy right eye offend thee, pluck it out, and cast it from thee: for it is profitable for thee that one of thy members should perish, and not that thy whole body should be cast into hell. And if thy right hand offend thee, cut it off, and cast it from thee: for it is profitable for thee that one of thy members should perish, and not that thy whole body should be cast into hell (Matthew 5:29–30).

Here we have the distinct teaching of Jesus that there is a hell. In fact, Jesus told stories and gave illustrations on the subject and warned men time after time about the folly of living a sinful and hypocritical life here on earth.

HELL ON EARTH

There is no doubt that wicked men suffer a certain hell here on earth. The Bible says, "Be sure your sin will find you out" (Numbers 32:23). Again the Bible says, "Whatsoever a man soweth, that shall he also reap" (Galatians 6:7). However, there is evidence all around us to show that some wicked men seem to prosper and the righteous suffer for their righteousness. The Bible teaches that there is going to be a time of equalization when justice shall be done.

Someone has said that "we are not punished for our sins but by them." Both are true.

Will a loving God send a man to hell? The answer is yes, because He is just, but He does not send him willingly. Man condemns himself by his refusal of God's way of salvation. In love and mercy, God is offering to men and women a way of escape, a way of salvation, a hope and anticipation of better things. Man in his blindness, stupidity, stubbornness, egotism, and love of sinful pleasure refuses God's simple method of escaping the pangs of eternal banishment.

Suppose I am sick and call a doctor, who comes and gives me a prescription. But, after thinking it over, I decide to ignore his advice and to refuse the medicine. When he returns a few days later he might find my condition much worse. Could I blame the doctor—could I hold him responsible? He gave me the prescription. He prescribed the remedy. But I refused it!

Just so, God prescribes the remedy for the ills of the human race. That remedy is personal faith and commitment to Jesus Christ. The remedy is to be born again, as we will discuss in another chapter. If we deliberately refuse it, then we must suffer the consequence; we cannot blame God. Is it God's fault because we refuse the remedy?

The man who refuses to believe in life after death, in heaven to gain or hell to shun the man who refuses to believe what God says in His Word about heaven and hell—awakes in the next life to find that he has been wrong, he has lost everything. In *People* magazine, one of the nation's leading gamblers, Lem Banker, has been quoted as saying, "Never bet what you want to win, only what you can afford to lose." Can you afford to lose your eternal soul?

There are others who ask, "What is the nature of hell?" There are four words that have been translated in our Bible as "hell." One word is *Sheol*, which is translated thirty-one times as "hell" in the Old Testament. It means an "unseen state." The concepts of sorrow, pain, and destruction are used in connection with it.

The second word is *Hades*, which is translated from the Greek and used ten times in the New Testament. It means the same as *Sheol* in the Old Testament. Judgment and suffering are always connected with it.

The third word is *Tartarus*, used only once in 2 Peter 2:4, where it says that disobedient angels are cast into Tartarus. It indicates a place of judgment, such as a prison, or dungeon, where there is intense darkness.

The fourth word is *Gehenna*, used eleven times and translated as "hell" in the New Testament. It is the illustration that Jesus used of the Valley of Hinnon, a place outside Jerusalem where rubbish and debris were burned continually.

Others ask, "Does the Bible teach literal fire in hell?" If it is not literal fire, it is something worse. Jesus would not have exaggerated. There is no doubt that the Bible many times uses the word *fire* figuratively. However, God does have a fire that burns and yet does not consume.

When Moses saw the bush of fire, he was amazed to find that the bush was not consumed. The three Hebrew children were put in a fiery furnace, but they were not consumed; in fact, not a hair of their heads was singed.

On the other hand, the Bible talks about our tongues being "set on fire of hell" (James 3:6) every time we speak evil about our neighbors. That does not mean that literal combustion takes place every time we say something against our neighbors. But whether it be literal or figurative does not affect its reality. If there is no fire, then God is using symbolic language to indicate something that could be far worse.

SEPARATION FROM GOD

Essentially, hell is separation from God. It is the second death, which is described as the eternal, conscious banishment from the presence of all that is light, joyous, good, righteous, and happy. The Bible has many fearful descriptions concerning this awful condition in which the soul will find itself one minute after death.

It is strange that men will prepare for everything except death. We prepare for education. We prepare for business. We prepare for our careers. We prepare for marriage. We prepare for old age. We prepare for everything except the moment we are to die. Yet the Bible says it is appointed unto all of us once to die.

Death is an occurrence that to each man seems unnatural when related to himself, but natural when related to others. Death reduces all men to the same rank. It strips the rich man of his millions and the poor man of his rags. It cools avarice and stills the fires of passion. All would like to ignore death, and yet all must face it—the prince and the peasant, the fool and the philosopher, the murderer and the saint alike. Death knows no age limits, no partiality. It is a thing that all men fear.

Toward the end of his life, Daniel Webster related how once he attended a church service in a quiet country village. The clergyman was a simple-hearted, pious old man. After the opening exercises he arose and pronounced his text, and then with the utmost simplicity and earnestness said, "My friends, we can die but once."

Daniel Webster, commenting on this sermon, later said, "Frigid and weak as these words might seem, at once they were to me among the most impressive and awakening I ever heard."

An Appointment with Death

It is easy to think of others having to keep this appointment with death, but it is difficult for us to remember that we, too, must keep this same appointment. When we see soldiers going to the front or read of a condemned prisoner or visit a dying friend, we are conscious of a certain solemnity that gathers about such persons. Death is appointed for all, and the question of its occurrence is merely a matter of time. Other appointments in life—the appointment of pleasure—we can neglect or break and take the consequence, but here is an appointment that no man can ignore, no man can break. He can meet it only once but meet it he must!

If physical death were the only consequence of a life lived apart from God, we would not have so much to fear, but the Bible warns that there is the second death, which is the eternal banishment from God.

However, there is a brighter side. As the Bible pronounces hell for the sinner, it also promises heaven for the saint. A saint has been described as a sinner who has been forgiven. The subject of heaven is much easier to accept than the subject of hell. And yet the Bible teaches both.

If you are moving to a new home, you want to know all about the community to which you are going. If you are transferring to another city, you want to know all about the city—its railroads, industries, parks, lakes, schools, etc. Since we are going to spend eternity someplace, we ought to know something about it. The information concerning heaven is found in the Bible. It is right that we should think about it and talk about it. In talking about heaven, earth grows shabby by comparison. Our sorrows and problems here seem so much less when we have keen anticipation of the future. In a certain sense, the Christian has heaven here on earth. He has peace of soul, peace of conscience, and peace with God. In the midst of troubles and difficulties he has an inner peace and joy, not dependent on circumstances.

THERE IS A HEAVEN

But the Bible also promises the Christian a heaven in the life hereafter. Someone asked John Quincy Adams at the age of ninety-four how he felt one morning. He said, "Quite well. Quite well. But the house I live in is not so good." Even though the house we live in may be sick and weak, we can actually feel strong and sure if we are Christians. Jesus taught there is a heaven.

There are a number of passages that could be quoted about heaven but the most descriptive is found in John 14:2: "In my Father's house are many rooms; if it were not so, would I have told you that I go to prepare a place for you? And when I go and prepare a place for you, I will come again and receive you to myself, that where I am there you may be also" (RSV). Paul was so certain of heaven that he could say, "We are confident, I say, and willing rather to be absent from the body and to be present with the Lord" (2 Corinthians 5:8).

How different is the anticipation of the Christian and that of the agnostic Bob Ingersoll, who said at the grave of his brother, "Life is a narrow veil between the cold and barren peaks of two eternities. We strive in vain to look beyond the heights. We cry aloud and the only answer is the echo of our wailing cry."

The apostle Paul said time after time, "We know," "We are confident," "We are always confident." The Bible says that Abraham "looked for a city which hath foundations, whose builder and maker is God."

Many people say, "Do you believe that heaven is a literal place?" Yes! Jesus said, "I go to prepare a place for you." The Bible teaches that Enoch and Elijah ascended in a literal body to a literal place that is just as real as Hawaii, Switzerland, the Virgin Islands, or more so!

Many people have asked, "Where is heaven?" We are not told in the Scripture where heaven is. Nor does it matter. It will be heaven and Christ will be there to welcome us home.

A Place of Beauty

The Bible teaches that this country will be a place of beauty. It is described in the Bible as "a building of God"—"a city"—"a better country"—"an inheritance"—"a glory."

You may ask, "Will we know each other in heaven?" The Bible

indicates in a number of places that it will be a time of grand reunion with those who have gone on before.

Others say, "Do you believe that children will be saved?" Yes. The Bible indicates that God does not hold a child accountable for his or her sins until he reaches the age of accountability. There seems to be plenty of indication that the atonement covers their sin until they reach an age at which they are responsible for their own right and wrong actions.

The Bible also indicates that heaven will be a place of great understanding and knowledge of things that we never learned down here.

Sir Isaac Newton, when an old man, said to one who praised his wisdom, "I am as a child on the seashore picking up a pebble here and a shell there, but the great ocean of truth still lies before me."

And Thomas Edison once said, "I do not know one millionth part of one percent about anything."

Many of the mysteries of God, the heartaches, trials, disappointments, tragedies, and the silence of God in the midst of suffering will be revealed there. Elie Wiesel said that eternity is "the place where questions and answers become one." And in John 16:23 Jesus says, "And in that day ye shall ask me nothing." All our questions will be answered!

Many people ask, "Well, what will we do in heaven? Just sit down and enjoy the luxuries of life?" No. The Bible indicates that we will serve God. There will be work to do for God. Our very beings will praise God. The Bible says, "And there shall be no more curse; but the throne of God and of the Lamb shall be in it; and his servants shall serve him" (Revelation 22:3).

It will be a time of total joy, service, laughter, singing, and praise to God. Imagine serving Him forever and never growing tired!

INTO THE PRESENCE OF CHRIST

Now the Bible teaches to be absent from the body is to be present with the Lord. The moment a Christian dies, he goes immediately into the presence of Christ. There his soul awaits the resurrection, when the soul and body will be rejoined.

Many people ask, "How can the bodies that have decayed or been cremated be raised?" God knows. But the new body that we will have will be a glorious body like the body of Christ. It will be an eternal body. It will never know tears, heartache, tragedy, disease, suffering, death, or fatigue. It will be a renewed body, but still recognizable.

Here we have a picture of two eternal worlds floating out into space. Every son of Adam will be on one or the other. There is a great deal of mystery surrounding both of them, but there are enough hints and implications in the Bible to give us light that one will be a world of tragedy and suffering and the other will be one of light and glory.

We have now seen the problems of the human race. Superficially, they are complex; basically, they are simple. We have seen that they could probably be summed up in one word—sin. We have seen that man's future is hopeless without God. But just to analyze our problems and have an intellectual understanding of God's plan is not enough. If God is to help man, then man must meet certain conditions. In the next few chapters we will survey these conditions.

Part Two

Advancing the Solution

8

Why Jesus Came

The Son of man is come to seek
and to save that which was lost.
Luke 19:10

We have seen that the most terrible, the most devastating fact in the universe is sin. The cause of all trouble, the root of all sorrow, the dread of every man lies in this one small word—sin. It has crippled the nature of man. It has destroyed the inner harmony of man's life. It has robbed him of his nobility. It has caused man to be caught in the devil's trap.

All mental disorders, all sicknesses, all perversions, all destruction, all wars find their *original* root in sin. It causes madness in the brain and poison in the heart. It is described in the Bible as a fatal disease that demands a radical cure. It is a tornado on the loose. It is a volcano gone wild. It is a madman escaped from the asylum. It is a gangster on the prowl. It is a roaring lion seeking its prey. It is a streak of lightning heading toward the earth. It is quicksand sucking man under. It is a deadly cancer eating its way into the souls of men. It is a raging torrent that sweeps everything before it. It is a cesspool of corruption contaminating every area of life.

But, as someone has said, "Sin can keep you from the Bible—or the Bible can keep you from sin."

For ages men were lost in spiritual darkness, blinded by the disease of sin, made to grope—searching, questing, seeking some way out. Man needed someone who could lead him out of the mental confusion and moral labyrinth, someone who could unlock the prison doors and redeem him from the devil's prison. Men with hungry hearts, thirsty minds, and broken spirits stood hopelessly with searching eyes and listening ears. Meanwhile, the devil gloated over his mighty victory in the Garden of Eden.

From the primitive man in the jungle through the mighty civilizations of Egypt, Greece, and Rome, bewildered men were all asking the same questions: "How can I get out? How can I be better? What can I do? Which way can I turn? How can I get rid of this terrible disease? How can I stop this onrushing torrent? How can I get out of the mess in which I find myself? If there is a way, how can I find it?"

THE BIBLE'S ANSWER

We have already seen how the Bible teaches that God was a God of love. He wanted to do something for man. He wanted to save man. He wanted to free man from the curse of sin. How could He do it? God was a just God. He was righteous and holy. He had warned man from the beginning that if he obeyed the devil and disobeyed God, he would die physically and spiritually. Man deliberately disobeyed God. Man had to die or God would have been a liar, for God could not break His word. His very nature would not allow Him to lie. His word had to be kept. Therefore, when man deliberately disobeyed Him, he was banished from the presence of God. He deliberately chose to go the devil's way.

There had to be some other way, for man was hopelessly involved and helplessly lost. Man's very nature was inverted. He opposed God. Many even denied that God existed, so blinded were they by the disease from which they suffered.

But even in the Garden of Eden, God gave a hint that He was going to do something about it. He warned the devil and promised man, "And I will put enmity between thee and the woman, and between thy seed and her seed; it shall bruise thy head, and thou shalt bruise his heel" (Genesis 3:15). "And thou shalt bruise his heel"—here was a brilliant flash of light from heaven. The head refers to a total permanent wound; the heel refers to a temporary injury. Here was a promise. Here was something that man could hold on to. God was promising that someday a Redeemer would come, a Deliverer would come. God gave man hope. Down through the centuries man held on to that one bit of hope!

That was not all. There were other occasions through the thousands of years of history when other flashes of light came from heaven. All through the Old Testament, God gave man the promise of salvation if by faith he would believe in the coming Redeemer. Therefore God began to teach His people that man could only be saved by substitution. Someone else would have to pay the penalty for man's redemption.

Go Back to Eden

Go back again with me in your imagination to Eden for a moment. God said, "In the day that thou eatest thereof thou shalt surely die." Man did eat of it. He died.

Suppose that God had said, "Adam, you must have made a mistake; that was a slight error on your part. You are forgiven. Please don't do it again." God would have been a liar. He would not have been holy, neither would He have been just. He was forced by His very nature to keep His word. God's justice was at stake. Man had to die spiritually and physically. His iniquities had separated him from his God. Thus man had to suffer. He had to pay for his own sins. As we have seen, Adam was the federal head of the human race. When Adam sinned, we all sinned. "Wherefore, as by one man sin entered into the world, and death by sin; and so death passed upon all men, for that all have sinned" (Romans 5:12).

The burning question became, "How can God be just and still justify the sinner?" It must be remembered that the word *justify* means the "clearance of the soul from guilt." Justification is far more than just forgiveness. Sin must be put away and made as though it had never been. Man must be restored so that there shall be no spot or blemish or stain. In other words, man must be taken back to the position he had before he fell from grace.

For centuries men in their blindness have been trying to get back to Eden—but they have never been able to reach their goal. They have tried many paths, but they have all failed. C. S. Lewis says that "All religions are either a preview or a perversion of Christianity."

Education is important, but education will not bring a man back to God. False religions are an opiate that attempt to keep men from present misery while promising future glory, but they will never bring man to the place of his goal. The United Nations may be a practical necessity in a world of men at war, and we are thankful for every step that can be taken in the field of international relations to settle disputes without recourse to war; but if the United Nations could bring lasting peace, man could say to God, "We do not need You anymore. We have brought peace on earth and have organized humanity in righteousness." All of these schemes are patchwork remedies that a sick and dying world must use while waiting for the Great Physician. Back in history we know that the first attempt of united man ended with the confusion of tongues at the Tower of Babel. Men have failed on every other occasion when they have tried to work without God, and they will continue to be doomed to such failures.

The question remains, "How can God be just—that is, true to Himself in nature and true to Himself in holiness—and yet justify the sinner?" Because each man had to bear his own sins, all mankind was excluded from helping, since each was contaminated with the same disease.

The only solution was for an innocent party to volunteer to die physically and spiritually as a substitution before God. This innocent party would have to take man's judgment, penalty, and death. But where was such an individual? Certainly there was none perfect on earth, for the Bible says, "All have sinned" (Romans 3:23). There was only one possibility. God's own Son was the only personality in the universe who had the capacity to bear in His own body the sins of the whole world. Certainly Gabriel or Michael the archangel might possibly have come and died for one, but only God's Son was infinite and thus able to die for all.

God in Three Persons

The Bible teaches that God is actually three Persons. This is a mystery that we will never be able to understand. The Bible does not teach that there are three Gods, but that there is one God. This one God, however, is expressed in three Persons. There is God the Father, God the Son, and God the Holy Spirit.

The Second Person of this Trinity is God's Son, Jesus Christ. He is coequal with God the Father. He was not *a* Son of God but *the* Son of God. He is the Eternal Son of God—the Second Person of the Holy Trinity, God manifested in the flesh, the living Savior.

The Bible teaches that Jesus Christ had no beginning. He was never created. The Bible teaches that the heavens were created by Him (John 1:1–3). All the myriads of stars and flaming suns were created by Him. The earth was flung from His flaming fingertip. The birth of Jesus Christ that we celebrate at Christmastime was not His beginning. His origin is shrouded in that same mystery that baffles us when we inquire into the beginning of God. The Bible only tells us, "In the beginning was the Word, and the Word was with God, and the Word was God" (John 1:1).

About Christ, the Bible teaches us, "Who is the image of the invisible God, the firstborn of every creature: For by him were all things created, that are in heaven, and that are in earth, visible and invisible, whether they be thrones, or dominions, or principalities, or powers: all things were created by him, and for him: And he is before all things, and by him all things consist" (Colossians 1:15–17).

That last phrase indicates that He holds all things together. In other words, the entire universe would smash into billions of atoms were it not for the cohesive power of Jesus Christ. The Bible again says, "And, thou, Lord, in the beginning has laid the foundation of the earth; and the heavens are the works of thine hands: They shall perish; but thou remainest; and they all shall wax old as doth a garment; And as a vesture shalt thou fold them up, and they shall be changed: but thou art the same, and thy years shall not fail" (Hebrews 1:10–12).

JESUS CHRIST, THE REDEEMER

Again Jesus said of Himself, "I am Alpha and Omega, the beginning and the end." He, and He alone, had the power and capacity to bring man back to God. But would He? If He did, He would have to come to earth. He would have to take the form of a servant. He would have to be made in the likeness of men. He would have to humble Himself and become obedient unto death. He would have to grapple with sin. He would have to meet and overcome Satan, the enemy of man's souls. He would have to redeem sinners out of the slave market of sin. He would have to loose the bonds and set the prisoners free by paying a price—that price would be His own life. He would have to be despised and rejected of men, a man of sorrows and acquainted with grief. He would have to be smitten of

God and separated from God. He would have to be wounded for the transgressions of men and bruised for their iniquities, His blood shed to atone for man's sin. He would have to reconcile God and man. He would be the great Mediator of history. He would have to be a substitute. He would have to die in the place of sinful man. All this would have to be done—voluntarily.

And that is exactly what happened! Looking down over the battlements of heaven He saw this planet swinging in space—doomed, damned, crushed, and bound for hell. He saw you and me struggling beneath our load of sin and bound in the chains and ropes of sin. He made His decision in the council halls of God. The angelic hosts bowed in humility and awe as heaven's Prince of princes and Lord of lords, who could speak worlds into space, got into His jeweled chariot, went through pearly gates and across the steep of the skies, and on a black Judean night, while the stars sang together and the escorting angels chanted His praises, stepped out of the chariot, threw off His robes, and became man!

It was as though I, while walking along a road, stepped on an anthill. I might look down and say to the ants, "I am terribly sorry that I've stepped on your anthill. I've disrupted your home. Everything is in confusion. I wish I could tell you that I care, that I did not mean to do it, that I would like to help you."

But you say, "That's absurd; that's impossible. Ants cannot understand your language!" That's just it! How wonderful it would be if I could only become an ant for a few moments and in their own language tell them of my concern for them!

That, in effect, is what Christ did. He came to reveal God to men. He it is who told us that God loves us and is interested in our lives. He it is who told us of the mercy and long-suffering and grace of God. He it is who promised life everlasting.

But more than that, Jesus Christ partook of flesh and blood in order that He might die (Hebrews 2:14). "He was manifested to take away our sins" (1 John 3:5). The very purpose of Christ's coming into the world was that He might offer up His life as a sacrifice for the sins of men. He came to die. The shadow of His death hung like a pall over all of His thirty-three years.

The night Jesus was born Satan trembled. He sought to slay Him before He was born and tried to slay Him as soon as He was born. When the decree went forth from Herod ordering the slaughter of all the children, its one purpose was to make certain of the death of Jesus.

THE SINLESS SON

All the days of His life on earth He never once committed a sin. He is the only man who ever lived who was sinless. He could stand in front of men and ask, "Which of you convinceth me of sin?" (John 8:46). He was hounded by the enemy day and night, but they never found any sin in Him. He was without spot or blemish.

Jesus lived a humble life. He made Himself of no reputation. He received no honor of men. He was born in a stable. He was reared in the insignificant village of Nazareth. He was a carpenter. He gathered around Him a humble group of fishermen as His followers. He walked among men as a man. He was one of the people. He humbled Himself as no other man has ever humbled himself.

Jesus taught with such authority that the people of His day said, "Never man spake like this man" (John 7:46). Every word that He spoke was historically true. Every word that He spoke was scientifically true. Every word that He spoke was ethically true. There were no loopholes in the moral conceptions and statements of Jesus Christ. His ethical vision was wholly correct, correct in the age in which He lived and correct in every age that has followed it.

The words of this blessed Person were prophetically true. He prophesied many things that are even yet in the future. Lawyers tried to catch Him with test questions, but they could never confuse Him. His answers to His opponents were clear and clean-cut. There were no question marks about His statements, no deception in His meaning, no hesitancy in His words. He knew, and therefore spoke with quiet authority. He spoke with such simplicity that the common people heard Him gladly. Though His words were profound, they were plain. His words were weighty, yet they shone with a luster and simplicity of statement that staggered His enemies. He dealt with the great questions of the day in such a way that, from simple to sophisticated, man had no difficulty in understanding Him.

The Lord Jesus cured the sick, the lame, the halt, and the blind. He healed the leper and raised the dead. He cast out demons. He quieted the elements. He stilled storms. He brought peace, joy, and hope to the thousands to whom He ministered.

He showed no sign of fear. He was never in a hurry. He met with no accidents. He moved with perfect coordination and precision. He had supreme poise of bearing. He did not waver or worry about His work. Though He did not heal all the sick, raise all the dead, open the eyes of all the blind, or feed all the hungry, at the end of His life He could say, "I have finished the work thou gavest me to do."

He stood before Pilate and quietly said, "Thou couldst have no power at all against me, except it were given thee from above" (John 19:11). He told the frightened people that angelic legions were at His command.

He approached His cross with dignity and calmness, with an assurance and a set purpose that fulfilled the prophecy written about Him eight hundred years earlier: "He is brought as a lamb to the slaughter, and as a sheep before her shearers is dumb, so he openeth not his mouth" (Isaiah 53:7).

Defeating the Devil

He moved supremely, gloriously, and with great anticipation toward the mission that He had come to accomplish. He had come to save sinful men. He had come to appease the wrath of God. He had come to defeat the devil forever. He had come to conquer hell and the grave. There was only one way that He could do it. There was only one course set before Him.

His death had been prophesied thousands of years before. First, as we have seen, in Eden's Garden; then, in sermon, story, and prophecy the death of Christ was set forth in the ages past. Abraham foresaw His death as the lamb was slain. The children of Israel symbolized His death in the slaughtered lamb. Every time blood was shed on a Jewish altar it represented the Lamb of God who was someday to come and take away sin. David prophesied

His death in detail in more than one prophetic psalm. Isaiah devoted whole chapters to predicting the details of His death.

Jesus Christ said that He had power to lay down His life when He said, "The good shepherd giveth his life for the sheep" (John 10:11). He said again, "Even so must the Son of man be lifted up: That whosoever believeth in him should not perish" (John 3:14–15). Jesus Christ had faced the possibility of the cross far back in eternity. During all the ages that preceded His birth, He knew that the day of His death was hastening on. When He was born of a virgin, He was born with the cross darkening His pathway. He had taken on a human body in order that He might die. From the cradle to the cross, His purpose was to die.

Someone has described how He suffered as no man has ever suffered:

> The night watches in Gethsemane, lighted by the flaming torches, the kiss of the traitor, the arrest, the trial before the high priest, the hour of waiting, the palace of the Roman governor, the journey to the palace of Herod, the rough handling by Herod's brutal soldiers, the awesome scenes while Pilate tried to save Him as priests and people clamored for His blood, the scourging, the howling multitudes, the path from Jerusalem to Golgotha, the nails in His hands, the spike through His feet, the crown of thorns upon His brow, the sarcastic and mocking cries of the two thieves on either side, "You have saved others; now save yourself."

Sometimes people have asked me why Christ died so quickly, in six hours, on the cross, while other victims agonized on the cross for two and three days—and longer. He was weak and exhausted when He came there. He had been scourged, He was physically depleted. But when Christ died, He died voluntarily. He chose the exact moment when He expired.

There He hung between heaven and earth. Having suffered unspeakably, He voiced neither complaint nor appeal but simply a statement by which He let us know in two words something of the terrible physical pain He suffered when he said, "I thirst."

Some unknown poet has put it this way:

> But more than pains wracked Him there
> Was the deep longing thirst divine
> That thirsted for the souls of men,
> Dear Lord—and one was mine!

Sinner or Substitute

God demands death, either for the sinner or a substitute. Christ was the substitute! Gabriel and ten legions of angels hovered on the rim of the universe, their swords unsheathed. One look from His blessed face and they would have swept the angry, shouting multitudes into hell. The spikes never held Him—it was the cords of love that bound tighter than any nails that men could mold. "But God commendeth his love toward us, in that, while we were yet sinners, Christ died for us" (Romans 5:8).

For you! For me! He bore our sins in His body upon the tree. As someone has said:

> Behold Him on the Cross, bending His sacred head, and gathering into His heart in the awful isolation of separation from God the issue of the sin of the world, and see how out of that acceptance of the issue of sin He creates that which He does not require for Himself that He may distribute to those whose place He has taken. Standing overwhelmed in the presence of this suffering, feeling our own inability to understand or explain, and with a great sense of might and majesty overwhelming us, we hear the next words that pass His lips, "It is finished."

But the physical suffering of Jesus Christ was not the real suffering. Many men before Him had died. Others had hung on a cross longer than He did. Many men had become martyrs. The awful suffering of Jesus Christ was His spiritual death. He reached the final issue of sin, fathomed the deepest sorrow, when He cried, "My God, why hast thou forsaken me?" This cry was proof that Christ, becoming sin for us, had died physically, and with it He lost all sense of the Father's presence at that moment in time. Alone in the supreme hour of mankind's history, Christ uttered these words! Light blazed forth to give us a glimpse of what He was enduring, but the light was so blinding, as G. Campbell Morgan says, "that no eye could bear to gaze." The words were uttered, as Dr. Morgan has so well expressed it, "that we men may know how much there is that may not be known."

He who knew no sin was made to be sin on our behalf that we might become the righteousness of God in Him (Galatians 3:13; Mark 15:34; 2 Corinthians 5:21). On the cross He was made sin. He was God-forsaken. Because He knew no sin there is a value beyond comprehension in the penalty He bore, a penalty that He did not need for Himself. If in bearing sin in His own body He created a value that He did not need for Himself, for whom was the value created?

How it was accomplished in the depth of the darkness man will never know. I know only one thing—He bore my sins in His body upon the tree. He hung where I should have hung. The pains of hell that were my portion were heaped on Him, and I am able to go to heaven and merit that which is not my own, but is His by every right. All the types, the offerings, the shadows, and the symbols of the Old Testament were now fulfilled. No longer do the priests have to enter once a year into the Holiest Place. The sacrifice was complete.

Now that the ground of redemption has been laid, all the guilty sinner has to do is believe on the Son, and he can have peace with God. "For God so loved the world, that he gave his only begotten Son, that whosoever believeth in him should not perish, but have everlasting life" (John 3:16).

Three Things in the Cross

In the cross of Christ I see three things: First, a description of the depth of *man's sin.* Do not blame the people of that day for hanging Christ on the cross. You and I are just as guilty. It was not the people or the Roman soldiers who put Him to the cross—it was your sins and my sins that made it necessary for Him to volunteer this death.

Second, in the cross I see the overwhelming *love of God.* If ever you should doubt the love of God, take a long, deep look at the cross, for in the cross you find the expression of God's love.

Third, in the cross is the only way of salvation. Jesus said, "I am the way, the truth and the life: no man cometh unto the Father but by me" (John 14:6). There is no possibility of being saved from sin and hell except by identifying yourself with the Christ of the cross. If there had been any other way to save you, He would have found it. If reformation or living a good moral and ethical life would have saved you, Jesus never would have died. A substitute had to take your place. Men do not like to talk about it. They do not like to hear about it because it injures their pride. It takes all self out.

Many people say, "Can I not be saved by living by the golden rule? Or following the precepts of Jesus? Or living the ethical life that Jesus taught?" Even if we could be saved by living the life that Jesus taught, we still would be sinners. We still would fail, because not one of us has ever lived the life that Jesus taught from the time we were born till the time we die. We have failed. We have transgressed. We have disobeyed. We have sinned. Therefore, what are we going to do about that sin? There is only one thing to do and that is to bring it to the cross and find forgiveness.

Years ago King Charles V was loaned a large sum of money by a merchant in Antwerp. The note came due, but the king was bankrupt and unable to pay. The merchant gave a great banquet for the king. When all the guests were seated and before the food was brought in, the merchant had a large platter placed on the table before him and a fire lighted on it. Then, taking the note out of his pocket, he held it in the flames until it was burned to ashes.

Just so, we have all been mortgaged to God. The debt was due, but we were unable to pay. Two thousand years ago God invited a morally corrupt world to the foot of the cross. There God held your sins and mine to the flames until every last vestige of our guilt was consumed.

The Bible says, "Without shedding of blood is no remission" (Hebrews 9:22). Many people have said to me, "How repulsive! You don't mean to tell us that you believe in a slaughterhouse religion!" Others have wondered, "I do not understand why God demands blood." Many people have wondered, "I cannot understand why Christ had to die for me." Today the idea of the shed blood of Christ is becoming old-fashioned and out of date in a lot of preaching. It is in the Bible. It is the very heart of Christianity. The distinctive feature of Christianity is blood atonement. Without it we cannot be saved. Blood is actually a symbol of the death of Christ.

Recently I was standing at the admissions desk at Mayo Clinic in Rochester, Minnesota. There, in a little box, were a number of folders entitled "A Gift of Blood" lettered in red forming a large drop of blood. My first reaction was that this must be a gospel tract, but on looking more closely I saw that it was a challenge to people to assist in the blood program. Blood could mean the difference between life and death for someone ill in the hospital. No one who has ever had to receive a blood transfusion will look upon that blood with anything but gratitude. Some might say that blood taken is somewhat revolting, but blood given is a blessing!

The fact remains that blood represents life, as Leviticus 17:11 says, "For the life of the flesh is in the blood and I have given it for you . . . to make atonement for your soul." So the blood sacrifice runs throughout the Old Testament—a foreshadowing or a symbol of Christ's perfect sacrifice.

FIVE THINGS BLOOD BRINGS

The Bible teaches that it first of all *redeems*: "Forasmuch as ye know that ye were not redeemed with corruptible things, as silver and gold, from your vain conversation received by tradition from your fathers; But with the precious blood of Christ, as of a lamb without blemish and without spot" (1 Peter 1:18–19). Not only are we redeemed from the hands of the devil, but from the hands of the law handed down by God through Moses. Christ's death on the cross brings me out from under the law. The law condemned me, but Christ satisfied every claim. All the gold and silver and the precious stones of earth could never have bought me. What they could not do, the death of Christ did. Redemption means "buying back." We had been sold for nothing to the devil, but Christ redeemed us and brought us back.

Second, it *brings us nigh*: "But now in Christ Jesus ye who sometimes were far off are made nigh by the blood of Christ" (Ephesians 2:13). When we were "aliens from the commonwealth of Israel, and strangers from the covenants of promise, having no hope, and without God in the world," Jesus Christ brought us nigh unto God. "There is therefore now no condemnation [judgment] to them which are in Christ Jesus" (Romans 8:1). The redeemed sinner will never have to face the judgment of Almighty God. Christ has already taken his judgment.

Third, it *makes peace*: "And, having made peace through the blood of his cross, by him to reconcile all things unto himself; by him, I say, whether they be things in earth, or things in heaven" (Colossians 1:20). The world will never know peace until it finds it in the cross of Jesus Christ. You will never know the peace with God, peace of conscience, peace of mind, and peace of soul until you stand at the foot of the cross and identify yourself with Christ by faith. There is the secret of peace. This is peace with God.

Fourth, it *justifies*: "Much more then, being now justified by his blood, we shall be saved from wrath through him" (Romans 5:9). It changes men's standing before God. It is a change from guilt and condemnation to pardon and forgiveness. The forgiven sinner is not like the discharged prisoner who has served out his term and is discharged but with no further rights of citizenship. The repentant sinner, pardoned through the blood of Jesus Christ, regains his full citizenship. "Who shall lay any thing to the charge of God's elect? It is God that justifieth. Who is he that condemneth? It is Christ that died, yea rather, that is risen again, who is even at the right hand of God, who also maketh intercession for us" (Romans 8:33–34).

Fifth, it *cleanses*: "But if we walk in the light, as he is in the light, we have fellowship one with another, and the blood of Jesus Christ his Son cleanseth us from all sin" (1 John 1:7). The key word in this verse is *all*. Not part of our sins, but *all* of them. Every lie you ever told, every mean, low-down dirty thing that you ever did, your hypocrisy, your lustful thoughts—all are cleansed by the death of Christ.

JUST AS I AM

The story has often been told that years ago, in London, there was a large gathering of noted people, and among the invited guests was a famous preacher of his day, Caesar Milan. A young lady played and sang charmingly and everyone was delighted. Very graciously, tactfully, and yet boldly the preacher went up to her after the music had ceased and said, "I thought as I listened to you tonight, how tremendously the cause of Christ would be benefited if your talents were dedicated to His cause. You know, young lady, you are as much a sinner in the sight of God as a drunkard in the ditch or a harlot on scarlet street. But I'm glad to tell you that the blood of Jesus Christ, His Son, can cleanse from all sin."

The young woman snapped out a rebuke for his presumption, to which he replied, "Lady, I mean no offense. I pray God's Spirit will convict you."

They all returned to their homes. The young woman retired but could not sleep. The face of the preacher appeared before her and his words rang through her mind. At two o'clock in the morning she sprang from her bed, took a pencil and paper, and with tears streaming down her face, Charlotte Elliott wrote her famous poem:

Just as I am, without one plea,
But that Thy blood was shed for me,
And that Thou bidd'st me come to Thee,
O Lamb of God, I come! I come!

Just as I am, and waiting not
To rid my soul of one dark blot,
To Thee, whose blood can cleanse each spot,
O Lamb of God, I come! I come!

But this is not the end. We do not leave Christ hanging on a cross with blood streaming down from His hands, His side, and His feet. He is taken down and laid carefully away in a tomb. A big stone is rolled against the entrance of the tomb. Soldiers are set to guard it. All day Saturday, His followers sit gloomily and sadly in the Upper Room. Two have already started toward Emmaus. Fear has gripped them all. Early on that first Easter morning, Mary, Mary Magdalene, and Salome make their way to the tomb to anoint the dead body. When they arrive, they are startled to find the tomb empty. As Alfred Edersheim, the Jewish scholar, writes, "There was no sign of haste, but all was orderly, leaving the impression of One Who had leisurely divested Himself of what no longer befitted Him." An angel is standing at the head of the tomb and asks, "Whom do you seek?" And they reply, "We seek Jesus of Nazareth." And then the angel gives the greatest, most glorious news that human ear has ever heard, "He is not here, He is risen."

THE FACT OF THE RESURRECTION

Upon that great fact hangs the entire plan of the redemptive program of God. Without the resurrection there could be no salvation. Christ predicted His resurrection many times. He said on one occasion, "For as Jonah was three days and three nights in the whale's belly; so shall the Son of man be three days and three nights in the heart of the earth" (Matthew 12:40). As He predicted, He rose!

There are certain laws of evidence that hold in the establishment of any historic event. There must be documentation of the event in question made by reliable contemporary witnesses. There is more evidence that Jesus rose from the dead than there is that Julius Caesar ever lived or that Alexander the Great died at the age of thirty-three. It is strange that historians will accept thousands of facts for which they can produce only shreds of evidence. But in the face of the overwhelming evidence of the resurrection of Jesus Christ they cast a skeptical eye and hold intellectual doubts. The trouble with these people is that they do not want to believe. Their spiritual vision is so blinded and they are so completely prejudiced that they cannot accept the glorious fact of the resurrection of Christ on Bible testimony alone.

The resurrection meant, first, that Christ was undeniably God. He was what He claimed to be. Christ was Deity in the flesh.

Second, it meant that God had accepted His atoning work on the cross, which was necessary to our salvation: "Who was delivered for our offenses, and was raised again for our justification" (Romans 4:25).

Third, it assures mankind of a righteous judgment. "For as by one man's disobedience many were made sinners, so by the obedience of one shall many be made righteous" (Romans 5:19).

Fourth, it guarantees that our bodies also will be raised in the end. "But now is Christ risen from the dead, and become the firstfruits of them that slept" (1 Corinthians 15:20). The Scripture teaches that as Christians, our bodies may go to the grave but they are going to be raised on the great resurrection morning. Then will death be swallowed up in victory. As a result of the resurrection of Christ the sting of death is gone and Christ Himself holds the keys. He says, "I am he that liveth, and was dead; and, behold, I am alive forevermore, Amen; and have the keys of hell and death" (Revelation 1:18). And Christ promises that "Because I live, ye shall live also."

Fifth, it means that death will ultimately be abolished. The power of death has been broken and death's fear has been removed. Now we can say with the Psalmist, "Yea, though I walk through the valley of the shadow of death, I will fear no evil: for thou art with me; Thy rod and thy staff they comfort me" (Psalm 23:4).

Paul looked forward to death with great anticipation as a result of the resurrection of Christ. He said, "For to me to live is Christ, and to die is gain" (Philippians 1:21). As Velma Barfield on Death Row in North Carolina said, "I love Him so much I can hardly wait to see Him."

Without the resurrection of Christ there could be no hope for the future. The Bible promises that someday we are going to stand face to face with the resurrected Christ, and we are going to have bodies like unto His own body.

Face to face with Christ my Savior,
Face to face, what will it be?
When with rapture I behold Him,
Jesus Christ who died for me?

Face to face I shall behold Him,
Far beyond the starry sky;
Face to face in all His glory
I shall see Him by and by.

Carrie E. Breck

9

How and Where to Begin

Except ye be converted, and become as little children,
ye shall not enter into the kingdom of heaven.
Matthew 18:3

We now recognize that there is a natural principle that pulls us down to the animal plane—blinding reason, searing conscience, paralyzing will. It is the pull of spiritual gravity. We stand condemned by our own deeds.

God is a holy and righteous God. He cannot tolerate sin. Sin separates from God. It brings the wrath of God upon the human soul. Man has lost his moral, intellectual, and spiritual sense of God because he has lost God. He will not find God until he finds the way back to God.

The way back to God is not an intellectual way. It is not a moral way. You cannot think your way back to God because human thought-life will not coordinate with divine thought-life, for the carnal mind is at enmity with God. You cannot worship your way back to God because man is a spiritual rebel from God's presence. You cannot moralize your way back to God because character is flawed with sin.

THE WAY BACK TO GOD

The natural questions come to you—What shall I do? Where shall I start? Where do I begin? What is my road back to God? There is only one way back to God. Jesus said, "Except ye be converted, and become as little children, ye shall not enter into the kingdom of heaven" (Matthew 18:3). It is significant that Jesus did not tell the little children to become as His disciples, but His disciples to become as little children. By childlike faith, everyone has a chance, from the feeble-minded to intellectuals. Thus Jesus demanded a conversion. This is how to begin! This is where it starts! You must be converted!

There are many people who confuse conversion with the keeping of the law. The law of Moses is set forth in specific terms in the Bible and the purpose of the law is made very clear. It was not offered at any time as a panacea for the world's ills. Rather, it was given as a diagnosis of the world's ills; it outlines the reason for our trouble, not the cure. The Bible says, "Now we know that what things soever the law saith, it saith to them who are under the law: that every mouth may be stopped, and all the world may become guilty before God" (Romans 3:19). The law has given a revelation of man's unrighteousness, and the Bible says, "By the deeds of the law there shall no flesh be justified in his sight" (Romans 3:20). It is impossible to be converted by the keeping of the law. The Bible says, "By the law is the knowledge of sin." The law is a moral mirror, the gauge by which man can see how far he has fallen. It condemns but does not convert. It challenges but does not change. It points the finger but does not offer mercy. There is no life in the law. There is only death, for the pronouncement of the law was, "Thou shalt die." It is the "straight stick" beside which the crookedness of human nature is obvious.

There are many people who say that their religion is the Sermon on the Mount, but the man or woman is yet to be born who has ever lived up to the Sermon on the Mount. The Bible says that all have sinned and come short of His glory.

Examine your own motives before you decide that you are above reproach and living a life that absolves you from all need of conversion. Look into your own heart fearlessly and honestly before you say religious conversion is alright for some but you certainly don't stand to benefit from it.

The Universal Question

When I was preaching in Hollywood, a group of movie people asked me to talk to them about religious experiences. After my address we had a discussion period and the very first question asked was, "What is conversion?"

Sometime later it was my privilege to address a group of political leaders in Washington. When the discussion period started, the first question again was, "What is conversion?"

In almost every university and college group where I have led discussions, this same question is invariably asked, "What do you mean by 'born again'?" In my book *How to Be Born Again* (Word, 1976), I described the process this way:

This new birth happens in all kinds of ways. It may seem to happen over a period of time or in a moment. The paths which people take to reach that point of decision may be very direct or very circuitous. Whatever the path, we always find Christ at the end to welcome us. That encounter with Christ, that new birth, is the beginning of a whole new path in life under His control. Lives can be remarkably changed, marriages excitingly improved, societies influenced for good—all by the simple, sweeping surge of individuals knowing what it is to be born again.

In today's economy we hear about "born again" cars, businesses, and fashions—but that is not what I'm talking about here. Probably the simplest way to state what it means to be "born again" is to refer to it as being born into God's family.

Probably there are more different answers to this query than to almost any other pertaining to religion. What is conversion? What is involved in it? How is it accomplished? What are its effects? Why must you be converted in order to get to heaven?

The idea of conversion is certainly not unusual in our society. Any good salesman knows that he must convert the prospect to his particular product or way of thinking. The chief business of advertising is to convert the buying public from one brand to another. We speak of political leaders being converted from their original political philosophy and adopting a different one. During the last war, we heard a great deal about peacetime industries converting to war production, and most of the oil furnaces in private homes were converted to coal and, more recently, converted from coal back to gas. We also talk about converting our money into foreign currency.

Actually, the word conversion means "to turn around," "to change one's mind," "to turn back," or "to return." In the realm of religion it has been variously explained as "to repent," "to be regenerated," "to receive grace," "to experience religion," "to gain assurance."

I remember one confirmed alcoholic who came to one of the opening meetings of a crusade and said to me, "Mr. Graham, I'm not sure there's a word of truth in what you're saying, but I'm going to give your Christ a trial, and if He works even a little bit the way you say He will, I'll come back and sign up for life!"

Weeks later he told me that he didn't quite understand it, but every time he started to take a drink it seemed as though something or someone stopped him. Christ had given him victory over his vicious habit. He returned to his family and is now living his life for Christ. In other words, he turned around, he changed his direction, he changed his way of thinking—he had been converted!

THE NATURE OF CONVERSION

Conversion can take many different forms. The way it is accomplished depends largely upon the individual—his temperament, his emotional balance, his environment, and his previous conditioning and way of life. Conversion may follow a great crisis in a person's life; or, it could come after all former values have been swept away, when great disappointment has been experienced, when one has lost one's sense of power through material possessions or lost the object of one's affections. A man or woman who has been focusing all attention on financial gains or business or social prestige, or centering all affection on one person experiences a devastating sense of loss when denied the thing that has given life its meaning.

In these tragic moments, as the individual stands stripped of all his worldly power, when the loved one is gone beyond recall, he recognizes how terribly and completely alone he really is. In that moment, the Holy Spirit may cause the spiritual bandages to fall from his eyes and he sees clearly for the first time. He recognizes that God is the only source of real power and the only enduring fountainhead of love and companionship.

Or again, conversion may take place at the very height of personal power or prosperity—when all things are going well and the bountiful mercies of God have been bestowed generously upon you. The very goodness of God can drive you to a recognition that you owe all to God; thus, the very goodness of God leads you to repentance (Romans 2:4).

Conversion at such a moment can be as sudden and dramatic as the conversion of Paul on the road to Damascus.

Not all conversions come as a sudden, brilliant flash of soul illumination that we call a crisis conversion. There are many others that are accomplished only after a long and difficult conflict with inner motives of the person. With others, conversion comes at the climactic moment of a long period of gradual conviction of their need and revelation of the plan of salvation. This prolonged process results in conscious acceptance of Christ as personal Savior and in the yielding of life to Him.

In his spiritual autobiography, C. S. Lewis describes his conversion experience:

> You must picture me alone in that room in Magdalen, night after night, feeling, whenever my mind lifted even for a second from my work, the steady, unrelenting approach of Him whom I so earnestly desired not to meet. That which I greatly feared had at last come upon me. In the Trinity Term of 1929 I gave in, and admitted that God was God, and knelt and prayed: perhaps, that night, the most dejected and reluctant convert in all England. I do not then see what is now the most shining and obvious thing; the Divine humility which will accept a convert even on such terms. The Prodigal Son at least walked home on his own feet. But who can duly adore that Love which will open the high gates to a prodigal who is brought in kicking, struggling, resentful, and darting his eyes in every direction for a chance of escape? The words *compelle intrare*, "compel them to come in," have been so abused by wicked men that we shudder at them; but, properly understood, they plumb the depth of the Divine mercy. The hardness of God is kinder than the softness of men, and His compulsion is our liberation.*

We may say, therefore, that conversion can be an instantaneous event, a crisis in which the person receives a clear revelation of the love of God; or, it can be a gradual unfolding accompanied by

---

* From *Surprised by Joy: The Shape of My Early Life*, copyright 1966 by Harcourt, Brace, Jovanovich, pp. 228–229.

a climactic moment at the time the line is crossed between darkness and light, between death and life everlasting.

It does not always happen in exactly this way. My wife, for example, cannot remember the exact day or hour when she became a Christian, but she is certain that there was such a moment in her life, a moment when she actually crossed the line. Many young people who have grown up in Christian homes and had the benefit of Christian training are unaware of the time when they committed their lives to Christ. Someone has said we may not know the exact moment when the sun rises—but we most certainly know once it has risen. Others remember very clearly when they made their public confession of faith. The reports of conversions in the New Testament indicate that most of them were the dramatic, crisis type.

Psychology Looks at Conversion

For many years, psychology left conversion and religious experience alone. In the last fifty years, however, psychologists have studied the whole process of conversion. They have pointed out that conversion is not only a Christian experience, but it is also found in other religions; it is not necessarily a religious phenomenon but it also occurs in nonreligious spheres. Students of psychology have agreed that there are three steps in conversion: First, a sense of perplexity and uneasiness; second, a climax and turning point; and, third, a relaxation marked by rest and joy.

In an article entitled "Why It's Good to Feel So Bad," The *New York Times* (29 November 1983) pointed out, "Guilt, the sense of anguish that we have fallen short of our own standards, is the guardian of our goodness. It is necessary to the development of conscience in children and to the avoidance of antisocial behavior." The article goes on to explain,

> In early childhood, good behavior is enforced mainly through parental introduction of guilty fear, the fear of punishment for violating a code of behavior. But as the child grows up, an 'ego ideal'—a form of father figure—becomes internalized as a model of correct behavior . . . and by adulthood, people seek to punish themselves when they betray that model. Dr. Gaylin sees the lack of appropriate role models or father figures as one cause of the growing rash of guiltless antisocial behavior among young people today."

It is this feeling of guilt that creates the hunger for something better—to be found only in a right relationship to Christ.

Psychologists say that there are two kinds of conversion. One is accompanied by a violent sense of sin, and the other by a feeling of incompleteness, a struggle after a larger life and a desire for spiritual illumination.

The value of psychological studies of conversion has been underestimated. We cannot brush them aside and ignore them. Psychologists shed a great deal of light, but most of them are unwilling to accept the biblical conversion as a supernatural experience.

Actually, biblical conversion involves three steps—two of them active and one passive. In active conversion, repentance and faith are involved. Repentance is conversion viewed from its starting point, the turning from the former life. Faith indicates the objective point of conversion, the turning of God. The third, which is passive, we may call the new birth, or regeneration, commonly called being "born again," which literally means being born into God's family.

In order to get to heaven, Jesus said that you must be converted. I didn't say it—Jesus said it! This is not man's opinion—this is God's opinion! Jesus said, "Except ye be converted, and become as little children, ye shall not enter into the kingdom of heaven" (Matthew 18:3).

True conversion will involve the mind, the affection, and the will. There have been thousands of people who have been intellectually converted to Christ. They believe the entire Bible. They believe all about Jesus, but they have never been really converted to Him. The Bible tells us "even the devils believe and tremble" (James 2:19).

The Difference Between Intellectual Belief and Conversion

In John there is a description of the hundreds of people who were following Jesus early in His ministry. The Bible says that "many believed in his name when they saw the miracles which he did. But Jesus did not commit himself unto them" (John 2:23–24) because He knew the hearts of all men. Why would Jesus not commit Himself to them? He knew that they believed with their heads and not with their hearts.

There is a vast difference between intellectual belief and the total conversion that saves the soul. To be sure, there must be a change in our thinking and intellectual acceptance of Christ.

There are thousands of people who have had some form of emotional experience that they refer to as conversion but who have never been truly converted to Christ. Christ demands a change in the way you live—and if your life does not conform to your experience, then you have every reason to doubt your experience! Certainly there will be a change in the elements that make up emotion when you come to Christ—hate and love will be involved, because you will begin to hate sin and love righteousness. Your affections will undergo a revolutionary change. Your devotion to Him will know no bounds. Your love for Him cannot be described.

Even if you have an intellectual acceptance of Christ and an emotional experience,—that still is not enough. There must be the conversion of the will! There must be that determination to obey and follow Christ. Your will must be bent to the will of God. Self must be nailed to the cross. Many of us can identify with the young woman who wrote us regarding this: "But I don't hang easy." None of us do, yet. Our main desire must be to please Him. It is a total commitment.

In conversion as you stand at the foot of the cross, the Holy Spirit makes you realize that you are a sinner. He directs your faith to the Christ who died in your place. You must open your heart and let Him come in. At that precise moment the Holy Spirit performs the miracle of the new birth. You actually become a new moral creature. There comes the implantation of the divine nature. You become a partaker of God's own life. Jesus Christ, through the Spirit of God, takes up residence in your heart.

Conversion is so simple that the smallest child can be converted, but it is also so profound that theologians throughout history have pondered the depth of its meaning. God has made the way of salvation so plain that "the wayfaring men, though fools, shall not err therein" (Isaiah 35:8). No person will ever be barred from the kingdom of God because he did not have the capacity to understand. The rich and the poor, the sophisticated and the simple—all can be converted.

To sum it up, conversion simply means "to change." When a person is converted he may continue to love objects he loved before, but there will be a change of reasons for loving them. A converted person may forsake former objects of affection. He may even withdraw from his previous companions, not because he dislikes them, for many of them will be decent and amiable, but because there is more attraction for him in the fellowship of other Christians of like mind.

The converted person will love the good he once hated, and hate the sin he once loved. There will even be a change of heart about God. Where he once may have been careless about God, living in constant fear, dread, and antagonism to God, he now finds himself in a state of complete reverence, confidence, obedience, and devotion. There will be a reverential fear of God, a constant gratitude to God, a dependence upon God, and a new loyalty to Him. Before conversion there may have been gratification of the flesh. Cultural and intellectual pursuits or the making of money may have been of first and supreme importance. Now, righteousness and holiness of heart and living the Christian life will be placed above all other concerns, for pleasing Christ will be the only goal of real importance. In other words, conversion means a complete change in the life of an individual.

A Case of Conversion

I remember so vividly a young New York career girl who came out to Los Angeles to be married. She and her fiancé had met when they were both working in a high-powered New York advertising agency, and their courtship had been conducted against a background of cocktail parties and night clubs. Filled with ambition and "on his way up," he had himself transferred to the California office, with the understanding that the girl would follow him in six months and they would be married.

About a week after she had arrived in Los Angeles, expecting to take up a joyous new life, she discovered that the man had fallen in love with a movie starlet and lacked the courage to write her about it before she left New York!

Here she was, alone in a city where she knew no one—all her plans in ruins, her pride crushed, and the future stretching ahead, bleak and empty. Her family had not been religious, and in this hour of extreme need she knew of nowhere to turn for comfort, advice, or guidance.

As she walked along the unfamiliar streets, trying to overcome her shock and humiliation, she came upon the "canvas cathedral" in which we were conducting our crusade. She said she was never sure what made her come inside, but she did, and sat glumly through the entire service. The next night she came again, and every night for the whole week, until through the cloud of bitterness and misery that surrounded her, God made His voice heard, and she came forward to confess her need of salvation.

With the burden of guilt and rejection lifted from her through faith in the Lord Jesus Christ, she came to see that the love she had lost was but a steppingstone to a far greater and much richer love. The sense of humiliation that prevented her from returning to her former New York job vanished, and rather than life being finished, she found upon her return that it was fuller than ever. Only instead of wasting her brains and organizational ability on an endless round of cocktail parties, she became extremely active walking with God and serving others.

The imagination she formerly devoted to entertaining the "office crowd" now goes into making Bible stories come alive for the young people. Her training as a fund-raiser is now being put to good use in the service of the Lord, and her minister says her ideas have been invaluable in increasing regular church attendance. Far from being rejected and unwanted, she is sought after constantly by her fellow church members. But, most important of all, her sense of loneliness has vanished, for she knows now that Jesus Christ is ever by her side, ready to comfort, to guide, and to protect her.

All this had come as a result of her conversion—her turning away from the bleak, empty, worldly road she was traveling so unhappily—to her Lord and Savior, Jesus Christ! She had found peace with God.

10

What Is Repentance?

Joy shall be in heaven over one sinner that repenteth, more than over ninety and nine just persons which need no repentance.
LUKE 15:7

We have now seen that Jesus demanded conversion. We have also seen that the three elements of conversion are repentance, faith, and regeneration. It may be debatable in which order these three should come, but it is generally agreed that they probably happen at the same time. Whether you are conscious or unconscious of it, in that critical moment of conversion these three take place simultaneously.

If repentance could be described in two words, I would use the words "turning around." Turn around from what? The answer can be given in one word—sin. The Bible teaches, as we have already seen, that sin is a transgression of the law. Sin is the rejection of all authority and the denial of all obligation to God. Sin is that evil principle that came into the Garden of Eden when Adam and Eve were tempted and fell. Ever since the disaster in Eden this evil poison has affected all men so that "all have sinned," and "there is none righteous, no, not one." Sin has destroyed our relationship with God, and as a consequence it has disturbed our relationships with each other, and even with ourselves.

We cannot possibly have peace with God or peace with each other in the world or even peace within ourselves until something is done about that "abominable thing which God hates." Not only are we told that we must renounce or turn our backs on sin, but we are also told to renounce *sins*—plural. We are to renounce the evil influence of the world, the flesh, and the devil. There can be no parleying, bargaining, compromise, or hesitation. Christ demands total loyalty.

REPENTANCE AND FAITH

But here again the principle of love is involved, because when you fall in love completely and absolutely with Jesus Christ you will not want to do the things that He hates and abhors. You will automatically renounce all the sins of your life when you surrender by faith to Him. Therefore repentance and faith go hand in hand. You cannot have genuine repentance without saving faith, and you cannot have saving faith without genuine repentance.

The word *repentance* is sadly missing today from the average pulpit. It is a very unpopular word. The first sermon Jesus ever preached was "Repent: for the kingdom of heaven is at hand" (Matthew 4:17). This was God speaking through His Son. Jesus had come with a heart filled with love and compassion, but He immediately began to press home man's guilt and sins. He called upon men to acknowledge their guilt and to turn from their ungodliness. He said repentance must come before He could pour out His love, grace, and mercy upon men. Jesus refused to gloss over iniquity. He insisted upon self-judgment, upon a complete right about-face. He insisted upon a new attitude before He would reveal the love of God.

The people came to Jesus one day and told Him of certain Galileans whose blood Pilate had mingled with sacrifices as his Roman legions quelled the Jewish uprising. They reported, too, how the falling of a tower in Siloam had killed many. In answer Jesus declared, "Suppose ye that these Galileans were sinners above all the Galileans . . . I tell you, Nay: but, except ye repent, ye shall all likewise perish" (Luke 13:3). In other words, Jesus said whether men are taken away by violence, by accident, or by natural death, their doom is the same unless they have turned to God in repentance. Until this is done, faith is absolutely impossible. This does not limit the grace of God, but repentance makes way for the grace of God.

Repentance and the Grace of God

We know that salvation is based entirely upon the grace of God. The Bible says that no man is justified by the law in the sight of God, and it also says, "The just shall live by his faith" (Romans 1:17). Salvation, forgiveness, and justification are based entirely upon the atoning work of Christ. However, if the sacrifice of

Christ on the cross is to be made effectual for any individual of any age, that individual must repent of sin and accept Christ by faith.

Jonah preached repentance in Nineveh until Nineveh repented. Ezekiel preached repentance when he said, "Therefore I will judge you, O house of Israel, every one according to his ways, saith the Lord God. Repent, and turn yourselves from all your transgressions; so iniquity shall not be your ruin" (Ezekiel 18:30).

The great message of John the Baptist was repentance when he said, "Repent ye: for the kingdom of heaven is at hand" (Matthew 3:2).

Repentance is mentioned seventy times in the New Testament. Jesus said, "Except ye repent, ye shall all likewise perish." The sermon that Peter preached on the Day of Pentecost was, "Repent, and be baptized every one of you in the name of Jesus Christ for the remission of sins" (Acts 2:38). Paul preached it when he said that he "testified both to the Jews, and also to the Greeks, repentance toward God, and faith toward our Lord Jesus Christ" (Acts 20:21). The Bible says God commands repentance, "And the times of this ignorance God winked at; but now commandeth all men everywhere to repent" (Acts 17:30). It is a command. It is an imperative. God says. "Repent! Or perish!" Have you repented? Are you sure of it?

There are many biblical examples of false repentance. For example, Pharaoh said to the children of Israel who were seeking to leave Egypt for the promised land, "I have sinned . . ." (Exodus 9:27). Obviously, it was an expression of regret or remorse but not an expression of true repentance. Saul did the same thing in 1 Samuel 15:24, 30 and 26:21. But when David said to the prophet

Nathan, "I have sinned" in 2 Samuel 12:13 and 20:10, 17, he was truly repentant (see Psalm 51).

JESUS' DEFINITION OF REPENTANCE

What did Jesus mean by the word *repent*? Why does it appear over and over throughout the Bible? If you look in a modern dictionary you will find that repent means "to feel sorry for, or to regret." But the original words that Jesus spoke meant a great deal more than that. They meant a great deal more than just regretting and feeling sorry about sin. The biblical word *repent* means "to change, or to turn." It is a word of power and action. It is a word that signifies a complete turnabout in the individual. When the Bible calls upon us to repent of sin, it means that we should turn away from sin, that we should do an about-face and walk in the opposite direction from sin and all that it implies.

Jesus told the parable of the Prodigal Son to dramatize what He meant by the word *repent*. When the Prodigal Son repented, he didn't just sit still and feel sorry about all his sins. He wasn't passive and limp about it. He didn't stay where he was, surrounded by the swine. He got up and left! He turned his feet in the other direction. He sought out his father and humbled himself before him, and then he was forgiven.

Too many modern Christians have lost sight of what the Bible means when it talks about repentance. They think that repentance is little more than shaking their heads over their sins and saying, "My, but I'm sorry I did that!" and then continuing to live just as they have lived before.

True repentance means "to change, to turn away from, to go in a new direction." To be sorry is not enough in repentance. Judas was sorry enough to hang himself. It was an admission of guilt without true repentance. Even reformation is not enough. There is no torture that you can give your body, no trials you can set for your mind that will be pleasing to Almighty God. Our sins were atoned for by Christ on the cross. There He suffered sin's penalty. No suffering that we can undergo will lead us to repentance.

Repentance Is Not Mere Emotion

When I speak of repentance, I am not speaking of the old-time mourners' bench. Many people have taught that to repent you must mourn for a stated time in order to be ready for salvation. One man told me the night he found Christ he went forward in an old-fashioned camp meeting some years ago. While he was kneeling at the altar trying to find God, some dear sister came and slapped him on the back and said, "Hold on, brother! If you want God, you'll have to hold on." A few minutes later a church officer came up and slapped him across the back and said, "Brother, turn loose!" Then another sister came up a few minutes later and said, "The night I was converted a big light hit me in the face and knocked me cold." He said, "I tried to turn loose and hold on at the same time while looking for the light. I almost never made it in the confusion!"

A very intelligent Christian leader once told me that at the time he was converted the demonstration of emotion expected of him by the preacher and congregation almost kept him from coming to God.

Falsely produced emotionalism in some revival meetings has been a stumbling block to many a sincere, searching soul. But the type of repentance I'm talking about is true biblical repentance, which involves three things: the intellect, the emotion, and the will.

THREE ASPECTS OF REPENTANCE

First, there must be a knowledge of sin. The Bible says, "All have sinned, and come short of the glory of God" (Romans 3:23). When Isaiah was convicted of his sins he said, " Woe is me! . . . I am a man of unclean lips" (Isaiah 6:5). When Job got a glimpse of God's holiness he said, "I abhor myself" (Job 42:6). When Peter was convicted of his sins he said, "I am a sinful man" (Luke 5:8). When Paul was convicted of his sins he called himself "the chief of sinners" (1 Timothy 1:15).

It is the Holy Spirit who brings about this conviction. Actually, repentance cannot take place unless first there is a movement of the Holy Spirit in the heart and mind. The Holy Spirit may use a mother's prayers, a pastor's sermon, a Christian radio program, the sight of a church steeple, or the death of a loved one to bring about this necessary conviction. However, I have seen men in some of our meetings stand trembling under conviction and still not repent of their sins. It is possible to be convicted of sin and know you are a sinner and even shed tears over your sins, and yet not repent.

Second, the emotions are involved in repentance, just as they are in all genuine experiences. Paul said there is a godly sorrow that worketh toward repentance. Someone has said, "Many people abhor all emotion, and some critics are suspicious of any conversion that does not take place in a refrigerator. There are many dangers in false emotionalism, produced for its own effect, but that does not rule out true emotion and depth of feeling."

As Dr. W. E. Sangster, the great British Methodist preacher, says in his book, *Let Me Commend*, "The man who screams at a football or baseball game but is distressed when he hears of a sinner weeping at the cross and murmurs something about the dangers of emotionalism hardly merits intelligent respect."

Horace Walpole once accused John Wesley of acting out very ugly emotionalism in his preaching, yet Wesley turned thousands to God.

Third, repentance involves the will. It is only when we come to the will that we find the very heart of repentance. There must be that determination to forsake sin—to change one's attitudes toward self, toward sin, and toward God—to change one's feeling; to change one's will, disposition, and purpose.

Only the Spirit of God can give you the determination necessary for true repentance. It means more than the little girl who prayed, "Make me good—not real good, but good enough so I won't get whipped."

There are thousands of people in America who have their names on church rolls. They go to church when it is convenient. They give their money to the church and support its activities. They shake hands with the minister after the service and tell him what a splendid sermon he preached. They may talk the language of the Christian and many of them can quote a fair amount of Scripture, but they have never really experienced true repentance.

They have a sort of "take-it-or-leave-it" attitude toward religion. They turn to God and pray when they get in a tight place, but the rest of the time they do not give God very much thought. The Bible teaches that when a person comes to Christ a change takes place that is reflected in everything he does.

REPENTANCE DEMANDS SURRENDER

There is not one verse of Scripture that indicates you can be a Christian and live any kind of a life you want to. When Christ enters into the human heart, He expects to be Lord and Master. He commands complete surrender. He demands control of your intellectual processes. He requires that your body be subject to Him. He expects you to surrender your talents and abilities to Him. He expects nothing less than that all your work and labor will be performed in His name.

Too many of today's professing Christians would give up going to church before they would give up getting a new refrigerator. Given a choice between making the down payment on a new car or contributing to the building of a new Sunday school, it is easy to guess what the decision of many would be. Thousands of so-called Christians are putting money and the things that make up our high standard of living ahead of the teachings of Christ. We can find time for the movies, baseball, or football games, but we can't find time for God. We can save toward a new home or a bigger television set, but we feel we no longer can afford to tithe. This is idolatry.

A change must take place! We point our fingers at the heathen and at the idol worshipers of old, but the only difference is that our graven images are made of gleaming chromium and steel and have thermostats and defrosting devices instead of jeweled eyes! Instead of gold, their surfaces are covered with easy-to-clean lifetime porcelain, but we worship them just the same and feel that our lives would be impossible without them. We have come to worship things, status, fame, popularity, money, security. Anything that comes between God and ourselves is idolatry.

Jesus demands lordship over all such things. He wants you to yield everything concerning your social life, your family life, your business life to Him. He must have first place in everything you do or think or say, for when you truly repent you turn toward God in everything.

We have the warning of Christ that He will not receive us into His kingdom until we are ready to give up all, until we are ready to turn from all sin in our lives. Don't try to do it partway. Don't say, "I'll give up some of my sins and hang on to some others. I'll live part of my life for Jesus and part for my own desires." Jesus expects 100 percent surrender, and when that is accomplished He rewards a thousandfold. But don't expect Jesus to hand out any 500 percent awards for 50 percent surrenders! God doesn't work that way. He demands all. When you have determined that you are renouncing sin, forsaking sin, and yielding all to Christ, you have taken another step toward peace with God.

The repentant thief on the cross said to Jesus, "Lord, remember me . . ." (Luke 23:42). His use of the word *Lord* implied his total submission to Jesus Christ. It implied his total surrender and true conversion. This is the result of true repentance.

With the hymn writer, the repentant sinner says:

All to Jesus I surrender, all to Him I freely give;
  I will ever love and trust Him, in His presence daily live.
All to Jesus I surrender, make me, Savior, wholly Thine.
  Let me feel the Holy Spirit, truly know that Thou art mine.

11

WHAT IS FAITH?

For by grace are ye saved through faith; and that not of yourselves: it is the gift of God: not of works, lest any man should boast.
EPHESIANS 2:8, 9

We are now ready to take up the next step in finding peace with God. You are now ready to forsake your past sinful life. You are determined that this change is going to take place in your life. You are no longer headed away from God, but you are moving toward His love and mercy and protection. You have made your decision. You have repented; you have chosen the right road, even though it may be a difficult one. You have chosen the road that Moses took almost 3,500 years ago when he renounced his right to the throne of Egypt and decided in favor of God!

Moses was forty years old when he fled Egypt for fear of his life. Forty years later he came back to lead the Israelites out of Egypt. What had changed? He had made his great decision. He concluded that faith and truth in company with agony and hardship were better than wealth and fame and the absence of God's love. Few men in history have been called upon to make a more difficult decision than his.

A MAN OF FAITH

Moses was a man of education and culture, a man of wealth and prominence. As the son of Pharaoh's daughter he had been accustomed to every honor, every luxury, and every privilege. The throne of Egypt, the richest, most powerful, most spectacularly successful country of its time, was within his grasp.

Yet the Bible records that:

> By faith Moses, when he was come to years, refused to be called the son of Pharaoh's daughter; choosing rather to suffer affliction with the people of God, than to enjoy the pleasures of sin for a season; esteeming the reproach of Christ greater riches than the treasures in Egypt: for he had respect unto the recompense of the reward. By faith he forsook Egypt, not fearing the wrath of the king: for he endured, as seeing him who is invisible. (Hebrews 11:24–27).

This passage was referring to Moses after his forty years in the wilderness with God—not the fiery young murderer who fled from Pharaoh in fear of his life.

Notice, it says that he "refused" and he "forsook"—this is true repentance. And then it says he did it "by faith"! This is the next step—*faith*. Moses made this decision not in a moment of overt emotionalism that some psychologists insist is necessary for religious experience. He was not motivated by frustration. He was not a hopeless misfit or an unfulfilled man. Moses was not choosing the path of God as a compensation for the rewards that he felt life had withheld from him, nor was he turning to the religious life out of boredom and apathy. He did not want for interest, entertainment, and amusement.

A Matter of Choice

None of these arguments, nor the many others so often advanced as reasons for seeking life with God, were valid in the case of Moses. He was not forced to run from the flesh and the devil. He did it from choice. Moses was certainly neither weak-minded nor weak-willed. He was not a child clinging to the security of an established order. He was not a nonentity seeking recognition and prestige. He was not any of the things that those who mock religion say one must be to feel the need of salvation. Moses had even more than the dreams to which most men would aspire; yet out of his mature judgment in the prime of life he turned his back on wealth, position, and esteem and chose instead faith in God. Every time I hear it said that only the hopeless and helpless, only the maladjusted need the comfort of "religion," I think of Moses.

It has been my privilege to talk to many men and women concerning their spiritual problems. I have learned that when men and women of sound judgment reject Christ as their Lord and Master, they do it not because they find Christian doctrines intellectually distasteful, but because they seek to avoid the responsibilities and obligations that the Christian life demands. Their faint hearts rather than their brilliant minds stand between them and Christ. They are not willing to submit themselves and surrender everything to Christ.

It is interesting to note that the two men most used of God in the Bible (one in the Old Testament and one in the New) were also the two best educated: Moses and Paul.

Moses considered the claims and obligations of God carefully. At forty he fled, a murderer. At eighty he returned, a leader. He realized that if he were to embrace God he would have to do it at the sacrifice of the things that men usually hold most dear. He made no hasty examination. He came to no half-considered conclusions under sudden impulse or emotional reaction. He knew how much was at stake, and he arrived at his decision with the full use of his well-trained and superior mental faculties. His final choice was not in the nature of a temporary experiment. He did not select faith as a tentative measure. It was a mature conviction with an unalterable purpose, a conviction not to be shaken by changes of fortune or the trials of long-endured privation. He carefully burned all the bridges and ships that might have made retreat possible from his new position. When Moses had his great crisis moment at the age of eighty, he committed himself totally and without reservation for all time and under all circumstances to God and His commands.

How different was the quality of Moses' decision from that of the famous biographer Gamaliel Bradford, who as he neared the end of his life said, "I do not dare read the New Testament for fear of awakening a storm of anxiety and doubt and dread, of having taken the wrong path, of having been a traitor to the plain and simple God."

Moses had no such fear. And neither should you fear if you turn yourself wholeheartedly to Christ now and forever by faith. Don't turn to Him saying, "I'll try Christianity for a while. If it works I'll go on with it, but if it doesn't I still have time to choose another way of life." When you come to Christ, every bridge has to be burned behind you, with no thought of ever turning back.

They Turned Back on Their Boats

Years ago, when the wings of the fierce Roman eagle cast an ominous shadow over the world, those audacious warriors whom Caesar led set out to conquer Britain. As the enemy vessels appeared on the horizon, thousands of Englishmen bravely gathered on the heights to defend their homeland. To their amazement, the tides and the sea destroyed most of the Roman ships. Thus the only avenue of retreat was cut off for the daring invaders. They fought with wild abandon, their escape route cut off. With such an indomitable spirit, how could they fail to conquer! Little wonder the petty village on the banks of the Tiber became the Mistress of the world!

Just so, Christ will accept nothing less than complete surrender and absolute devotion: "And Jesus said unto him, No man, having put his hand to the plow, and looking back, is fit for the kingdom of God" (Luke 9:62).

Moses made his soul-shaking choice as he stood at the fork of life's highway. His judicial mind weighed all the facts that bore upon his decision. He looked long and carefully down each road to its termination. He considered all the pros and cons, and only then did he decide to put his trust and faith in God.

Moses Burned His Bridges

First he looked down the broad road, the bright road filled with power and luxury, filled with gaiety and wine, rich in the things the world counts as pleasure. It was a familiar road. He knew it well. He had traveled it for forty years and he knew that it ended in destruction, knew that it could only lead to hell.

Then Moses looked down the other road, the narrow road, the more difficult road. He saw the suffering, the affliction, the humiliation and disappointment. He saw the hardships and the trials, the sorrows and the pains, but by faith he saw also the triumphs and the reward of eternal life.

A man of lesser judgment, a man of lesser experience than Moses, might have been tempted to take the first road. Egypt was then the greatest power on earth. It held command of the fertile Nile valley, the granary of the world. Its armies were invincible, its colleges and universities were setting the pattern that other centuries would follow.

Few of us are ever asked to give up as much for God as Moses did. Few of us are ever shown temptation in such abundance and variety and asked to withstand it. Few of us have such earthly delights and pleasures spread before our eyes, and even the Scriptures admit that there is pleasure in sin, if only for a season. The pleasure is fleeting and leaves no comfort in its wake.

In choosing God, Moses made a great sacrifice, but he also won a great reward. Great fortunes were rare in Moses' time, and few men indeed had the opportunity that he had to become the wealthiest man on earth.

The Wealth of the World

Today, many men can amass great fortunes. In 1923 (when fortune gathering was this country's major interest) a group of the world's most successful financiers gathered at the Edgewater Beach Hotel in Chicago. Even in the fabulous twenties, the meeting was an impressive array of wealth and power. Seated at a single table were the president of the world's largest independent steel company, the president of the largest utility company, the president of the New York Stock Exchange, a member of the cabinet of the president of the United States, the president of the Bank of International Settlements, the man who was known as the biggest trader on Wall Street, and another who headed the world's most powerful monopoly. Together, these men controlled more wealth than the United States Treasury! Their success stories were known to every schoolboy. They were the models whom other men tried to copy. They were the financial and industrial giants of America!

In 1923 the widely publicized stories of these men were glamorous and exciting. They fired the imagination! They kindled envy! They inspired other men to try to be as they were! But in 1923 their stories were only half told—the closing chapters were yet to be written.

At the time these eight men sat down together at the hotel in Chicago they were each at the place in their individual lives where Moses had been when he stood at the crossroads. These men were at the crossroads also, and two paths stretched out before each of them. Perhaps they were paths they could not see, paths about which they did not care. Certainly they were paths they didn't choose to follow, and today their stories are complete. Today we know those final chapters. We can review their lives, just as we can review the life of Moses, and see which seems the wisest and the best.

Charles Schwab, president of the steel company, lived the last years of his life on borrowed money and died penniless. Arthur Cutten, greatest of the wheat speculators, died abroad insolvent. Richard Whitney, president of the New York Stock Exchange, served a term in Sing-Sing Penitentiary. Albert Fall, the cabinet member, was pardoned from prison so he could die at home. Jessie Livermore, the "bear" of Wall Street; Leon Frazer, president of the Bank of International Settlements; and Ivon Kreuger, head of the world's largest monopoly, all committed suicide!

These men all had money, power, fame, prestige, intelligence, and education—but every one of them lacked the one attribute that gives life its real meaning and purpose. They lacked the one attribute that is essential to the Christian creed and conduct—the attribute that makes conversion possible, that makes regeneration real. They refused to believe! Compare their lives with those of missionaries who have left all to follow Christ. They may die penniless and in pain, but they have died for something!

These wealthy men had no faith, or if they did have faith, they refused to act upon it. How different the closing chapters of their lives would have been if they had been able to count faith in Christ among their treasuries.

MOSES TURNED HIS BACK ON THE WORLD'S WEALTH

Notice it was through faith that Moses renounced the wealth of Egypt. It was his faith that made him know that, even though he might suffer privation and humiliation all the rest of his life on earth, in the end he would receive the greatest of rewards—eternal life.

Men like Cutten and Schwab might have thought Moses a fool. They would have said, "A bird in the hand is worth far more than two in the bush." They would have said, "Look, you know what you have in Egypt. You know what a man of your brains can do to manipulate this wealth and power. Play your cards right and Egypt will control the world. You can put all the lesser countries out of business. You can get rid of all the competition and run things your own way." That's what they would have said, because that's the way they thought, that's the way they operated, that's the way many of them amassed their fortunes. They would have laughed at a person who said he believed God or had faith in Christ. They would have said, "Faith isn't good business. It isn't smart."

The Bible teaches that faith is the only approach to God. "For he that cometh to God must believe that he is, and that he is a rewarder of them that diligently seek him" (Hebrews 11:6). The

Bible also teaches that faith pleases God more than anything else. "Without faith it is impossible to please him" (Hebrews 11:6).

People all over the world torture themselves, clothe themselves in strange garments, disfigure their bodies, deny themselves the necessities of life, spend much time in prayer and self-sacrifice in an effort to make themselves acceptable in God's sight. This may be all well and good, but the greatest thing we can do to please God is to believe Him.

I might go to a friend and flatter him, but, if after all my flowery phrases I were to tell him I did not believe him, every flattering thing I said would have been in vain. I would have built him up only to let him down.

BELIEF IS ESSENTIAL

The greatest way we can please God is to *believe* His Word. It would seem that Christ was almost pleading for faith on the part of His hearers when He said, "Believe me that I am in the Father, and the Father in me: or else believe me for the very works' sake" (John 14:11).

The Bible declares that *faith* is absolutely essential. You ask, "Well, if faith is so important, what is faith? What do you mean by *faith*? What is a definition of faith? How can I know if I have proper faith? How much faith must I have?"

Wait just a minute—not so many questions at a time! I'll try to answer them as we go along.

The Bible teaches, time and time again, that we can have salvation only through faith:

> Believe on the Lord Jesus Christ, and thou shalt be saved, and thy house (Acts 16:31).

> But as many as received him, to them gave he power to become the sons of God, even to them that believe on his name (John 1:12).

> And by him all that believe are justified from all things, from which ye could not be justified by the law of Moses (Acts 13:39).

> But to him that worketh not, but believeth on him that justifieth the ungodly, his faith is counted for righteousness (Romans 4:5).

> Therefore being justified by faith, we have peace with God through our Lord Jesus Christ (Romans 5:1).

> But we are not of them who draw back unto perdition; but of them that believe to the saving of the soul (Hebrews 10:39).

> For by grace are ye saved through faith; and that not of yourselves: it is the gift of God (Ephesians 2:8).

THE NATURE OF FAITH

Are we actually saved by faith? No, we're saved by grace *through faith.* Faith is simply the channel through which God's grace to us is received. It is the hand that reaches out and receives the gift of His love. In Hebrews 11:1, we read, "Now faith is the substance of things hoped for, the evidence of things not seen." Weymouth has translated it this way, which makes it easier to understand, "Now faith is a confident assurance of that for which we hope, a conviction of the reality of things which we do not see." Faith literally means "to give up, surrender, or commit." Faith is complete confidence.

I have never been to the North Pole, and yet I believe there is a North Pole. How do I know? I know because somebody told me. I read about it in a history book, I saw a map in a geography book, and I believe the men who wrote those books. I accept it by faith.

The Bible says, "Faith cometh by hearing, and hearing by the word of God" (Romans 10:17). We believe what God has to say about salvation. We accept it without question.

Martin Luther has translated Hebrews 11:27 this way, "For he held on to Him whom he saw not just as though he saw Him."

It is not some peculiar, mysterious quality for which we must strive. Jesus said we must become as little children, and just as little children trust their parents, so we must trust God.

Suppose I were driving along the road at fifty miles an hour and I came to the crest of a hill. Would I immediately slam on my brakes, stop my car, get out, walk up to the top of the hill, and look over to see if the road continues? No, I wouldn't do that. I would trust the highway department of the particular state in which I was driving. I would continue at my normal rate of speed, secure in the knowledge that the road continued on ahead even though I couldn't see it. I would accept it on faith. So it is with saving faith in Christ!

THREE ASPECTS OF FAITH

Again, as in repentance, there are three things involved in faith. First, there must be a *knowledge* of what God has said. That's why it's so important for you to read the Bible. That's why it's important for you to know something of the teaching of the Bible concerning the salvation of the soul. Just to know that you are a sinner and that Christ died for you is enough knowledge. Knowing no more than John 3:16 could be enough knowledge. Many have been converted on less. But on anything as important as this you should be as well informed as possible, and the only place to learn about salvation is in the Bible!

Many people say, "But I cannot understand much of the Bible, therefore I don't try to read it." That is not the wise attitude. There are many things in the Bible that I do not understand. My finite mind will never understand all about the infinite. I do not understand all about television, but I do not refuse to turn on my television set. I accept it by faith.

But God does not ask the impossible. He does not ask you to take a leap in the dark concerning conversion. Believing in Christ is based on the best evidence in the world, the Bible. Even though you do not understand it all, you can accept it at face value because God said it. One of the first attacks the devil makes on man is to get him to doubt the Word of God: "Yea, hath God said?" (Genesis 3:1). If you begin doubting and putting question marks over God's Word, then you're in trouble. There must be a knowledge that you are a sinner. You must have the knowledge that Christ died for your sins and that He rose again for your justification. The death, burial, and resurrection of Jesus Christ is the very heart of the Gospel. That must be believed and accepted as a minimum for conversion.

Second, the *emotions* again are involved. The Bible says, "The fear of the Lord is the beginning of wisdom" (Proverbs 1:7). Paul said, "The love of Christ constraineth us" (2 Corinthians 5:14). Desire, love, fear—all are emotions. Emotion cannot be cut out of life. No intelligent person would think of saying, "Let's do away with all emotion." To remove all personality from deep feeling is impossible. We cannot imagine life without the warm overtones of feeling. Suppose we had a family in which everyone acted only from a cold sense of duty. Suppose I asked my wife to marry me after I had explained to her first of all that I had no feelings for her at all.

As Dr. Sangster says, "Carry the same principle over into religion. Require that the Herald of God announce the offer of His King, freely to pardon and fully to bless, but firmly forbid that any transport of joy should accompany either the announcement of the news or its glad reception, and you ask the impossible."

There is going to be a tug at the heart. Emotion may vary in religious experience. Some people are stoical and others are demonstrative, but the feeling will be there.

When Churchill gave his masterful speeches to the British people during the war, he appealed to logic, but at the same time he made his audience feel. I remember hearing him one time in Glasgow. He challenged my thinking, but he made me feel like standing up and shouting and waving a flag! When you fall in love with Jesus Christ, your emotions are bound to be stirred.

Third, and most important of all, is the *will*. It's like three little men—one is named "Intellect," the second is named "Emotion," and the third is named "Will." Intellect says that the gospel is logical. Emotion puts pressure upon Will and says, "I feel love for Christ," or "I feel fear of judgment." And then the middleman, called Will, is the referee. He sits there with his hand on his chin, in deep thought, trying to make up his mind. It is actually the will that makes the final and lasting decision. It is possible to have the intellectual conviction and the emotional feeling and still not be properly converted to Christ. Faith has legs. "Faith without works is dead" (James 2:20).

AN EXAMPLE OF FAITH

I heard about a man some years ago who was rolling a wheelbarrow back and forth across Niagara River on a tightrope. Thousands of people were shouting him on. He put a two-hundred-pound sack of dirt in the wheelbarrow and rolled it over, and then he rolled it back. Then he turned to the crowd and said, "How many of you believe that I can roll a man across?"

Everybody shouted! One man in the front row was very excited in his professed belief. The man pointed to this excited professor and said, "You're next!"

You couldn't see that man for dust! He actually didn't believe it. He said he believed it, he thought he believed it—but he was not willing to get in the wheelbarrow.

Just so with Christ. There are many people who say they believe on Him, who say they will follow Him. But they never have gotten into the wheelbarrow. They actually never have committed and surrendered themselves wholly, 100 percent to Christ.

There are many people who ask, "Well, how much faith does it take?" Jesus said only the faith as of "a grain of mustard seed."

Others ask, "What kind of faith?" It is not a matter of any special kind of faith. There is only one kind, really. It is the object of the faith that counts. What is the object of your faith? The object of your faith must be Christ—not faith in ritual, not faith in sacrifices, not faith in morals, not faith in yourself—not faith in anything but Christ!

Now the Bible teaches that faith will manifest itself in three ways. It will manifest itself in doctrine—in what you believe. It will manifest itself in worship—your communion with God and the fellowship of the church. It will manifest itself in morality—in the way you live and behave, which we will discuss in other chapters.

The Bible also teaches that faith does not end with trust in Christ for your salvation. Faith continues. Faith grows. It may be weak at first, but it will become stronger as you begin to read the Bible, pray, go to church, and experience God's faithfulness in your Christian life. After you have repented of sins and accepted Him by faith, then you must trust Him to keep you, strengthen you, enable you, sustain you. You will learn more and more how to rely on Christ for every need, in meeting every circumstance and every trial. You will learn to say with Paul, "I am crucified with Christ; nevertheless I live; yet not I, but Christ liveth in me: and the life which I now live in the flesh I live by the faith of the Son of God, who loved me, and gave himself for me" (Galatians 2:20).

When you have saving faith in Jesus Christ, you have taken an additional step toward having peace with God.

12

THE OLD AND THE NEW

Except a man be born again
he cannot see the kingdom of God.
JOHN 3:3

If I could come and have a heart-to-heart chat with you in your living room, you perhaps would turn to me and confess, "I am perplexed, confused, and mixed up. I have transgressed God's laws. I have lived contrary to His commandments. I thought I could get along without God's help. I have tried to make up my own rules and I've failed. The bitter lessons that I've learned have come through suffering and tragic experience. What wouldn't I give to be born again! What wouldn't I give to be able to go back and start all over—what a different road I'd travel if I could!"

If those words strike a familiar chord in your heart, if they echo the thoughts that have been moving through your mind, I want to tell you some glorious news. Jesus said you can be born anew! You can have the fresh and better start for which you've prayed. You can lose your despised and sinful self and step forth a new person, a clean and peaceful being from whom sin has been washed away.

A Way Out

No matter how soiled your past, no matter how snarled your present, no matter how hopeless your future seems to be—there is a way out. There is a sure, safe, everlasting way out—but there is only one! You have only one choice to make. You have only one path to follow, other than the torturous, unrewarding path you've been treading.

You can go on being miserable, discontented, frightened, unhappy, and disgusted with yourself and your life; or you can decide right now that you want to be born again. You can decide right now to wipe out your sinful past and make a new start, a fresh start, a right start. You can decide now to become the person that Jesus promised you could be.

How Do I Find It?

The next logical question that you may ask is, "How can I have this rebirth? How can I be born again? How can I start afresh?"

This is the question that Nicodemus asked Jesus that night two thousand years ago under an Oriental sky. Being born again, however, means a great deal more than just a fresh start, or turning over a new leaf, or reforming. As we have already seen, the Bible teaches that you were born the first time into the physical world but your spiritual nature was born in sin. The Bible declares that you are "dead in trespasses and sins" (Ephesians 2:1).

The Bible teaches that there is nothing in your dead and sinful nature that can originate life. Being dead in sin, you cannot produce a life of righteousness. Many people are trying to produce a good, holy, and righteous life without being born again, but they can do nothing but fail. A corpse cannot reproduce. The Bible teaches that "sin, when it is finished, bringeth forth death" (James 1:15). All of us are dead spiritually.

Your old nature cannot serve God. The Bible says, "The natural man receiveth not the things of the Spirit of God . . . neither can he know them" (1 Corinthians 2:14). In our natural state we are actually at enmity with God. We are not subject to the laws of God, neither indeed can we be, according to Romans 8:7.

The Bible also teaches that our old nature is totally corrupt. From its head to its feet "there is no soundness in it"; it is full of "wounds, and bruises, and petrifying sores" (Isaiah 1:6). Its heart is "deceitful above all things, and desperately wicked" (Jeremiah 17:9). It is corrupt, subject to deceitful lust.

The Bible also teaches that our old nature is a self-nature. It is incapable of being renovated. The Bible teaches that when we are born again, we put off the old man—we do not patch him up. The old self is to be crucified, not cultivated. Jesus said the cleansing of the outside of the cup and the platter leaves the inside just as dirty as before.

YOU MUST BE BORN AGAIN!

The Bible also teaches that unless we have experienced this new birth we cannot get into the kingdom of heaven. Jesus made it even stronger. He said, "Ye must be born again" (John 3:7). There is nothing indefinite, nothing optional about that. He who would enter the kingdom of God must be born again.

Salvation is not just repairing the original self. It is a new self created of God in righteousness and true holiness. Regeneration is not even a change of nature, or a change of heart. Being born again is not a change—it is a regeneration, a new generation. It is a second birth. "Ye must be born again."

There is nothing about the old nature that God will accept. There is no soundness in it. The old nature is too weak to follow Christ. Paul said, "Ye cannot do the things that ye would" (Galatians 5:17). Those who are in the flesh cannot serve God. "Doth a fountain send forth at the same place sweet water and bitter? Can the fig tree, my brethren, bear olive berries?" asked James (James 3:11–12).

The old man is described in Romans as "Their throat is an open sepulchre; with their tongues they have used deceit; the poison of asps is under their lips: Whose mouth is full of cursing and bitterness: Their feet are swift to shed blood: Destruction and misery are in their ways: . . . There is no fear of God before their eyes" (Romans 3:13–18).

How are you going to reform or patch up or change such throats and tongues and lips and feet and eyes as these? It is impossible. Jesus, knowing that it was impossible to change, patch up, and reform, said you must have a total new birth, "Ye must be born again." Jesus said, "That which is born of the flesh is flesh." On another occasion the Bible says, "Can the Ethiopian change his skin, or the leopard change his spots?" (Jeremiah 13:23). Again in Romans the Bible says, "They that are in the flesh cannot please God." "In me (that is, in my flesh) dwelleth no good thing" (Romans 7:18). Again the Bible says, "Without holiness no man shall see the Lord" (Hebrews 12:14).

The life that comes from the new birth cannot be obtained by natural development or self-effort. Man does not by nature have this holiness that God requires for heaven. In the new birth alone is the beginning of such a life to be found. To live the life of God we must have the nature of God.

What God Does

The whole matter of receiving new life is like a coin. A coin has two sides. The receiving of new life has a divine side and a human side. We have seen the human side in our chapter on conversion, we have seen what we must do. Now let's see what God does.

Being born again is altogether a work of the Holy Spirit. There is nothing we can do to obtain this new birth. The Bible says, "But as many as received him, to them gave he power to become the sons of God, even to them that believed on his name: Which were born, not of blood, nor of the will of the flesh, nor of the will of man, but of God" (John 1:12–13). In other words, we cannot be born of blood; that means we cannot inherit the new birth. God has no grandchildren.

We cannot inherit Christianity. We might have had a Christian father and mother, but that does not necessarily produce a Christian child. I could be born in a garage, but that doesn't make me an automobile! God has no grandchildren.

We cannot be born of the will of the flesh, the Scripture says. In other words, there is nothing we can do about it. The unbeliever is dead. A dead man has no life to do anything.

Nor can one be born of the will of man. This new birth cannot be produced by human devices or schemes. Many people think they are automatically born again when they join a church or go through some religious ritual or make some New Year's resolution or give a large gift to an outstanding charitable institution. All of these are fine and right, but they do not produce the new birth.

A Divine Work

Jesus told us we must be born again. The infinitive *be* is passive. It shows that it is something that must be done for us. No man can "born" himself. He must *be* born. The new birth is wholly foreign to our will. In other words, the new birth is a divine work—we are born of God.

Nicodemus could not understand how he could be born the second time. In perplexity he asked twice, "How?"

Even though the new birth seems mysterious, that does not make it untrue. We may not understand the how of electricity, but we know that it lights our homes, runs our television and radio sets. We do not understand how the sheep grows wool, the cow grows hair, or the fowl grows feathers—but we know they do. We do not understand many mysteries, but we accept by faith the fact that at the moment we repent of sin and turn by faith to Jesus Christ we are born again.

It is the infusion of divine life into the human soul. It is the implantation or impartation of divine nature into the human soul whereby we become the children of God. We receive the breath of God. Christ through the Holy Spirit takes up residence in our hearts. We are attached to God for eternity. That means that if you have been born again you will live as long as God lives, because you are now sharing His very life. The long-lost fellowship man had with God in the Garden of Eden has been restored.

THE RESULTS OF THE NEW BIRTH

When you are born again, several results follow: First, it will increase your vision and *understanding*. The Bible says, "God, who commanded the light to shine out of darkness, hath shined in our hearts, to give the light of the knowledge of the glory of God in the face of Jesus Christ" (2 Corinthians 4:6). Again the Bible says, "The eyes of your understanding being enlightened" (Ephesians 1:18). Things that you used to laugh at as foolishness you now accept by faith. Your whole mental process is changed. God becomes the hub of your intellectual thinking. He becomes the center. The ego has been dethroned.

Second, your *heart* undergoes a revolution. The Bible says, "A new spirit will I put within you: and I will take away the stony heart out of your flesh, and I will give you an heart of flesh" (Ezekiel 36:26).

Your affections have undergone a radical change. Your new nature loves God and the things pertaining to God. You love the finest and highest things in life. You reject the lower and baser. You discover a new appreciation for the social problems around you. Your heart beats with compassion for those who are less fortunate.

Third, your *will* undergoes a tremendous change. Your determinations are different. Your motives are changed. The Bible says, "Now the God of Peace . . . make you perfect in every good work to do his will, working in you that which is well-pleasing in his sight" (Hebrews 13:20, 21).

This new nature that you receive from God is bent to the will of God. You will want to do only His will. You are utterly and completely devoted to Him. There is a new self-determination, inclination, disposition, a new principle of living, new choices. You seek to glorify God. You seek fellowship with other Christians in the church. You love the Bible. You love to spend time in prayer with God. Your whole disposition is changed. Whereas your life once was filled with unbelief, the root and foundation of all sin, and you once doubted God, now you believe Him. Now you have utmost confidence and faith in God and His Word.

There may have been a time when pride was the very center of your life. You had ambitious thoughts of yourself, your powers, desires, and aims; but now that will begin to change. There may have been a time when there was hatred in your life. Envy, discontent, and malice filled your thoughts toward others. That, too, will gradually change.

There was a time when you could easily tell a lie. There were falsehoods and hypocrisies in many of your thoughts, words, and deeds. That is now all changed. There was a time when you gave in to the lust of the flesh. That is now changed. You have been born again. You may stumble into some of these traps that the devil puts out for you, but immediately you will be sorry, confess your sins, and ask forgiveness, because you have been born again. Your very nature has changed.

THE PIG AND THE LAMB

There is an old story about the pig and the lamb. The farmer brought the pig into the house. He gave it a bath, polished its hoofs, put some Chanel No. 5 on it, tied a ribbon around its neck, and placed it in the living room. The pig looked fine. It almost seemed to be acceptable to society and to friends who might come in, it was so fresh and clean. It made a very nice and companionable pet for a few minutes. But as soon as the door was opened, the pig left the living room and jumped into the first mud puddle it could find. Why? Because it was still a pig at heart. Its nature had not been changed. It had been changed outwardly but not inwardly.

Take a lamb, on the other hand. Put a lamb in a living room and then turn it out into the yard, and it will try its best to avoid all mud puddles. Why? Because its nature is that of a lamb.

You can take a man—dress him up, put him in the front row in church, and he almost looks like a saint. He may fool even his best friends for a while. But then put him in his office the next day, or put him at home or put him in the club on Saturday night, and you will see his true nature come out again. Why does he act that way? Because his nature has not been changed. He has not been born again.

THE MEANING OF JUSTIFICATION

Now the moment you receive the new birth, the moment you are born again, the moment you receive this divine impartation of a new nature, you are justified in the sight of God. By being justified is meant "just-as-if-I'd" never sinned. Justification is that act of God whereby He declares an ungodly man to be perfect while he is still ungodly. God places you before Him as though you had never committed a sin.

As Paul says, "Who shall lay anything to the charge of God's elect? It is God that justifieth" (Romans 8:33). Your sins have been forgiven. God has buried them in the depths of the sea and placed them behind His back of forgetfulness. Every sin is completely wiped out. You stand before God as a debtor, and you have received your discharge, you have become reconciled to God. You were actually an enemy of God before. The Bible says, "And all things are of God, who hath reconciled us to himself by Jesus Christ, and hath given to us the ministry of reconciliation" (2 Corinthians 5:18).

But more than all of that, you have been adopted into the family of God. You are now a child of God. "Having predestinated us unto the adoption of children by Jesus Christ to himself, according to the good pleasure of his will" (Ephesians 1:5). You are now a member of the royal family of heaven. You have royal blood in your veins. You are a child of the King. Even your friends will begin to notice the change that has taken place in your life. You have now been born again.

THE OLD AND THE NEW

Certain changes will take place once you have been born again. First, there will be a different attitude toward sin. You will learn to hate sin as God hates it. You will detest it and abhor it.

Down in Houston, Texas, a man was born again in one of our meetings. He owned a liquor store. The next morning he had a sign on the front of his door saying, "Out of business."

I heard about a man some time ago who had been born again in an evangelistic service. He was known as the city drunk. He was called "Old John." Somebody spoke to him the next morning on the street and said, "Good morning, Old John."

He said, "Who are you talking to? My name is not Old John. I'm new John." A complete revolution had taken place in his life.

Second, you will know that you have been born again because you will want to obey God. "And hereby we do know that we know him, if we keep his commandments" (1 John 2:3).

Third, you will be separated from the world. The Bible says, "Love not the world, neither the things that are in the world. If any man love the world, the love of the Father is not in him" (1 John 2:15). An unknown poet explains it this way:

All the water in the world,
However hard it tried,
Could never sink a ship
Unless it got inside.
All the evil in the world,
The wickedness and sin,
Could never sink the soul's craft
Unless it got inside.

Fourth, there will be a new love in your heart for other people. The Bible says, "We know that we have passed from death unto life, because we love the brethren" (1 John 3:14).

Fifth, we will not practice sin. The Bible says, "We know that whosoever is born of God sinneth not" (1 John 5:18). We will not engage in sinful practices.

In Texas they tell a story about a man who used to hitch his horse every morning in front of the saloon. One morning the saloonkeeper came out and found that the horse was hitched in front of the Methodist Church. He saw the man walking down the street and called out, "Say, why is your horse hitched in front of the Methodist Church this morning?"

The man turned around and said, "Well, last night I was converted in the revival meeting, and I've changed hitching posts."

That's what it means to be born again. That's what it means to be converted. That's what it means to be separated from the world. It means that you change hitching posts.

13

How to Be Sure

These things have I written unto you that believe on the name of the Son of God; that ye may know that ye have eternal life, and that ye may believe on the name of the Son of God.
1 John 5:13

Every week I receive scores of letters from those who say they have doubts and uncertainties concerning the Christian life. Many come from genuine Christians who seem to have none of the joy of Christian faith, or the assurance, because they have failed to understand a basic truth of Christian experience. Even though the Bible says, "But these [the Bible] are written that ye might believe that Jesus is the Christ, the Son of God; and that believing ye might have life through his name" (John 20:31), many are unsure.

Now let's use this chapter to sum up what has happened to us. We have seen what it means to repent, to have faith, and to be born again. Now, how can I be certain, how can I be sure that all of this has happened to me? Many people with whom I talk have repented and have believed and have been born again, but they often lack the assurance of their conversion. Let's go over a few things that we've learned. First of all, becoming a Christian can be a crisis experience in your life, or it can be a process with a climactic moment of which you may or may not be conscious. Do not misunderstand me; you do not become a Christian as a result of a process of education. Some years ago a great preacher said, "We must so educate and train our youth in the Christian way of life that they will never know when they were not Christians." Much of the philosophy of religious education has been based upon this premise, and perhaps many have missed the essence of Christian experience because nothing more than religious training took its place. No change took place in the heart.

At the turn of the century, Professor Starbuck, a leading thinker in the field of psychology, observed that Christian workers generally were recruited from the ranks of those who had had a vital experience of conversion. He also observed that those who had a clear concept of what it means to be converted were mainly those who had come out of rural areas where in the early days they had had either little or no carefully planned religious training.

This is not a criticism of religious training, but it may be taken as a warning of the dangers involved in improper use of religious training that becomes a substitute for the experience of the new birth.

RELIGION IS NOT REBIRTH

To Nicodemus, one of the most religious men of his times, Jesus said, "Except a man be born again, he cannot see the kingdom of God" (John 3:3). Nicodemus could not substitute his profound knowledge of religion for spiritual rebirth, and we have not progressed beyond this point in our generation.

The ugly larva in its cocoon spends much time in almost unnoticeable growth and change. But no matter how slow that growth may be, the moment comes when it passes through a crisis and emerges a beautiful butterfly. The weeks of silent growth are important, but they cannot take the place of that experience when the old and the ugly are left behind and the new and the beautiful come into being.

It is true that thousands of Christians do not know the exact day or hour that they came to know Christ. Their faith and lives testify that consciously or unconsciously they have been converted to Christ. Whether they can remember it or not, there was a moment when they did cross over the line from death to life.

Probably everyone has had doubts and uncertainties at times in his religious experience. When Moses went up on Mount Sinai to receive the tables of the law from the hand of God, he was lost for some time to the sight of the Hebrews who stood anxiously waiting his return. They finally became doubtful and said among themselves, "As for this Moses, the man that brought us up out of the land of Egypt, we wot not what is become of him" (Exodus 32:1). Their defection was a result of their doubting and uncertainty.

The dreadful uncertainty that haunts the souls of multitudes grows out of a misunderstanding of what constitutes true Christian experience. Many do not seem to understand the nature of Christian experience, while others have been misinformed and are seeking something for which we are not warranted by Scripture to expect.

More than three hundred times the word *faith* is mentioned in the New Testament with reference to man's salvation, and many more times it is implied. The writer of the book of Hebrews said, "He that cometh to God must believe that he is, and that he is a rewarder of them that diligently seek him." And again he said that "Without faith it is impossible to please him" (Hebrews 11:6).

It is because we have confused faith with feeling that many experience the difficulty and uncertainty that is so common among professing Christians today.

Faith always implies an object—that is, when we believe, we must believe something. That something I call the *fact*. Let me give you, then, three words, three words that must always be kept in the same order and never rearranged. Let me give you these three words that will point the way, for you, out of uncertainty to a confident Christian life. These three words are *fact*, *faith*, and *feeling*. They come in this order and the order is essential. If you confuse them, eliminate one, or add one, you will end up in the mire of despair and continue to grope about in semidarkness, without the joy and confidence of one who can say, "I know him in whom I have believed" (2 Timothy 1:12).

FACT

If you are saved from sin at all, you are saved through a personal faith in the gospel of Christ as defined in the Scriptures. Though it may at first seem dogmatic and narrow to you, the fact remains that there is no other way. The Bible says, "I delivered unto you first of all that which I also received, how that Christ died for our sins according to the Scriptures; and that he was buried, and that he arose again the third day according to the Scriptures" (1 Corinthians 15:3–4). The Bible says that we are saved when our faith is in this objective fact. The work of Christ is a fact, His cross is a fact, His tomb is a fact, and His resurrection is a fact.

It is impossible to believe anything into existence. The gospel did not come into being because men believed it. The tomb was not emptied of its deposit that first Easter because some faithful persons believed it. The fact always preceded the faith. We are psychologically incapable of believing without an object of our faith.

The Bible does not call upon you to believe something that is not credible, but to believe in the fact of history that in reality transcends all history. The Bible calls upon you to believe that this work of Christ, done for sin and for sinners, is effective in all who will risk their souls with Him. Trusting in Him for your eternal salvation is trusting in a fact.

Faith

Faith is second in this order of three words. Faith is rationally impossible where there is nothing to believe. Faith must have an object. The object of Christian faith is Christ. Faith means more than an intellectual assent to the claims of Christ. Faith involves the will. It is volitional. Faith demands action. If we actually believe, then we will live. Faith without works is dead. Faith actually means surrender and commitment to the claims of Christ. It means an acknowledgment of sin and a turning to Christ. We do not know Christ through the five physical senses, but we know Him through the sixth sense that God has given every man—which is the ability to believe.

THE EXPERIENCE OF FAITH

In reading carefully through the New Testament to see just what kind of an experience you can expect, I find that the New Testament sets forth only one. There is just one experience for which you can look—only one feeling you can expect—and that is the experience of faith. Believing is an experience as real as any experience, yet many are looking for something more—some dramatic sensation that will bring a physical thrill, while others look for some spectacular manifestation. Many have been told to look for such sensations, but the Bible says that a man is "justified by faith" and not by feeling. A man is saved by trusting in the finished work of Christ on the cross and not by physical excitement or religious ecstasy.

But you may say to me, "What about feeling? Is there no place in saving faith for any feeling?" Certainly there is room for feeling in saving faith, but we are not saved by it. Whatever feeling there may be is only the result of saving faith, but it in itself is not what does the saving!

FEELING

Feeling is the last of the three words and is the least important. I believe that much religious unrest and uncertainty is caused by earnest, honest seekers after salvation who have a predetermined idea that they must be in some kind of an emotional state before they can experience conversion.

Those who are seeking salvation as it is presented through the Scriptures will want to know what kind of an experience the Bible leads you to expect. I speak to those who have gone often to an altar, or to an inquiry room, or perhaps have knelt beside a radio or television set when an invitation has been given to receive Christ. You have heard the message, you have known that you were a sinner in need of the Savior, you have recognized that your life is a spiritual wreck, you have tried every man-made scheme for self-improvement and for reformation, but they all failed. In your lost and hopeless condition you looked to Christ for salvation. You believed that He could and would save you. You have often read His invitation to sinners when He said, "Come unto me, all ye that labor and are heavy laden, and I will give you rest" (Matthew 11:28). You have read the promise that says, "Him that cometh unto me, I will in no wise cast out" (John 6:37). You have read how He said, "If any man thirst, let him come unto me and drink" (John 7:37).

Feeling Comes after Faith

When I understand something of Christ's love for me as a sinner, I respond with a love for Christ—and love has feeling.

But love for Christ is a love that is above human love, though there is a similarity. It is a love that frees us from self. In marriage there is commitment. There is also feeling. But feelings come and go. Commitment stays. We who have committed ourselves to

Christ have feelings that come and go—joy, love, gratitude, and so on. But the commitment remains unchanged. Feelings are important but not essential. The Bible says, "Perfect love casteth out fear" (1 John 4:18). And those who love Christ have that confidence in Him that raises them above fear. Psychologists tell us there is destructive fear and healthy fear. Healthy fear is *instructive*, causing us to care for our bodies and our loved ones—Jesus told us to *fear* Satan.

When I understand that Christ in His death gained a decisive victory over death and over sin, then I lose the fear of death. The Bible says that "He also himself likewise took part of the same that through death he might destroy him that had the power of death, that is, the devil; And deliver them who through fear of death were all their lifetime subject to bondage" (Hebrews 2:14–15). Surely this also is a feeling. Fear is a kind of feeling, and to overcome fear with boldness and confidence in the very face of death is feeling and experience. But again I say, it is not the feeling of boldness and confidence that saves us, but it is our faith that saves us, and boldness and confidence result from our having trusted in Christ. From Genesis to Revelation we are told to fear the Lord. It is the fear of the Lord that puts all other fears in proper perspective.

The Part Guilt Plays

To have a guilty conscience is an experience. Psychologists may define it as a guilt experience and may seek to rationalize away the sense of guilt; but once this has been awakened through the application of the law of God, no explanation will quiet the insistent voice of conscience. Many a criminal has finally given himself over to the authorities because the accusations of a guilty conscience were worse than prison bars.

In an article on guilt that appeared in the *New York Times* (29 November 1983) Dr. Helen Block Lewis, a psycho-analyst and psychologist at Yale University, described guilt as a feeling that "helps people stay connected" to their fellow human beings. "Guilt is one of the cements that binds us together and keeps us human," she explained. "If it occurs to you that you've done something to injure someone else, guilt compels you to do something to fix it, to repair the bond."

Samuel Rutherford said to "Pray for a strong and lively sense of sin; the greater the sense of sin, the less sin." A sense of sin and guilt is the same thing. It not only tells you when you are in trouble, but like the sense of pain it can keep you out of it. Without a sense of pain one could put his hand on a hot stove and feel nothing. The vital part that a sense of pain plays in keeping us healthy is explored in the book, *Fearfully and Wonderfully Made*, by Paul Brand and Philip Yancey. They explain that it is not the disease of leprosy itself that causes the deformation so common among lepers. It is the absence of a sense of pain when the extremities are injured (for instance, the hand in a fire) which causes the horrible mutilation associated with leprosy.

The Bible teaches that Christ cleanses the conscience. The Bible says, "For if the blood of bulls and of goats and the ashes of an heifer sprinkling the unclean sanctifieth to the purifying of the flesh: How much more shall the blood of Christ, who through the eternal Spirit offered himself without spot to God, purge your conscience from dead works to serve the living God?" (Hebrews 9:13–14).

To have a guilty conscience cleansed and to be free from its constant accusation is an experience, but it is not the cleansing of the conscience that saves you; it is faith in Christ that saves, and a cleansed conscience is the result of having come into a right relationship with God.

Joy is a feeling. Inward peace is a feeling. Love for others is a feeling. Concern for the lost is a feeling.

Finally, someone may say, "I believe the historic facts of the gospel, but still I am not saved." Perhaps so, for the faith that saves has one distinguishing quality—saving faith is a faith that produces obedience, it is a faith that brings about a way of life. Some have quite successfully imitated this way of life for a time, but for those who trust Christ for salvation, that faith brings about in them a desire to live out that inward experience of faith. It is a power that results in godly living and surrender.

Let that intellectual faith, that historical faith that you may now have, yield itself to Christ in full surrender, earnestly desiring His salvation, and upon the authority of the Word of God you will become a child of God. "But as many as received him, to them gave he the right to become the sons of God, even to them that believe on his name" (John 1:12).

PART THREE

APPLYING THE ANTIDOTE

14

Enemies of the Christian

For we wrestle not against flesh and blood, but against principalities, against powers, against the rulers of darkness of this world, against spiritual wickedness in high places.
Ephesians 6:12

Now that you have made your decision—now that you have been born again—now that you have been converted—now that you have been justified—now that you are a child of God—what next? Is that all there is to it? Just one moment of decision and then it is all over? "Do I have any more responsibilities?" you ask.

Ah yes, you have just begun the Christian life. You have just been born into a new world—the spiritual world. Everything is brand-new. You are actually a spiritual baby. You need tenderness, love, care, nurture. You need to be fed. You need protection. That is one of the reasons Christ established the church. It is nearly impossible to live the Christian life alone. Most of us need help and fellowship.

The newborn Christian is like a newborn baby in his need for love. While revising this book, my wife and I took an island vacation with our oldest daughter, her husband, and their seventh child, little three-month-old Anthony—our sixteenth grandchild. In the week we were together he cried only twice. Why? He was surrounded by tenderness, love, care, nurture. All he did was eat, sleep, and smile. Ideally, at the outset of their spiritual experience, "baby" Christians need this kind of nurture, but unfortunately our world is not geared to that kind of beginning for the Christian life. The church is the place where that beginning takes place, in the plan and purpose of God.

Possibly you have already found that you have enemies. These are dangerous, vicious enemies who will use any method to defeat you in your Christian life. Within minutes after you made your decision you found these enemies already at work: either you were tempted to commit some sin, or you had a moment of depression and discouragement. To be sure, everything is exciting and thrilling just after you have made your decision for Christ! But it is also natural to have doubts, problems, questions, temptations, discouragements, and even difficulties.

The Bible teaches that you have three enemies that will be warring against you as long as you live. You must be prepared. They must be warded off.

First, let's look at these enemies we must face. Let's unmask them and see what they are, and who they are, and how they operate.

The Devil

First—*the devil.* We have already seen that the devil is a mighty being who opposes God and tempts God's people. We have found that even though he was beaten at the cross by Christ, he still has power to influence men for evil. The Bible calls him "the wicked one," "the devil," "a murderer," "a liar, and the father of lies," "an adversary" who seeks to devour, "that old serpent," and "accuser of our brethren" (Matthew 13:19; Luke 4:33; John 8:44; 1 Peter 5:8; Revelation 12:9–10).

The moment you made your decision for Christ, Satan suffered a tremendous defeat. He is angry now. From now on he is going to tempt you and try to lead you into sin. Don't be alarmed. He cannot rob you of your salvation, and he need not rob you of your assurance and victory. He will do everything in his power to sow seeds of doubt in your mind as to whether your conversion is a reality or not. You cannot argue with him, for he is the greatest debater of all time.

The moment of test has come with the first temptation. Remember to refuse any reliance upon your feelings; they will change like a weather vane in a whirlwind. His next approach probably will be to make you feel proud and important—to make you confident of your own powers, ambitions, desires, and aims. On another occasion he will put hatred in your heart. He will tempt you to say unkind and ungenerous things about others. He will put envy, discontent, and malice in your heart. Then, on another occasion, he will tempt you to lie, and you could easily find yourself being a hypocrite. Lying is one of the worst of all sins and can be committed by a thought, word, or deed. Anything that is intended to deceive another person is lying. The devil will do his best to make a liar of you. He also will try to get you to work for him to tempt others to sin—to try to lead other Christian friends astray. If you are not careful, you will find yourself actually in the employ of the devil. He is powerful, slick, crafty, wily, and subtle. He is called the "god of this world," "the prince of this world," "the prince of the power of the air" (2 Corinthians 4:4; John 12:31; Ephesians 2:2).

The devil will try to discourage you, to divert you; he will seek to dilute your testimony; he will attempt anything to destroy your relationship to Christ and your influence upon others.

You ask, "How can I overcome him? What can I do? Which way can I turn? Is there any escape?"

"There hath no temptation taken you but such as is common to man: but God is faithful, who will not suffer you to be tempted above that ye are able; but will with the temptation also make a way to escape, that ye may be able to bear it" (1 Corinthians 10:13).

Years ago I heard my friend J. Edwin Orr compare the Christian attacked by Satan to a mouse being attacked by a housewife wielding a broom. The mouse does not sit there contemplating the housewife or the broom. It is busy looking for a hole—a way to escape. So we Christians under satanic attack should look for our "way of escape."

God says in this verse that He has made a way of escape. Now remember this: Temptation of the devil is not a sign that your life is not right with God. It is actually a sign that you are right with God. Temptation is not sin. Also remember that God never tempts His own children. It never causes His children to doubt. All doubts and temptations come from the devil. Remember also that Satan can only tempt. He can never compel you to yield to the temptation. Remember also that Satan has already been conquered by

Christ. His power is made inoperative in the life of a fully trusting and yielded Christian who is completely dependent upon God.

The poet put it this way:

> The devil trembles when he sees
> the weakest saint upon his knees.

To say that Satan will be defeated when we read or quote Scripture and will run like a scalded dog when we resist him is an oversimplification. But we can depend upon the blood of Christ when we are under attack. There are times when we simply must hide behind the Person of Christ and ask Him to handle our problems. Jude says, "Yet Michael the archangel, when contending with the devil he disputed about the body of Moses, durst not bring against him a railing accusation, but said, The Lord rebuke thee" (v. 9). That's what we need to do—call upon God.

Now the Bible says that we are to "resist the devil and he will flee" from us (James 4:7). But before that, God says "Submit yourselves . . . to God." If you have fully submitted, 100 percent yielded and surrendered yourself to Christ, then you can "resist the devil," and the Bible promises he will flee from you. The devil will tremble when you pray. He will be defeated when you quote or read a passage of Scripture to him, and will leave you when you resist him.

THE WORLD

Your second enemy is the world. The world means the cosmos, this world system. The world has a tendency to lead us into sin—evil companions, pleasures, fashions, opinions, and aims.

You will find in your born-again experience that your pleasures have been lifted into an entirely new and glorious realm. Many non-Christians have accused the Christian life as being a set of rules, taboos, vetoes, and prohibitions. This is another lie of the devil. It is not a series of "don'ts," but a series of "dos." You become so busy in the work of Christ and so completely satisfied with the things of Christ that you do not have time for the things of the world.

Suppose someone should offer me a hamburger after I had eaten a T-bone steak. I would say, "No, thank you, I am already satisfied." Young Christian, that is the secret. You are so filled with the things of Christ, so enamored of the things of God, that you do not have time or taste for sinful pleasures of this world. The Bible says, "The full soul loatheth an honeycomb; but to the hungry soul every bitter thing is sweet" (Proverbs 27:7).

Worldliness, however, has been vastly misunderstood on the part of thousands of Christians. It needs a little clarification. It is probably one of the greatest difficulties that meets a young and inexperienced Christian.

Dr. W. H. Griffith Thomas has said:

> There are certain elements of daily life which are not sinful in themselves, but which have a tendency to lead to sin if they are abused. Abuse literally means extreme use, and in many instances overuse of things lawful becomes sin. Pleasure is lawful in use but unlawful in its overuse. Ambition is an essential part of true character, but it must be fixed on lawful objects and exercised in proper

> proportion. Our daily occupation, reading, dress, friendships and other similar phases of life are all legitimate and necessary, but can easily become illegitimate, unnecessary and harmful. Thought about the necessities of life is absolutely essential, but this can easily degenerate into anxiety, and then as Christ reminds us in the parable, the cares of this life choke the spiritual seed in the heart. Making of money is necessary for daily living, but money-making is apt to degenerate into money-loving and then the deceitfulness of riches enters into and spoils our spiritual life. Worldliness is thus not confined to any particular rank, walk, or circumstance of life so that we cannot separate this class from that and call one worldly and the other unworldly . . . one spiritual and the other unspiritual. Worldliness is a spirit, an atmosphere, an influence permeating the whole of life and human society, and it needs to be guarded against constantly and strenuously.

The Bible says, "Love not the world, neither the things that are in the world" (1 John 2:15). The Bible also warns that the world and the "lust thereof" shall pass away, "but he that doeth the will of God abideth forever" (1 John 2:17). However, under certain conditions these can become perplexing problems in our modern-day living. Many young people come to me and ask, "Is this wrong?" or "Is that wrong?" "Is this sinful?" or "Is that sinful?" One simple question, earnestly and prayerfully asked, will settle about 90 percent of your problems along this line. Just ask this question to yourself every time: "What would Christ have me to do?" Another question you can ask is, "Can I ask His blessing upon this particular thing for me?" "What would Christ think about my amusements, recreation, books, companions, and television programs?" "Could I ask Christ to go along with me to this particular event?" Being omnipotent, He'll be there anyway. The point is, should you?

It does not mean that in society we are snobs or have a superiority complex, lest we be in danger of spiritual pride—which would be far worse than any worldliness. But today there are so many professing Christians who are walking hand in hand with the world that you cannot tell the difference between the Christian and the unbeliever. This should never be.

The Christian should stand out like a sparkling diamond against a rough background. He should be more wholesome than anyone else. He should be poised, cultured, courteous, gracious, but firm in the things that he does and does not do. He should laugh and be radiant, but he should refuse to allow the world to pull him down to its level.

The Bible says that "whatsoever is not of faith is sin" (Romans 14:23), and the Bible again says that he who doubts is condemned if he does it. In other words, we are never to do anything of which we are not perfectly clear and certain. If you have a doubt about that particular thing that is bothering you, as to whether it is worldly or not, the best policy is "don't do it."

The Flesh

The third enemy that you will face immediately is the lust of the flesh. The flesh is that evil tendency of your inward self. Even after you are converted, sometimes your old, sinful cravings will return. You become startled and wonder where they come from. The Bible teaches that the old nature, with all its corruption, is still there and that these evil temptations come from nowhere else. In other words, "a traitor is living within." "That wretched bent toward sin is ever present to drag you down." War has been declared! You now have two natures in conflict, and each one is striving for dominance.

The Bible teaches "the flesh lusteth against the Spirit, and the Spirit against the flesh" (Galatians 5:17). It is the battle of the self-life and the Christ-life. This old nature cannot please God. It cannot be converted, or even patched up. Thank God, when Jesus died He took you with Him, and the old nature can be made inoperative and you can "reckon ye also yourselves to be dead indeed unto sin" (Romans 6:11). This is done by faith.

However, you must distinguish very carefully again between use and abuse—between that which is lawful and that which is unlawful. Some of these things that will be cropping up may be sinful lusts, or they may not be.

As Dr. W. H. Griffith Thomas says:

> The original meaning of the word lust is 'strong desire' and not necessarily a sinful desire, since there are certain desires of our physical nature—such as hunger and thirst—which we have in common with the animal world and which, in themselves, are natural and not sinful. It is only their abuse that is evil. Hunger is a natural lust. Gluttony is a sinful lust. Thirst is a natural lust. Intemperance is a sinful lust. Sloth should not be confused with exhaustion or illness. Marriage is according to the will of God and the dictates of human

> nature, physical, mental and social. Adultery is a sin and is opposed to the will of God and to all that is pure in body, mind and heart. But there are other lusts of the flesh which are sensually and inherently sinful. Such as, for instance, the desire to gratify at all cost our hatred and revenge. We must, therefore, distinguish carefully between the lust which is simply a strong desire, and the same lust as a sinful desire. Sins of the flesh are in some respects the most terrible of all because they represent the yearnings of the nature to do evil. Neither the devil nor the world, nor even our own evil heart can compel us to sin. It must be by our consent and will and it is at this point that our evil nature comes in with its awful power and possibility of evil.

Paul said he had no confidence in the flesh. On another occasion he said, "I make no provision for the flesh" (Romans 13:14). On another occasion he said, "I keep my body under" (1 Corinthians 9:27). We are so to reyield and resurrender ourselves to God that we can, by faith, reckon the old nature dead indeed unto sin.

FIGHTING OUR FOES

These, then, are our three foes: the devil, the world, and the flesh. Our attitude toward them as Christians can be summed up in one word—renounce. There can be no bargaining, compromise, or hesitation. Abiding in Christ, as taught in John 15, is the only possible course for the Christian who has to be "in" the world but does not want to be "of" it. Someone has said that the apostle Paul was dealing with this dilemma when he wrote to the

Ephesians, "Paul, an apostle of Jesus Christ . . . to the saints . . . at Ephesus and to the faithful in Christ Jesus" (Ephesians 1:1). Ephesus was their business address, but "in Christ" was their home address! In relation to the devil, we resist him only as we submit ourselves to God. In relation to the world, the Bible says, "This is the victory that overcometh the world, even our faith" (1 John 5:4). In relation to the flesh, the Bible says, "Walk in the Spirit, and ye shall not fulfill the lust of the flesh" (Galatians 5:16).

Here is glorious news to you who have already been fighting these battles and temptations: You are not asked to fight the battle alone. The Bible says in Romans 8:13 that you, by the Spirit, shall put to death the deeds of the body. Remember, Jesus promised that He would never leave us or forsake us. Remember, Jesus promised us that after He left the earth He would send Another—the Third Person of the Trinity—the Holy Spirit, who is called a Comforter (which actually means "one who comes alongside to help"), that He may abide with us forever (John 14:16). Jesus said, "I am not going to leave you alone. I will come to you in the person of the Holy Spirit." Jesus is the vine and believers are the branches is the way Jesus put it (see John 15).

The Holy Spirit is the most powerful Being in the world today. The time of the Old Testament was an age of God the Father. During the time that Jesus was on earth it was an age of God the Son. Now we are living, since Pentecost, in the age of God the Holy Spirit. The Bible says, "Be filled with the Spirit" (Ephesians 5:18), which reads literally, "Be being filled . . . ." It's a continuous and ongoing process. Just as Christ came to make God visible and redeem mankind, so the Holy Spirit came to make Christ visible in the life of the believer and enable the individual Christian to offer Christ's redemption to a lost and dying world.

The Bible says that the moment you accepted Christ as Savior the Holy Spirit took up residence in your heart. Your body is now "the temple of the Holy Ghost which is in you" (1 Corinthians 6:19). Paul even warned that if any man has not the Spirit of Christ he is none of His.

You say, "But I don't feel anything down in my heart. I don't feel the Spirit of God in me."

FAITH IS A FACT

Disregard feelings. You're not saved by feeling, and you may or may not feel the Spirit. Accept Him by faith as a fact. He lives within you right now to help you live the Christian life. He is living in you in order to magnify, glorify, and exalt Christ in you so that you can live a happy, victorious, radiant, Christ-honoring life.

The Bible commands, "Be filled with the Spirit" (Ephesians 5:18). If you are filled with the Spirit, then you are going to produce the fruit of the Spirit, which is "love, joy, peace, longsuffering, gentleness, goodness, faith, meekness, temperance" (Galatians 5:22–23). To be filled with the Spirit is not optional. It is a command to be obeyed—a duty to be done.

How do you know that you are filled? And how can you be filled? Is it some emotional experience through which you must pass? Not necessarily. When you give all you know of yourself to all that you know of Him, then you can accept by faith that you are filled with the Spirit of God. That means that He can have all of you. Commitment actually is surrender—total, absolute, unconditional, irreversible surrender. "I beseech you, therefore, brethren, by the mercies of God, that ye present your bodies a living sacrifice, holy, acceptable unto God, which is your reasonable service" (Romans 12:1).

It is only the consecrated, Spirit-filled Christian who can have victory over the world, the flesh, and the devil. It is the Holy Spirit who will do the fighting for you. "We wrestle not against flesh and blood, but against principalities, against powers, against the rulers of darkness" (Ephesians 6:12). This is a spiritual warfare. You cannot fight against these three enemies with normal weapons. Only as we become channels and let the Holy Spirit do the fighting through us are we going to get complete victory. Don't hold back anything from Christ. Let Him be completely the Lord and Master of your life. He said, "Ye call me Master and Lord: and ye say well; for so I am" (John 13:13).

I believe unself-consciousness is characteristic of the fruit of the Holy Spirit. The person who says, "I am Spirit-filled" sets himself up for some pretty uncomfortable scrutiny. Did any apostle or disciple say of himself, "I am filled with the Holy Spirit"? But of many it was said, "They were filled with the Holy Spirit." The person who is self-consciously loving, self-consciously joyful, self-consciously peaceful, has about him the odor of self. And as one Christian sanely observed, "Self is spiritual B.O."

A little child playing one day with a very valuable vase put his hand into it and could not withdraw it. His father, too, tried his best, but all in vain. They were thinking of breaking the vase when the father said, "Now, my son, make one more try. Open your hand and hold your fingers out straight as you see me doing, and then pull."

To their astonishment the little fellow said, "Oh no, father. I couldn't put my fingers out like that, because if I did I would drop my penny."

Smile, if you will—but thousands of us are like that little boy, so busy holding on to the world's worthless penny that we cannot accept liberation. I beg you to drop that trifle in your heart. Surrender! Let go, and let God have His way in your life.

Now, after you have given yourself completely to Christ in consecration, remember that God has accepted what you have presented. "Him that cometh unto me I will in no wise cast out" (John 6:37). You have come to Him; now He has received you. And He will in no wise cast you out!

THE FRUIT OF THE SPIRIT

Not only will you have boldness, but you will produce the fruit of the Spirit. Keep in mind that these fruits of the Spirit are of the Spirit. One does not produce them himself. They are supernatural in origin. The first is, according to Galatians 5, love, and from this root will grow all the others. Jesus said, "This is my commandment, that ye love one another, as I have loved you. . . . If ye keep my commandments ye shall abide in my love; even as I have kept my Father's commandments, and abide in his love" (John 15:12, 10). We must differentiate between the gifts of the Spirit and the fruit of the Spirit. Gifts are given—fruits are grown. To grow something there must be a close, intimate, personal relationship between the vine and the branch. A person must be rooted and grounded in Christ.

As we pointed out earlier, one of the characteristics of the Holy Spirit is unself-consciousness. Whenever a person is self-conscious of spiritual fruit there goes up the odor of self.

Another fruit of the Spirit is joy. One of the characteristics of the Christian is an inward joy that does not depend upon circumstances. Nehemiah says, "For the joy of the Lord is your strength" (8:10). S. D. Gordon, the well-known devotional writer of a past generation, said of joy: "Joy is distinctly a Christian word and a Christian thing. It is the reverse of happiness. Happiness is the result of what happens of an agreeable sort. Joy has its springs deep down inside. And that spring never runs dry, no matter what happens. Only Jesus gives that joy. He had joy, singing its music within, even under the shadow of the cross. It is an unknown word and thing except as He has sway within."

"Real joy comes not from ease or riches or . . . the praise of men, but from doing something worthwhile," said the missionary Sir Wilfred Grenfell. And Alexander MacLaren said, "To pursue joy is to lose it. The only way to get it is to follow steadily the path of duty, without thinking of joy, and then, like sheep, it comes most surely, unsought, and we 'being in the way' the angel of God, fair-haired joy, is sure to meet us."

There will be peace. Paul said, "Troubled on every side, yet not distressed; we are perplexed, but not in despair; persecuted, but not forsaken; cast down, but not destroyed" (2 Corinthians 4:8–9). We could go through all the rest of the supernatural list—longsuffering, gentleness, goodness, faith, meekness, and temperance—and see how all of this fruit flourishes in the lives of those who are truly yielded and Spirit-filled.

The victory is yours. Claim it! It is your birthright. Browning said, "The best is yet to be." This doesn't mean the Christian can never suffer defeat or experience low periods in life. But it does mean that the Savior goes with you no matter the problem. The peace comes in the midst of problems and in spite of them.

15

GUIDELINES FOR CHRISTIAN LIVING

And as ye would that men should do
to you, do ye also to them likewise.
LUKE 6:31

Whether we are playing a game, driving a car, or baking a cake, there are certain rules that must be followed for our safety as well as our success.

I well recall what happened near my home in Montreat, North Carolina, some years ago. The road between Black Mountain and Asheville was being widened from two lanes to four. For several weeks during the construction period there were no lane markers. One night there was a tragic head-on collision and five people were killed—because the "road rules" had not been clearly marked.

The Bible teaches that the Christian life is one of constant growth. When you were born again, you were born into God's family. My wife, Ruth, and I now have nineteen grandchildren. And each of them is precious to us. Each is an accepted, treasured member of our family. And that's the way God feels about you. It is God's purpose that you will grow into full stature and become mature in Christ. It would be against the law of God and nature if you were to remain a baby and thus become a spiritual dwarf. In 2 Peter 3:18, the Bible says that we are to grow. This implies steady development, constant enlargement, increasing wisdom.

READ THE BIBLE DAILY

For one to grow properly, certain rules must be observed for good spiritual health. First, *read your Bible daily*. It is one of your greatest privileges. Your spiritual life needs food. What kind of food? Spiritual food. Where do you find this spiritual food? In the Bible, the Word of God. The Bible reveals Christ, who is the Bread of Life for your hungry soul, and the Water of Life for your thirsty heart. If you fail to partake of daily spiritual nourishment, you will starve and lose your spiritual vitality. The Bible says, "Desire the sincere milk of the Word, that ye may grow thereby" (1 Peter 2:2). Read it, study it, meditate on it, memorize it. Ninety-five percent of the difficulties you will experience as a Christian can be traced to a lack of Bible study and reading.

Suppose an archaeologist discovered the original diary of Genghis Khan, or Alexander the Great, or the love letters of Cleopatra? Or what if our astronauts had discovered a mysterious manuscript during their moon walk? Imagine the stampede into the bookstores across America to get copies of such books. Yet we have here a Book that God Himself has written for mankind—and think how it is either ignored or attacked by many so-called civilized people.

Some parts of our world do not enjoy the freedom we have to read the Bible and study it together with fellow Christians. In most of the world, in fact, there's a veritable famine for the Word of God! I recall the story of a Chinese musician in the People's Republic of China. He was converted and strengthened spiritually through the reading of individual pages of the Scripture torn from a Bible and slipped to him by an unknown friend. There are other stories of prisoners who survived twenty to thirty years at hard labor—and sometimes terrible torture—and came out with their minds intact, totally lacking in bitterness toward their captors.

One more story of the Bible's power comes from a mental hospital here in this country. A young man, an inmate of the hospital, wrote to our organization requesting a copy of the Bible. His recovery and subsequent complete rehabilitation date back to his receipt of that Bible—and his reading of its pages. Today he is married and self-supporting!

Do not be content to skim through a chapter merely to satisfy your conscience. Hide the Word of God in your heart. A little portion well digested is of greater spiritual value to your soul than a lengthy portion scanned hurriedly. Do not be discouraged because you cannot understand it all. Some excuse themselves saying, "It's too hard to understand." Any book is difficult to understand if you don't read it! Read simple portions of the Bible first. You do not feed a baby beefsteak the first day—you give him milk.

I would suggest that you start by reading the Gospel of John.

As you read, the Holy Spirit will enlighten the passages for you. He will illuminate the difficult words and make obscure meanings clear. Even though you cannot remember all you have read, or understand it all, go on reading. The very practice of reading in itself will have a purifying effect upon your mind and heart. Let nothing take the place of this daily exercise.

Scripture memorized can come to mind when you do not have your Bible with you—on sleepless nights, when driving a car, traveling, when having to make an instantaneous important decision. It comforts, guides, corrects, encourages—all we need is there. Memorize as much as you can.

LEARN TO PRAY

Second, *learn the secret of prayer*. Your prayers may falter at first. You may be awkward and inarticulate. But the Holy Spirit who lives within you will help you and teach you. Every prayer that you pray will be answered. Sometimes the answer may be "Yes" and sometimes "No," and sometimes it is "Wait," but nevertheless it will be answered.

Prayer is communicating. A baby's first response is to his parents. He isn't asking for anything. He is simply smiling back when his parents smile, cooing when they talk to him. What a thrill his first response brings to the entire family! In the same way, can you imagine the joy our first response to Him brings to God?

Your petitions should always be conditioned by "Thy will be done." "Delight thyself also in the Lord and he shall give thee the desires of thine heart" (Psalm 37:4). But the delighting of oneself in Him precedes the fulfillment of our desires. Delighting ourselves in Him will direct our desires, so God can answer our petitions.

Remember that you can pray anytime, anywhere. Washing dishes, digging ditches, working in the office, in the shop, on the athletic field, even in prison—you can pray and know God hears! We have a friend on Death Row who prays for us every morning between four and six. How often this fact has encouraged and cheered us on.

Try to have a systematic method of prayer. Prayer combined with Bible study makes for a healthy Christian life. The Bible says, "Pray without ceasing." If you have special prayer periods that you set aside during the day, your unconscious life will be saturated with prayer between the prayer periods. It is not enough for you to get out of bed in the morning and just bow your knee and repeat a few sentences. There should be stated periods in which you slip apart with God. For the overworked mother or one living under extremely busy circumstances, this may be impossible. But here is where "prayer without ceasing" comes in. We pray as we work. As we have said, we pray everywhere, anytime.

The devil will fight you every step of the way. He will cause the baby to cry, the telephone to ring, someone to knock at the door—there will be many interruptions, but keep at it! Don't be discouraged. Soon you will find that these periods of prayer are the greatest delight of your life. You will look forward to them with more anticipation than to anything else. Without constant, daily, systematic prayer your life will seem barren, discouraging, and fruitless. Without constant prayer you never can know the inner peace that God wants to give you.

RELY ON THE HOLY SPIRIT

Third, *rely constantly on the Holy Spirit.* Remember that Christ dwells in you through the Holy Spirit. Your body is now the dwelling place of the Third Person of the Trinity. Do not ask Him to help you as you would a servant. Ask Him to come in and do it all. Ask Him to take over in your life. Tell Him how weak, helpless, unstable, and unreliable you are. Stand aside and let Him take over in all the choices and decisions of your life. We know that the Holy Spirit prays for us (Romans 8), and what a comfort that should be to the weakest of us.

It is impossible for you to hold out in your Christian life—but He can hold you. It is very difficult for Him to hold you if you are struggling, fighting, and striving. Just relax and rest in the Lord. Let go all those inner tensions and complexes. Rely completely on Him. Do not fret and worry about important decisions—let Him make them for you. Do not worry about tomorrow—He is the God of tomorrow, He sees the end from the beginning. Do not worry about the necessities of life—He is there to supply and provide. A true victorious Christian is one who, in spite of worries, inner conflicts, and tensions, is confident that God is in control and will be victorious in the end. In reliance on the Holy Spirit, you will find that many of your physical and mental ailments will disappear along with many worries, inner conflicts, and tensions. Whatever our difficulties, whatever our circumstances, we must remember, as Corrie ten Boom used to say, "Jesus is victor!"

ATTEND CHURCH REGULARLY

Fourth, *attend church regularly*. Christianity is a religion of fellowship. Following Christ means love, righteousness, service; and these can only be achieved and expressed through social relations. These social relationships are to be found in the church.

There is a visible church and there is an invisible church. The invisible church is made up of true believers down through the centuries and the world over. The visible church is made up of both Catholic and Protestant—the latter with its various denominations. But we are told in the Scriptures, "Forsaking [not] the assembling of ourselves together . . ." (Hebrews 10:25). Christians need fellowship—the fellowship of fellow believers.

The visible church is Christ's organization upon earth. It is a place where we gather to worship God, learn from His Word, and fellowship with other Christians. The Bible calls the church "a holy nation," "God's own people," "the household of God," "a holy temple in the Lord," "a dwelling place of God in the Spirit," "the body of Christ." These are all figures of speech, symbols, or pictures used to indicate the spiritual reality of the church.

Nothing can take the place of church attendance. If you are a true follower of Christ you will scorn such flimsy excuses as the weather being too hot or too cold, rain or snow, as unworthy of a true follower of Christ. There are many people who say they can stay at home on Sunday morning and worship God in their own minds. The person who does only this fails to give God the complete worship to which He has a right, for God is the Creator of our bodies, no less than of our minds and souls; therefore both the mind and the body should participate in rendering to God a complete act of worship.

In certain countries today, however, church gatherings are not encouraged. For years people have been forced to meet privately in homes, perhaps just a single family or perhaps a few Christian friends gathering together. In the People's Republic of China the government has reopened some of the old churches. The packed buildings prove that what I have said above is true. Christians need one another; we need to gather together to worship God, and nothing can take the place of church attendance.

At the same time I think we should be grateful for the electronic church. There are many in hospitals, institutions, like old people's homes, or even prisons where the only way they have to attend a church service is by television or even radio.

On the other hand, there are many who claim they can stay at home and listen to a sermon on the radio or television and that this takes the place of a church service. That is not enough. You do not go to church to hear a sermon. You go to church to worship God and to serve Him in the fellowship of other Christians. You cannot be a successful and happy Christian without being faithful in church. In the church you will find your place of service. We are saved to serve. The happy Christian is the serving Christian.

BE A WITNESSING CHRISTIAN

Fifth, *be a witnessing Christian.* If you are faithfully practicing the four preceding rules this one will take care of itself—just as it follows naturally that if a cup is being filled continually it is bound to overflow.

Sometime ago I came across the question, which is more important, to witness by one's life or to witness by the Word? And the answer was, "Which is more important, the left or right wing of an airplane?" Thinking this very clever, I repeated it one day in a car as I was driving some missionaries out to lunch. One of them spoke up and said, "That's very clever. But it's just not true." Surprised, I asked what she meant. "All the way through the Scriptures," she replied, "God has promised to bless His Word, not our lives: 'My Word shall not return unto me void but shall accomplish . . . He that hath my word let him preach my word faithfully, for what are the tares to the wheat, saith the Lord.'" I realized she was speaking the truth. We are responsible to God for the way in which we live, but it is His Word that He has promised to bless and this explains why a musician in a communist country can pick up a page torn from the Bible and be converted. That is why a surgeon general in Portugal, returning home on a muddy day and finding a piece of paper stuck to his shoe, can pull it off and read a portion of the Word of God and be converted.

We Christians are now duly appointed and commissioned ambassadors of the King of kings. We are to let our flag fly high over our embassy. Suppose our ambassador to Russia should order the American flag pulled down because it is not popular in Russia—we would soon call him home! He would not deserve to represent the United States.

If we are not willing to let our flags fly in the home, in the office, in the shop, on the campus—then we are not worthy to be ambassadors for Christ! We are to take our stand and let all those around us know that we are Christians. We are to bear witness for Christ.

We witness in two ways: by life and by word—and the two, where possible, should go hand in hand. God's purpose for you and me after we have been converted is that we be witnesses to His saving grace and power. We are to be commandos for Christ. We are to be Minutemen for Him.

Christ said, "Whoever therefore shall confess me before men, him will I confess also before my Father which is in heaven" (Matthew 10:32). Acts 28:23 presents a thrilling scene. Paul, held in bonds at Rome, persuaded men concerning Jesus, from morning to evening. Concerning each of us it should be said every day, "Behold a sower went forth to sow."

Very little originality is permitted a Western Union messenger boy. His sole obligation is to carry the message he receives from the office to the person to whom it is addressed. He may not like to carry that message. It may contain bad news or distressing news for the person to whom he carries it. He cannot stop on the way, open the envelope, and change the wording of the telegram. His duty is to take the message.

We Christians have the Word of God. Our Great Commander has said, "Go, and take this message to a dying world." Some are neglecting it. Some are tearing up the message and substituting one of their own. Some are taking out a part of it. Some are telling the people that the Lord does not mean what He says. Others are saying that He really did not write the message but that it was written by ordinary men who are mistaken about the meaning of it.

Let us remember that the apostle Paul exhorted the Christians centuries ago to teach only the Word. Remember we are sowing seed. Some indeed may fall on beaten paths and some among thorns, but it is our business to keep on sowing. We are not to stop sowing because some of the soil looks unpromising.

We are holding a light. We are to let it shine! Though it may seem but a twinkling candle in a world of blackness, it is our business to let it shine.

We are blowing a trumpet. In the din and noise of battle the sound of our little trumpet may seem to be lost, but we must keep sounding the alarm to those who are in danger.

We are kindling a fire. In this cold world full of hatred and selfishness our little blaze may seem to be unavailing, but we must keep our fire burning.

We are striking with a hammer. The blows may seem only to jar our hands as we strike, but we are to keep on hammering. Amy Carmichael of India once asked a stone-cutter which blow broke the stone. "The first one and the last," he replied, "and every one in between."

We have bread for a hungry world. The people may seem to be so busy feeding on other things that they will not accept the Bread of Life, but we must keep on giving it, offering it to the souls of men.

We have water for famishing people. We must keep standing and crying out, "Ho, every one that thirsteth, come ye to the waters." Sometimes they can't come and we must carry it to them.

We must persevere. We must never give up. Keep using the Word!

Jesus said that much of our seed will find good soil and spring up and bear fruit. We must be faithful witnesses. The most thrilling experience known to man is to win another to Jesus Christ. It has been my privilege to win others to a saving knowledge of Christ. I never cease to thrill at hearing of one who has listened, accepted Christ, and been transformed by His grace. This is worth more than all the money in all the world. There is no happiness, no experience, no romantic adventure comparable to the thrill of winning another person to Christ.

The Bible says, "He that winneth souls is wise" (Proverbs 11:30). "And they that be wise shall shine as the brightness of the firmament; and they that turn many to righteousness as the stars for ever and ever" (Daniel 12:3).

"Ye are the salt of the earth" (Matthew 5:13). Salt makes one thirsty. Does your life make others thirsty for the water of life?

LET US LOVE

Sixth, *let love be the ruling principle of your life*. Be ruled by love. Jesus said to those who followed Him, "By this shall all men know that ye are my disciples, if ye have love one to another." In another part of the Bible we find the same thing stated:

> Beloved, let us love one another, for love is of God; and every one that loveth is born of God, and knoweth God. He that loveth not knoweth not God, for God is love. In this was manifested the love of God toward us, because that God sent his only begotten Son into the world, that we might live through him. Herein is love,

not that we loved God, but that he loved us, and sent his Son to be the propitiation for our sins. (1 John 4:7–10).

Love does not necessarily imply approval of the one loved. If God had waited until He could approve of us before He sent His Son to redeem us, where would we be?

Of all the gifts God offers His children, love is the greatest. Of all the fruits of the Holy Spirit, love is the first.

The Bible declares that we who follow Christ should love one another as God loved us when He sent His Son to die on the cross. The Bible says that the moment we come to Christ He gives us supernatural love and that His love is shed abroad in our hearts by the Holy Spirit. The greatest demonstration of the fact that we are Christians is that we love one another. If we learn this secret of God early in our Christian experience, we will have gone a long way toward a mature, happy Christian life.

Be an Obedient Christian

Seventh, *be an obedient Christian*. Let Christ have first place in all the choices of your life. Make Him Lord and Master.

Learn How to Meet Temptation

Eighth, *learn how to meet temptation*. As we have already learned, temptation is natural. Temptation is not sin. It is yielding that is sin. God never brings temptation to us. He allows it to test us. It is the work of the devil. Recognize it as such. One way to meet temptation is to quote a verse of Scripture at the Tempter—he will always run, for he cannot stand the Word of God.

When Jesus was tempted in the wilderness, the only resource that He had was the Word of God. He said three times, "It is written."

Say to the devil, "Thus saith the Lord," and he will flee. At the same time let Christ through the Holy Spirit do the fighting for you. Be like the little girl who said, "Every time I hear the devil knock, I send Jesus to the door."

Everyone has temptations but some folks entertain them. They seem to enjoy being tempted. Chase a mouse with a broom and you will notice that he isn't eying the broom. He is looking for a hole. Get your eyes off the temptation and onto Christ!

I once asked an army officer which he would rather have on the field of battle—courage or obedience. He flashed right back, "Obedience!"

God would rather have your obedience than anything else. In order to be obedient you must know His commands. That is another reason for the necessity of studying and reading the Bible. The Bible is your compass and rule book. Obey what God tells you.

BE A WHOLESOME CHRISTIAN

Ninth, *be a wholesome Christian.* It has been well said that "Some Christians are so heavenly minded they are no earthly good."

Certainly the Bible teaches separation from sin, but the Bible says nowhere that we are to be peculiar or unnatural. We are to be radiant. We should be chivalrous, courteous, clean of body, pure of mind, poised, and gracious. Silly flirtations, unhealthy gossip, shady conversations, suggestive amusements should be avoided like rattlesnakes. We should be neat in appearance, clean, attractive, and as much as possible in style, with good taste. Extremes should be avoided. Our lives and appearance should commend the gospel and make it attractive to others. As the late Dr. Barnhouse once said, "Men may not read the gospel in sealskin, or the gospel in morocco, or the gospel in cloth covers; but they can't get away from the gospel in shoe leather."

LIVE ABOVE YOUR CIRCUMSTANCES

Tenth, live above your circumstances. God made you as you are! He placed you where you are! So you can best serve and glorify Him just as you are, where you are. Some people are always looking on the other side of the fence because they think the grass is greener. They spend so much time wishing things were different, and thinking up alibis for why they are not, that they overlook all the advantages and opportunities open to them right where they are.

Be as the apostle Paul when he said, "But none of these things move me" (Acts 20:24). Paul said he had learned how to abound and how to be abased. He had learned to be every inch a Christian even in prison. Don't let your circumstances get you down. Learn to live graciously within them, realizing the Lord Himself is with you.

These principles and suggestions may seem simple, but keep

them—they work. I have seen them tested in the lives of thousands. I have tested them in my own life. Properly and faithfully kept, they will give you peace of soul, happiness, peace of mind, and pleasure, and you will have learned the secret of living life with satisfaction.

16

The Christian and the Church

In whom ye also are builded together for an habitation of God through the Spirit.
Ephesians 2:22

Man is a social animal, gregarious by nature, and finds his greatest sense of security and satisfaction in the company of others who share his interests and attitudes. Of all the many groups into which humans have collected themselves, of all the many tribes, clans, organizations, and societies throughout history, none has been so powerful, so far-reaching, or more universal than the church.

In primitive times, men gathered together for mutual protection, and at a far later date they learned to join together for mutual benefit and pleasure. With more advanced civilization, secret societies came into being, to give their members a sense of belonging, a feeling of being "set apart" and therefore distinguished from nonmembers. Special oaths, rituals, and codes were established and given great significance.

Racial and national groups were established with membership restricted to those of similar place of origin, or with allegiance to a common flag. Country clubs, college fraternities, lodges, literary societies, political parties, military organizations—all of these, from the most select "gentlemen's club" to the high-school "gang," represent man's need to find comfort and reassurance in the company of others who approve of his way of life because their own way of life is similar.

Nowhere, however, has man found this comfort, this reassurance, this peace to the extent that he has found it in the church, for all other groups are obviously man-inspired. They draw artificial boundaries and set up only the illusion of protection, while the church provides a living, vibrant organism that draws its power from God Himself instead of relying upon outside sources to give it meaning and vitality.

ORIGIN OF THE CHURCH

The word *church* is an English translation of the Greek word *ecclesia*, which means "the called-out ones," or an assembly of people. Although church soon became a distinctively Christian word, it has a pre-Christian history. Throughout the Greek world the word *church* was the designation of the regular assembly of the whole body of citizens in a free city-state. A group of the citizens would be called out by the herald for the discussion and decision of public business. This same word *church* was also the Hebrew equivalent in the Old Testament and is translated in English as "congregation" or "community" of Israel in which members were designated as the called-out people of God. Thus we find Stephen in the book of Acts using it when he describes Moses as "he that was in the church in the wilderness" (Acts 7:38). In the first century, therefore, the word *church* would suggest to the Greek a self-governing, democratic society; to the Jew, a theocratic society whose members were the subjects of God.

The word *church* as applied to the Christian society was first used by Jesus Himself when He told Peter, "Upon this rock I will build my church, and the gates of hell shall not prevail against it" (Matthew 16:18). Thus Jesus Christ Himself founded the church. He is the great cornerstone upon which the church is built. He is the foundation of all Christian experience, and the church is founded upon Him. "For other foundation can no man lay than that is laid, which is Jesus Christ" (1 Corinthians 3:11). Jesus proclaimed Himself to be the founder of the church and the builder of the church. The church belongs to Him and to Him alone. He has promised to live with, and in, all those who are members of His church. Here is not only an organization but an organism which is completely unlike anything else that the world has ever known: God Himself living with, and in, ordinary men and women who are members of His church.

JESUS CHRIST ITS HEAD

The New Testament teaches that while there is actually only one universal church there can be any number of local churches formed into various denominations and societies or councils. These local churches and denominational groups may be divided along national and theological lines or according to the temperament of their members. However, the New Testament teaches that even though there may be many cleavages and divisions within the structure of the church, yet we have only "one Lord." As the hymn puts it, "The church's one foundation is Jesus Christ her Lord."

Jesus Christ is the head of this great universal church. From Him must spring all the activities and teachings of the church, for He is the fountainhead of all Christian experience.

In this day of electronics it is easy to draw a comparison with a far-flung communications system in which there is one central station toward which all light or sound waves converge and from which all connections are made. In a railroad system there is always one central office from which orders governing the operations of all trains originate. In the army, one commanding general issues orders to the many groups under his jurisdiction. His various subordinates may interpret his orders in slightly different ways, but his orders still remain the basis for their conduct.

In relation to the church, Jesus Christ stands in the position of the commanding general. It is upon His orders that the church has its existence. Its very power comes directly from Him, and it is up to every church group to follow His commands as closely as possible. Just as the commanding general expects to have his orders carried out faithfully, so does Jesus expect every branch of the church to abide by His teachings to the fullest.

The church has been widely criticized for many internal squabbles, much hair-splitting, and apparent lack of unity. These, however, are superficial things; these are the conflicts that come from the slightly varying interpretations of the general's orders and in no way reflect upon the wisdom of the general or His absolute authority in issuing His orders!

Study the underlying beliefs of the various denominations and you will find that basically and historically they are almost identical. They may differ widely in ritual, they may seem to lock horns over theological technicalities, but fundamentally they all recognize Jesus Christ as God incarnate, who died upon the cross and rose again that man might have salvation—and that is the all-important fact to all humanity.

THE CHURCH—OR CHURCHES?

Now that you have accepted Christ as your Savior and put your trust and confidence in Him, you have already become a member of the great church invisible. You are a member of the household of faith. You are a part of the body of Christ. Now you are called upon to obey Christ, and if you obey Christ, you will follow His example of joining with others in the worship of God. "Not forsaking the assembling of ourselves together, as the manner of some is" (Hebrews 10:25).

It is true that we are now talking about the local church, the one in your own community, of whose many imperfections and shortcomings you may be well aware. But we must remember that perfection does not exist among human beings, and the institutions they create to the greater glory of God are filled with these self-same flaws. Jesus is the only perfect Man who ever lived. The rest of us are at best but repentant sinners, try as we may to follow His magnificent example; and the church is but turning a blind eye toward itself when it claims infallibility or perfection for itself or any of its members.

Samuel Rutherford at one point received a complaint from some church members who were unhappy with their pastor and the local church situation. He wrote them a very stern reply, telling them that they were not responsible for the life of their pastor. But they were responsible to pray for him, and to remain in the church, and to work for the Lord. And that the Lord would honor and bless them for it.

The tabernacle under Eli had degenerated so terribly that the people despised the sacrifice of the Lord because Eli's "sons made themselves vile, and he restrained them not" (1 Samuel 3:13). But little Samuel was left in that environment and grew up to be a great prophet.

In the New Testament, it was the temple leaders who had Christ crucified, yet after His resurrection and ascension, the disciples were "continually in the temple, praising and blessing God" (Luke 24:53).

When Jesus founded the church, He intended His followers to join it and remain faithful to it. Today, if you are among the more than 50 percent of the population of this country who have no active formal church affiliation, you may stand in bewilderment before the number whose membership is open to you. In selecting one you may well have a natural tendency to return to the church of your childhood, or you may feel you want to make a choice based on your more spiritually mature judgment. A church affiliation is not something to be entered into lightly, for if the church is to be of the greatest service to you, and even more important, if it is to give you the greatest possible opportunity to be of service to others, you must prayerfully select the one where you feel you can be of the most service to God.

A Church for Everyone

Some people find it easier to draw closer to God in magnificent buildings and with some form of ritual. Others find they can seek God only in stark simplicity. Some people find themselves more comfortable with formality; others feel more at home with informality. The important thing is not how we do it, but the sincerity and depth of purpose with which we do it, and we should each find and join the church in which as individuals we can best accomplish this.

Do not make the mistake of attaching yourself to a particular minister rather than to the body of the church itself. The ministry may change—it is healthy and stimulating that it should—but the tenets of the church remain the same, and it is to the church and its Christ that you owe allegiance. A stable church is built up when the members of the congregation recognize that it is their mutual love of Jesus Christ and the sincere desire to follow in His steps that hold them together.

The true Christian goes to church not only for what he gets out of it, but also for what he can put into it. He goes to add his prayers to those of others, he goes to add his voice to the other voices raised in praise of the Lord, he goes to add his strength in beseeching the Lord's blessing, he goes to add his weight of testimony to the possibility of salvation through the Lord Jesus Christ. He goes to join with others in the worship of God, in the contemplation of His boundless mercy and love. He also goes for the necessary companionship of fellow believers.

Christians who are not actively involved in the life of a local church remind me of what happens when a burning coal is removed from the fire. You've seen it happen. The coal gradually cools and its flame dies once it is removed from the bed of glowing coals.

In the far west, when the wolves attack a flock of sheep, the first thing they do is try to scatter them. Then, they close in for the kill on one of the isolated sheep.

THE CHURCH IS A CHANNEL

The church should be the means of channeling your funds for Christian work and the needs of fellow Christians. The Bible teaches tithing. A tithe is one-tenth of your net income. That one-tenth of your income belongs to the Lord. In addition to your tithe, you should give as the Lord has prospered you. Giving is a Christian grace that should be woven into the fabric of our daily lives until it becomes a part no longer distinguishable from the rest. Generosity should motivate us in all things.

Christ said, "It is more blessed to give than to receive" (Acts 20:35). He knew how giving warms the heart and satisfies the soul. He coveted for you that particular blessing. Selfishness is caused by fear—and a Christian should stand forth unafraid. Jesus stood always with hands that were open—not with hands that were clenched tight with selfishness and greed. As far as possible, one should give inconspicuously and quietly. Jesus also said that when giving, "let not thy left hand know what thy right hand doeth" (Matthew 6:3).

Giving cannot be measured in dollars and cents. It cannot be measured in boxes of old clothes. Sometimes the greatest gift is the gift of friendship and neighborliness. A kind word, a friendly greeting, an evening spent with someone who is lonely can reap rich harvest for the kingdom of God. It is impossible for you to become a soul winner unless you are prepared to give something of yourself. Not only your money, but your time, your talents, your very self—everything is to be given to the service of Christ.

The giving of your offering which is above the tithe should not be limited by set rules or organized methods. It should be governed by the need that is brought to your attention according to the rules set down by Christ in Matthew 6:14. It might be a neighbor, the newsboy who brings the daily paper, or someone in far-off Africa or South America. Our giving is the expression of our love for God. We give back to Him in return for the great love He has bestowed on us, and in that way we spread His love abroad.

The Christian should also share in community responsibilities as time and money allow. The people to whom the money is given should know that you are giving it in the name of Christ. The letter accompanying the financial gift to the social or charitable organization should say something like, "As a Christian, believing the Lord would have me assist my community as I am able, I send this gift. God bless your efforts."

Be careful that you do not become guilty of the sin of robbing God. The Bible says, "Bring ye all the tithes into the storehouse, that there may be meat in mine house, and prove me now herewith, saith the Lord of hosts, if I will not open you the windows of heaven, and pour you out a blessing, that there shall not be room enough to receive it" (Malachi 3:10).

Dr. Louis Evans has said, "The gospel is free, but it costs money to provide the pails in which to carry the water of salvation."

The act of giving is just as much an act of worship as praying or singing. The United States government now allows individuals to give up to 50 percent of adjusted gross income to charitable institutions and/or religious organizations. It is deductible from our income tax, and yet it is estimated that less than 10 percent of the American people take advantage of this. Corporations are allowed to give up to 10 percent, and yet only about 15 percent of them are taking advantage of this provision of the government. Yet even if our government made no such allowance, 10 percent still belongs to God.

The Church Spreads the Gospel

The church is for the spreading of the gospel. The church is commanded to "Go ye into all the world, and preach the gospel" and to baptize those who believe. The basic and primary mission of the church is to proclaim Christ to the lost. The need of the world today is sending forth its S.O.S., asking the church to come to its help. The world is being overwhelmed by social, moral, and economic problems. Its people are going down, swept under the waves of crime and shame. The world needs Christ. The mission of the church is to throw the lifeline to the perishing sinners everywhere.

Jesus said, "Ye shall receive power, after that the Holy Ghost is come upon you: and ye shall be witnesses unto me" (Acts 1:8). With the power of the Holy Spirit we can join hands with other Christians to win people to Christ. Sixty-five percent of the world have yet to hear the gospel of Jesus Christ. In this generation we have failed miserably to fulfill our mission to evangelize the world. According to the Wycliffe Bible translators, there are still more than three thousand languages and dialects into which the Bible has not been translated.

The early church had no Bibles, no seminaries, no printing presses, no literature, no educational institutions, no radio, no television, no automobiles, no airplanes; and yet within one generation the gospel had been spread to most of the known world. The secret of the spread of this gospel was the power of the Holy Spirit.

Today in the face of vastly improved methods of communication the power of the Holy Spirit is the same. We need not do things in our own strength and, as a result, fail.

Today the only feet that Christ has are our feet. The only hands, our hands. The only tongues, our tongues. We must use every talent, facility, and method possible to win men to Christ. This is the great mission of the church. Our methods may vary. We may use visitation evangelism, educational evangelism, preaching missions, industrial evangelism, cell evangelism, radio and television evangelism, movie evangelism, or so-called mass evangelism.

I am aware today that in many parts of the world the church is outlawed, discredited, and at times virtually destroyed. Yet again and again it has been proven "The blood of the martyrs is the seed of the church." And God's church is a Bible-centered church, and it grows strong under persecution. "Where two or three are gathered, there am I in the midst of them" has become literally true in some parts of the world. In such places where believers in Christ live in abject poverty, they still tithe. And when one member suffers, the others come to that one's aid. Unable to preach openly, they look for opportunities to witness by life. So, for instance, when one is punished harshly for some unjust reason and bears it cheerfully, a curious observer will slip up to him and say, "I saw that. It was unfair. And yet you remain cheerful." And the Christian has the opportunity to share his faith in Christ.

So even where Christ's church suffers, she grows. What a challenge to us to do likewise!

17

Am I My Brother's Keeper?

And forgive us our debts, as we forgive our debtors.
Matthew 6:12

Since you have made your decision for Christ and have begun studying the Bible, you find yourself confronted with various social obligations and problems. You have made your peace with God. You are no longer at war and at enmity with God. Sin has been forgiven. You have new horizons for your thinking—new perspectives for your life. The whole world has changed. You now begin to see others through the eyes of Jesus. Old ideas and ideals have changed. Prejudices that you once held are beginning to slip away. Selfishness that was once characteristic of you in many areas of your life has now disappeared. Suddenly you understand what the little story means: Someone asked, "Am I my brother's keeper?" And the reply came, "No, I am my brother's brother."

Many people have refused the Christian life because it has been presented to them in its negative rather than its positive aspect. They say that Christian conduct is against everything pleasant and profitable. They say Christians are like the woman who complained that everything worth doing in this life was either immoral, illegal, or fattening!

Contrary to worldly belief, being a true Christian does not mean the forfeiting of all real pleasure. Only sinful pleasure that has been forbidden by God is to be given up. The full acceptance of Christ and the determination to be guided by God's will draws you almost immediately to the source of the only true pleasure—fellowship with Christ. To you who have not been born again this may seem a far cry from pleasure, but those who have actually experienced daily fellowship with Christ know that it surpasses all worldly activities.

In his introduction to his anthology on George MacDonald, C.S. Lewis writes, "He seems to have been a . . . playful man, deeply appreciative of all the really beautiful and delicious things that money can buy and no less deeply content to do without them."

George MacDonald himself wrote: "I would, if I may, be ever greeted in my study in winter by a glowing hearth, and in the summer by a bowl of flowers. But if not, then let me think how nice they would have been and let me bury myself in my work. I do not think that contentment lies in despising what you have not got."

Even as the psalmist says, "They shall be abundantly satisfied with the fatness of thy house; and thou shalt make them drink of the river of thy pleasures" (Psalm 36:8). God has also said, "No good thing will he withhold from them that walk uprightly" (Psalm 84:11). Paul said that "[God has] given us richly all things to enjoy" (1 Timothy 6:17).

The fact that we have daily fellowship with Christ should enable us to live realistically. Christ's way of life does not require that a man renounce legitimate interests or ambitions. Though the Scriptures may teach that Christ may return at any time, the Scripture also exhorts us to carry on business as usual until He comes.

For example, there was nothing wrong about the eating, drinking, marrying, and giving in marriage in Noah's day except that the people had become totally preoccupied with these activities to the neglect of the spiritual dimension of life (Luke 17:27). Nor was there anything wrong about the buying, selling, planning, and building in Lot's day except that they were carried on by sinful methods (Luke 17:28). What seems to have been fundamentally wrong in the days of Noah and Lot was that men made these the sole interest of their lives. They thought of nothing but their personal pleasures, their personal property, and the material profits they were amassing. They became so absorbed in the things of this life that they had no time for God. This was displeasing to God, and He visited the offenders with judgment.

As someone has said, "The Bible was not written to encourage people to take an interest in the affairs of this life. It assumes that they already have more than their share of interest of that. The Bible aims to encourage man to see his worldly affairs in the light of the greater importance and value of spiritual things."

The Bible teaches that we are to perform our daily tasks and that we are to take pride in performing them well. We were put here on earth and given certain work to do, and those who claim to be Christians are taught not only to labor but to labor to the best of their ability.

The Bible speaks approvingly of Bezaleel as a worker in metals, stone, and wood. He was filled with the Holy Spirit for craftsmanship: "And I have filled him with the spirit of God, in wisdom, and in understanding, and in knowledge, and in all manner of workmanship . . . to work in gold, and in silver, and in brass, and in cutting of stones, to set them, and in carving of timber, to work all manner of workmanship" (Exodus 31:3–5). Jacob and his sons were shepherds. Joseph was a prime minister. Daniel was a statesman. Both Joseph and Jesus were carpenters, and some of the disciples were fishermen. We are told of the Ethiopian eunuch who was treasurer under Candace; of Lydia, the seller of purple; of Paul, Priscilla, and Aquila who were tentmakers; and Luke, the beloved physician.

The Christian ideal certainly does not demand that a person renounce all interest in the affairs of this life; but rather that we seek God's guidance in performing our daily work to the best of our ability and that we keep both our work and our ambitions in subordination to the Lord at all times. Thus we find that Christ offers positive help in our daily living here on earth. He inspires us in our gifts, helps us in our work, and blesses us in our pleasure.

In one of his delightful essays, F. W. Boreham, quoting Isaiah, goes on to recount how the carpenter of Nazareth has encouraged the goldsmiths of the ages. The world's greatest writers have been inspired by Jesus of Nazareth; the greatest artists, musicians, and sculptors have also been illumined by Him.

He also helps in facing the social problems that confront us, and it is here that we may become confused. For it is in our daily tasks and in the way we face the social problems around us that the world will see Christ in us.

As my father-in-law, the late Dr. L. Nelson Bell, once wrote in the *Southern Presbyterian Journal*:

> If you are in church on Sunday the people who see you there may presume that you are a Christian. But what about the people with whom you come in contact during the week on the street, in your office, in your store, and the multiple places where you make these inevitable daily contacts? Orthodox Christian profession has its place. Attendance at, and active participation in, the program and activities of the church are an inescapable part of Christian living. But we all know the business of making a living, the responsibilities of a home, the daily routine all combine to test the reality of our Christian experience and faith. In these daily contacts what do others see? Can our weekday associates tell that we are Christians? Do casual acquaintances see anything in us to suggest that we are different from those who do not know Christ? Certainly one of the real tests of Christian character is to be found in the lives we live from day to day.

The reality of our Christian profession is shown in many ways: the things we say, as well as the things we do not say; the things we do, as well as the things we do not do. For while Christianity is not primarily a matter of externals, nevertheless it does find expression in conversation, habits, recreation, emphasis, and ambitions to be noted in our daily life. Does our conversation honor Christ? Are our habits those of which He approves? Are our sources of recreation those in which His presence can be a part? Do we bow our heads in a word of thanks when eating in a public place? Can people tell from the emphasis we attach to material things whether we have set our affection on things above, or whether we are primarily attached to this world? Do people see in us an ambition for place and position out of accord with that of a Christian? We should ask ourselves these and many other questions, for in such things men judge whether we are Christians or not.

Sometime after my father-in-law's death, my wife hired a man to help with some road work on our mountain property. One day, on the way to town, she stopped to speak to him. Suddenly he asked, "Is you Dr. Bell's daughter?" She admitted she was, whereupon the man exclaimed with deep appreciation, "Law! He was the awfullest Christian I ever knowed!"

What is our attitude toward those of other races? What is our attitude toward sex? What is our attitude toward the labor-management problems? What is our attitude toward the abortion issue, sexual deviation as an acceptable alternate lifestyle, drug and alcohol abuse and the problems inherent in them? All of these are very real and practical questions that must be answered, interpreted, and lived before our fellow men.

The guiding principle of our relation to the world about us should be, as Jesus said, "And as ye would that men should do to you, do ye also to them likewise" (Luke 6:31).

Many people have criticized the so-called "social gospel," but Jesus taught that we are to take the gospel to the world. Actually there is no such thing as a "social gospel." It is a misnomer. There is only one gospel. "If any man preach any other gospel to you, let him be accursed" (Galatians 1:9). At the same time, in 1 Timothy

5:8 we are told, "If any provide not for his own, and especially for those of his own house, he hath denied the faith, and is worse than an infidel." What a relief to the federal government if Christians made themselves responsible for the needs of their own!

My son, Franklin, is deeply involved in social work, heading up a Christian relief agency. In a recent interview he was quoted as saying that "proclaiming the gospel must always have priority." He urged evangelical relief and development agencies not to lose sight of the need to reach people for Christ. "The gospel—not development—is the Christian's mandate," he said.

The cup of cold water comes after and sometimes before rather than instead of the gospel. Christians, above all others, should be concerned with social problems and social injustices. Down through the centuries the church has contributed more than any other single agency in lifting social standards to new heights. Child labor has been outlawed. Slavery has been abolished in Britain, the U.S.A., and some other parts of the world. The status of women has been lifted to heights unparalleled in history, and many other reforms have taken place primarily as a result of the influence of the teachings of Jesus Christ. The Christian is to take his place in society with moral courage to stand up for that which is right, just, and honorable.

BE A GOOD CITIZEN

First, *the Christian should be a good citizen.* The Bible teaches that the Christian should be law-abiding. The Bible also teaches loyalty to country. A loyalty and love of country does not mean that we cannot criticize unjust laws. The Bible says that God is no respecter of persons. All should have equal opportunities. The government of God should be our model.

The Bible also teaches that we are to cooperate with the government. The apostle Paul exhorted Timothy to "supplications, prayers, intercessions . . . for all men; for kings, and for all that are in authority" (1Timothy 2:1, 2). Jesus was asked, "Is it lawful to give tribute?" Then He set the example forever by paying taxes. It takes money to run a government and to maintain law and order. The tax dodger is a civic parasite and an actual thief. No true Christian will be a tax dodger. Jesus said, we are to "render to Caesar the things that are Caesar's" (Mark 12:17). We ought to be more than taxpayers. To be simply law-abiding is not enough. We ought to seek and work for the good of our country. Sometimes we may be called upon to die for it. We are to be conscientious in our work as good citizens.

We should be generous and give to those who are in need and to those organizations who are faithfully and honestly ministering to those in need. We should enter into various activities such as the Red Cross, the Salvation Army, World Vision, Samaritan's Purse, the Tear Fund, and other good, constructive, and helping-hand organizations. At the same time, as responsible stewards we are to check our various organizations for trustworthiness and honesty and also to find if the relief given certain governments is given where designated.

Christians should be interested in orphanages, hospitals, asylums, prisons, and all social institutions. Jesus said, "Love thy neighbor as thyself" (Matthew 22:39). Think of a country without any philanthropic enterprises whatever! No one would want to live in it.

I recall visiting a country in which there were both government and Christian homes for the elderly. In the Christian home we saw love in action, but in the government home the care was impersonal and perfunctory. The doctor who served both homes said that the people in the Christian home were not only happier but lived longer. We want to live where neighborly love prevails. We are to take our place in the community. Those in positions of responsibility are entitled to respect, support, and cooperation. "Let every soul be subject unto the higher powers. For there is no power but of God: the powers that be are ordained of God" (Romans 13:1).

BE HOSPITABLE

Second, *Christians should be "given to hospitality"* (1 Timothy 3:2). The Bible teaches that our homes should be hospitable and that those who come in and out of our homes should sense the presence of Christ. The happiest Christian homes I know are those given to hospitality, where neighbors feel at home, where young people are welcome, where the elderly are respected, where children are loved. That which God has given to us should be shared with others. In doing so God will bless and prosper our homes.

A PROPER VIEW OF SEX

Third, *we should have the Christian attitude toward sex.* Nowhere does the Bible teach that sex in itself is a sin, although many interpreters of the Bible would try to make it appear so. The Bible teaches that the *wrong use* of sex is sinful. For sex, the act by which all life on this earth is created, should be a wonderful, meaningful, and satisfying human experience.

Man, with his vile, self-destructive nature, however, has taken what was intended to be the most glorious and complete act of love between two people and made of it something low and cheap and filthy. Sex, stripped of total commitment, of mutual love, respect, and the sincere desire to give joy and fulfillment to the other person, becomes simply an animal act, about which the Bible warns us in no uncertain terms!

It is significant that the Bible is one of the world's most outspoken books on the subject of sex. It does not try to gloss over sex in either its right or wrong aspects. The sly, secret, embarrassed, let's-pretend-it-doesn't-exist attitude about sex is purely man-made.

In trying to overcome the mysterious let's-not-talk-about-it approach to sex, our present civilization has put far too much emphasis on the mechanics of it and far too little insistence on the spiritual atmosphere in which this overwhelming expression of human love must have its origin.

Our divorce courts bear tragic testimony to the inability of men and women to achieve this lasting and ever more beautiful relationship without a firm foundation of spiritual values.

Sex is a part of life that we cannot abolish, even if we would, for without it all life would cease. For sex, the act by which all life on this earth is perpetuated, should be a wonderful and meaningful human experience. Used rightly it can bring joy into the home. Used wrongly it can make it a hell. Use it wisely and it will become a wonderful servant. Use it wrongly and it will be a terrible taskmaster.

Christians feel a sense of outrage, a sense of violation, when they see sex emblazoned in newspaper headlines, exploited in advertisements, and used as a cheap lure outside theaters. They blush for their fellowmen that they can be so stupid, so gross, so indecent as to defile and distort the act by which all God-given life is bestowed.

A Christian View of Marriage

Fourth, it follows naturally that *those who take a Christian view of sex will take a Christian view of marriage*. Before you enter into a marriage, consider the real spiritual implications that make an earthly marriage binding in heaven. Little by little as we grow toward maturity, we learn to love, first our parents and our friends, and later the one person who is to share our life. We have already seen how difficult this process is, for it is passion and not love that comes naturally to the unregenerate sinner.

Many have the terrible misfortune of selecting their mates while they are still in the toils of the world, the flesh, and the devil, and while the man or woman they select is also still in the same condition. Is it any wonder then that so many marriages contracted by two spiritually ignorant souls, who most of the time are incapable of real and lasting love, end up in the divorce courts?

Marriage is a holy bond because it permits two people to help each other work out their spiritual destinies. God declared marriage to be good because He knew that man needed a helpmate and woman needed a protector. He desires that husbands and wives never lose sight of the original purpose of marriage. It is woman's role to love and help and reassure her husband in every way she can, and it is man's role to love and protect and provide for his wife and the children she bears, so that the home may be filled with God's peace and harmony. They are to submit to each other—to love each other.

Marriages entered into with a clear understanding of God's purpose and God's laws have no need for divorce courts. Marriages that fall short of this ideal (and it is appalling how many of them do) should first seek to learn what God expects of the husband and the wife and then pray for God's help and guidance in carrying out His commands.

A Christian Approach to Labor Management Problems

Fifth, *we are to take the Christian attitude in labor-management relationships*. The Bible says,

> Whatever you do, put your whole heart and soul into it, as into work done for God, and not merely for men—knowing that your real reward, a heavenly one, will come from God, since you are actually employed by Christ, and not just by your earthly master. But the slacker and the thief will be judged by God Himself, Who naturally has no distinction to make between master and man. Remember, then, you employers, that your responsibility is to be fair and just towards those whom you employ, never forgetting

that you yourselves have a Heavenly Employer'. (Colossians 3:23–25, Phillips).

If Christ could prevail in all labor-management relations we would rarely have strikes. There would not be these long drawn-out arguments in which both sides are unwilling to concede the rights of the other. Management would treat employees with generosity, and employees would be eager to put in a full day's work for their hire or what their contract calls for—for they would be working not only for wages. We can learn from the attitude of both employer and employees in Japan toward one another in this regard.

The Bible teaches that all honest work is honorable, and the Christian should be the most faithful, the most willing and efficient worker of all. He should stand out in a factory or shop as one who wants justice, but one who would not stoop to take unfair advantage.

By the same token, the Christian employer should treat his employees with a respect and generosity that will become an example for other employers. A man of real Christian concepts cannot help being concerned about safety precautions, good working conditions, and the well-being of those in his employ. He will not only see his workers as "manpower," but also as human beings.

Both management and labor should remember that the improved conditions and better understanding they now enjoy had their beginnings as the result of a great spiritual revival. The heritage of labor unions comes from the church and the mighty Wesleyan revivals of the eighteenth century. Social liberty for the working classes began when a Christian leader, Lord Shaftesbury, in the face of bitter family opposition, led a lifelong crusade for better working conditions, shorter hours, more pay, and fair treatment for the working man.

Had it not been for the spiritual revival of the eighteenth century, the gains that labor has made might not have been achieved, or might have been delayed until much later in our history. When some labor leaders talk of outlawing religion, disregarding God, the Bible, and the church, they should remember how much of what they have today is due to the power of the gospel of Christ.

Some labor leaders, as well as industrialists, have grown haughty, proud, rich, self-satisfied, and power-seeking. All of them should humble themselves before God, seek to recognize the needs of each other and their extreme dependence on each other, and, above all, try to apply the golden rule in its most practical and realistic sense.

A Christian View of Other Races

Sixth, *the Christian looks through the eyes of Christ at the race question* and admits that the church has only partially solved this great human problem. We have let the sports world, the entertainment field, politics, the armed forces, education, and industry outstrip us. The church should have been the pacesetter. The church should voluntarily be doing what the federal courts in America are doing by pressure and compulsion. But in the final analysis the only real solution will be found at the foot of the cross where we come together in brotherly love. The closer the people of all races get to Christ and His cross, the closer they will get to one another.

The Bible says in Christ there is neither Jew nor Gentile, there is neither male nor female, neither Greek nor barbarian, neither rich nor poor. The Bible indicates that we are all one in Christ. The ground is level at the foot of the cross. When Christ opens our spiritual eyes we behold not color, nor class, nor condition, but simply human beings with the same longings, fears, needs, and aspirations as our own. We begin to see people through the Master's eyes. Become friends—invite them to your home.

A Christian View of Materialism

Seventh, *the Christian attitude should prevail in the matter of economics*. Jesus said a man's life does not consist in the abundance of the things which he possesses. Money is a good slave but a bad master. Property is to be used, enjoyed, shared, given, but not hoarded. Paul said that the love of money was the "root of all evil" (1 Timothy 6:10). Wealth has its place and its power, but it is not entitled to occupy the throne or swing the scepter. Covetousness puts money above manhood. It shackles its devotee and makes him its victim. It hardens the heart and deadens the noble impulses and destroys the vital qualities of life.

Beware of covetousness in every phase and form! All of us should keep ourselves from it through vigilance, prayer, self-control, and discipline. Life is not a matter of dollars and cents, houses and lands, earning capacity and financial achievement. Greed must not be allowed to make man the slave of wealth.

When Jesus was asked to settle an inheritance dispute between two brothers, He declined with a word of warning and with one of the magnificent parables with which He so frequently pointed out the earthly applications of heavenly messages. He told the story of the wealthy landowner who, in the midst of prosperity, envisioned even greater wealth and made long-range plans which would fill his life with all the physical comforts and personal glory that he held most dear. Apparently he was talented, economical, industrious, prudent, honest, and moral in all his dealings—but he was the victim of ambition and self-interest, as are so many others.

He measured his success in broad fields and full barns, and fed his soul on human vanities. His life was wrapped up in his riches and centered in himself, and he made his plans without thought of God or the uncertainty of life.

But God spoke the final word, and the plans that extended for years ahead were cut short by sudden death. The property he had amassed so painstakingly slipped through his cold fingers to be divided, scattered, and squandered by others, while he was left to stand before God with nothing to show for the life he had led on earth.

The Christian, above all others, should realize that we come into life with empty hands—and it is with empty hands that we leave it. Actually we can possess nothing—no property and no person—along the way. It is God who owns everything, and we are but stewards of His property during the brief time we are on earth. Everything that we see about us that we count as our possessions only comprises a loan from God, and it is when we lose sight of this all-pervading truth that we become greedy and covetous.

When we clutch an object or a person and say, "This thing is mine," when we look with envious eyes at what another person has and plan to "get it by fair means or foul," we are forgetting that no matter what we get, we can't take it with us when we go to make our final accounting before the seat of judgment.

This does not mean that earthly riches in themselves are a sin—the Bible does not say that. The Bible makes it clear that God expects us to do the best we can with the talents, the abilities, the situations with which life endows us. But there is a right way and a wrong way to acquire money and a right way and a wrong way to achieve power. Too many Christians have misunderstood this and taken a most sinful and damaging spiritual pride in being poverty-stricken, in standing by helplessly and saying, "God's will be done," as their children suffered and went untended. The apostle Paul said, "But if any provide not for his own, and especially for those of his own house, he hath denied the faith, and is worse than an infidel" (1 Timothy 5:8).

Jesus told one of His most revealing parables to illustrate this very point when He recited the story of the rich man who gave each of his servants a certain amount of money to invest while he was away in a far land. When he returned he found that some servants had made wise investments and his money was multiplied, and he praised them for their sound judgment and prudence; but the frightened, unimaginative servant who could think of nothing to do with the money but to hide it from thieves, he condemned.

Earn your money, as much as you can, according to God's laws, and spend it to carry out His commands. Give one-tenth of it to the Lord, the firstfruits (Proverbs 3:9), tithe faithfully, for the Bible says that this is right and just. After you have given a tithe—gifts and offerings. Whenever you have any doubts about material values, get out your Bible and read what Jesus taught about money, read what He had to say about the earning of money and the use and distribution of wealth. Just ask yourself, "What would Jesus have done in this situation?" and be guided by that and that alone.

It was my privilege at one time to have among my close friends an extremely wealthy industrialist. One day as we were lunching together he calmly announced that the day before he had sold a certain product, his family clearing $13,000,000 on the deal. "But let me tell you what I discovered in the Scriptures this morning!" he exclaimed, changing the subject abruptly to his deepest interests. This man had his priorities in order.

A Christian View of Those Who Suffer

Eighth, *a Christian will be concerned about suffering humanity around him*. The great slum areas of your own country will become a burden to you. The poverty and suffering of thousands of people in your own neighborhood will become a concern to you. You will join with organizations and associations to help alleviate the suffering of humanity around you. Many people spend so much time in lofty enterprises that they make no contribution to suffering immediately at hand. Who is our neighbor? Whoever is closest to us. It could be a wife, a husband, a child, or those living next door. Our neighbor is that one closest to us—then in our city or country—then the world.

The Bible says the common people heard Jesus gladly. Wherever He went, He healed the sick. He comforted the sorrowful, He gave practical encouragement. Years ago, an Anglican bishop told me that he could think of no social organization in England which did not have its roots in some evangelical awakening (including the SPCA!). The Christian will be interested in helping build and develop hospitals, orphanages, old people's homes, and other charitable institutions that are trying to help the less fortunate. The Christian will be interested in doing his part to help share the great wealth of this country with the needy in other parts of the world. He will be a supporter of reputable national or international social organizations helping the unfortunate of the world. A word of caution here. When we're giving God's money to an organization, it behooves us as good stewards to check out how this money is being spent. There are many responsible, worthwhile charitable ministries deserve our support and prayers—there are others we should not support.

Nowhere in the Bible does it teach that we are to withdraw ourselves from society. Rather, it teaches quite the contrary. We are to join with others who are working to good purpose to help lift the unfortunate. God needs social workers, prison guards, policemen, doctors, hospital attendants, nurses, charity workers, and many other types of people who can help alleviate human suffering.

The motto of the Rotary Club is "Service above self." The motto of the Kiwanis Club is "We build." The motto of the Lions Club is "Liberty, intelligence, our nation's safety." All of these ideas originated in Christianity. Lots of the pagan religions never had a service club. All of these organizations are really by-products of Christianity even when some of their members are not

Christians. The perfume of Christ is in the fragrance of any and all social service.

LOVE FOR THE BRETHREN

Ninth, *the Christian has a special obligation to fellow Christians.* Fellow Christians are in a special class. We are to have supernatural love for them. "We know that we have passed from death unto life, because we love the brethren. He that loveth not his brother abideth in death" (1 John 3:14).

We are to love our enemies. We are even to love those who persecute us and say "all manner of evil against us, falsely" (Matthew 5:11).

But the greatest of our human love is for those other believers. Jesus said, "This is my commandment, that ye love one another, as I have loved you" (John 15:12).

We are told to serve one another: "Brethren, through love be servants of one another."

> Lord, help me to live from day to day
> In such a self-forgetful way
> That even when I kneel to pray
> My prayers shall be for others.
> Help me in all the work I do
> Ever to be sincere and true,
> And know that all I do for Thee
> Must needs be done for others.
> Others Lord; yes, others.

Let this my motto be.
Let me live for others
That I may live like Thee.
—C. D. Heigs

The Bible says that our obligation to each other as Christians is such that we should be examples to each other. Paul said. "Be thou an example of the believers, in word, in conversation, in charity, in spirit, in faith, in purity" (1 Timothy 4:12). This is not a suggestion—it is a command! It is not a recommendation but an obligation. We are to be model Christians.

The Bible also says we are to forgive one another. "And be ye kind one to another, tenderhearted, forgiving one another, even as God for Christ's sake hath forgiven you" (Ephesians 4:32). Jesus said that if you will not forgive, neither will your Father which is in heaven forgive your sins. He also said, "When ye stand praying, forgive, if you have ought against any; that your Father also may forgive you" (Mark 11:25).

We are told as Christians not to judge one another, but rather decide never to put a stumbling block or hindrance in the way of a brother.

The Bible says that we are to be subject one to another; we are to clothe ourselves with humility toward each other. We are to be "in honor, preferring one another." We are to put others first, and ourselves last.

During the last six years of her life my mother-in-law was confined to a wheelchair as a result of a stroke. My father-in-law, Dr. L. Nelson Bell, who had been an extremely active athlete, physician, missionary, and writer (for the last year of his life he also served as moderator of the Southern Presybterian Church before its union), devoted himself totally and lovingly to her care. One day he said to my wife, "You know, these are the happiest days of our lives! Taking care of your mother is the greatest privilege of my life." And those of us who watched him care for her knew that he meant it.

As Christians we are to bear one another's burdens. There are burdens that every man must bear for himself, for no one can do it for him, and if he neglects them they will not be borne. However, there are other burdens that our friends can help us bear, such as sorrow, misfortune, trials, loneliness, family cares, spiritual difficulties, a son or daughter on drugs or in prison—or a child who has disappeared. But we are not to worry about our burdens. We are to roll them on to God's shoulders, looking to Him for power to sustain and strengthen us. However, it is our duty to help our fellow man bear his own burden.

The Bible says as Christians, also, we are to be generous with each other. God says it is our duty as Christians to take care of widows and orphans and to help the poor within the Christian society. The Bible says: Contribute to the needs of the saints . . . practice hospitality . . . lodge strangers . . . wash the saints' feet . . . relieve the afflicted . . . be not forgetful to entertain strangers. And Jesus said, "Inasmuch as ye have done it unto one of the least of these my brethren, ye have done it unto me. . . . It is more blessed to give than to receive." "God loveth a cheerful giver." All of these are our social obligations one to another as Christians.

GRACE IN ACTION

Last, *Christians ought to be gracious*, and this is one of the most important of Christian virtues—and one of the greatest.

The very power of our conviction sometimes inclines us toward feeling that we are right and that all other people are wrong. This is well and good when our convictions are based upon the "Thou shalts" and the "Thou shalt nots" of Scripture rather than our own ideas. The many different and frequently warring factions within the church emphasize the terrible human tendency to gather into select little groups, built upon profound convictions on trivial matters, each insisting that they and they alone have the right answer.

As the late Dr. Harry Ironside once said: "Beware lest we mistake our prejudices for our convictions."

To be sure we must deplore wickedness, evil, and wrongdoing, but our commendable intolerance of sin too often develops into a deplorable intolerance of sinners. Jesus hates sin but loves the sinner.

I was amused and shocked to hear a man of considerable religious background declare on television not long ago that "you didn't catch Jesus associating with questionable people or those whose basic ideas and attitudes were at variance with what Jesus knew to be honorable and right!"

Such a man should have known that Jesus wasn't afraid to associate with anyone! One of the things the scribes and Pharisees criticized most bitterly was His willingness to help and talk to and exchange ideas with anyone, be they publicans, thieves, learned professors or prostitutes, rich or poor! Even His own followers decried some of the people with whom He was seen in public, but this did not lessen the compassion that Jesus felt for all the members of poor, blinded, struggling humanity.

Jesus had the most open and all-encompassing mind that this world has ever seen. His own inner conviction was so strong, so firm, so unswerving that He could afford to mingle with any group secure in the knowledge that He would not be contaminated. It is fear that makes us unwilling to listen to another's point of view, fear that our own ideas may be attacked. Jesus had no such fear, no such pettiness of viewpoint, no need to fence Himself off for His own protection. He knew the difference between graciousness and compromise, and we would do well to learn of Him. He set for us the most magnificent and glowing example of truth combined with mercy of all time and in departing said: "Go ye and do likewise" (Luke 10:37).

These are just a few of the scores of things that could be mentioned that are the social obligations of the Christian. He cannot withdraw himself as a hermit and live a solitary life. He is a member of society. Therefore, the teachings of Jesus deal frequently with our attitudes toward our fellow men.

Study the Bible, read it—and then live by it. Only then can you demonstrate to a confused world the transforming power of the indwelling Christ.

18

Hope for the Future

For the Lord himself shall descend from heaven with a shout,
with the voice of the archangel, and with the trump of God:
and the dead in Christ shall rise first: then we which are alive and
remain shall be caught up together with them in the clouds,
to meet the Lord in the air: and so shall we ever be with the Lord.
Wherefore comfort one another with these words.
1 Thessalonians 4:16–18

Some time ago the book review section of one of the great newspapers of America ran an article entitled "The Literature of Doom." In it, they listed all the titles of books today that are dealing with the end of the world. Also a number of movies are coming out today that are called "Armageddon" movies. This concern about the last days has dramatically invaded the entertainment world. People are wondering whether there's going to be a world of tomorrow or not. There is concern about what is going to happen by the year 2000—or if we'll even reach that landmark year. Because of the tension in the world, the turmoil on almost every continent, some world leaders doubt we will survive beyond the year 2000—we seem to be getting worse and worse every day.

Some people ask the question, "When is Jesus Christ coming back?" He told us not to speculate about a certain day, but He did leave some signs that we'll discuss later. The coming again of Jesus Christ is mentioned in the Scripture more than 300 times in the New Testament alone. This shows that the Holy Spirit, who directed the writing of the Bible, puts tremendous stress on the fact that Christ is coming back to this earth again.

C. S. Lewis, the great Cambridge and Oxford professor, once said that there are three things that keep people from believing in the coming of Christ. First, he said Jesus didn't come when they expected Him to come in that first century. So people say, "Well, things are going on just as they have always gone, and He hasn't come. Why hasn't He come?" The second reason, he said, was the theory of evolution—the idea that we are making progress on our own, and we really don't need Christ. We're doing it ourselves! And the third reason, Lewis added, is that the coming of Christ cuts across our materialism and our good times—all the things that we like the most in this world. Even though he has been dead for some years now, Lewis saw our day with a perceptive eye.

Just a few days before president-elect John F. Kennedy was to be inaugurated, I was invited to join him and Senator George Smathers in Florida for a golf game and an evening visit at the Kennedy compound in Palm Beach. As we were driving back from the golf course, President Kennedy parked the car, turned to me, and asked, "Do you believe Jesus Christ is coming back to earth again?" I was dumbfounded at his question. For one thing, I never dreamed that Mr. Kennedy would ask a question like that, and for another, I wasn't even sure that he knew Jesus was supposed to come back! Having only been with him a few times prior to that incident I had no grasp of his religious knowledge. "Yes, sir, I do," I replied.

"All right," he said. "Explain it to me." So for several minutes I had the opportunity to talk to him about the second coming of Jesus Christ. I have often wondered why he asked that question, and I think part of the answer came a thousand days later when he was assassinated. Cardinal Cushing read the verses I've quoted at the beginning of this chapter at President Kennedy's funeral, and millions of people watched and heard the services around the world.

That statement in verse 17 especially stands out: We who are alive on that day will be caught up together with those who have gone before to meet the Lord in the air. That phrase, "caught up," is the translation of a Greek word which means to snatch away. The day is fast approaching when Jesus Christ will come back to "snatch away" His followers from all the graveyards of the world, and those of us who are alive and remain will join them in the great escape! That is the hope of the future for the Christian.

BECAUSE OF THE PROMISES OF THE OLD TESTAMENT

Why is Christ going to come? There are five reasons Christ has to come back to this earth. First, He must come back because of the promises of the Old Testament that have yet to be fulfilled. Scores of prophecies were fulfilled at His first coming. But some prophecies still remain to be fulfilled. For example, the Scripture says, "For unto us a child is born, unto us a son is given: and the government shall be upon his shoulder: and his name shall be called Wonderful, Counselor, The mighty God, The everlasting Father, The Prince of Peace. Of the increase of his government and peace there shall be no end, upon the throne of David and upon his Kingdom, to order it and to establish it with judgment and justice from henceforth even forever" (Isaiah 9:6, 7). Someone has said, "When our government is upon His shoulder, of its increase and of our peace there shall be no end."

That portion has not been fulfilled to completion. A child was born. A Son was given. But the government is not upon His shoulder. He did not bring world peace in that first coming, nor did He bring world justice at His first coming. But He's going to bring it the second time, because the Scripture teaches that all of these prophecies are going to be fulfilled. In Micah the prophet says, "He shall judge among many people, and rebuke strong nations afar off; and they shall beat their swords into plowshares, and their spears into pruning hooks: nation shall not lift up sword against nation, neither shall they learn war any more" (4:3). But consider the wars that are being fought right now. Look at the armament race that is escalating. Someday, however, men are going to make spears into pruning hooks; and some day, nation will not lift up sword against nation. Why? Because the Prince of Peace is coming back—He's going to be the world ruler.

Because of His Own Statements

Second, Christ has to return because of His own statements. He is absolute truth. Matthew 24 and 25 are entirely given over to statements about His coming again. For example, Matthew 24:27: "For as the lightning cometh out of the east, and shineth even unto the west; so shall also the coming of the Son of man be." The Bible again says in Matthew 25:31–32, "When the Son of man shall come in his glory, and all the holy angels with him, then shall he sit upon the throne of his glory: and before him shall be gathered all nations. . . ." This prophecy has yet to be fulfilled, but He said it and I believe it will be.

Jesus didn't lie to us. He said, "I go to prepare a place for you. And if I go and prepare a place for you, I will come again, and receive you unto myself; that where I am, there ye may be also" (John 14: 2, 3). He's going to come back in person. The Lord Jesus is coming back Himself! That's how much He loves us. The plan of salvation is not only to satisfy us in this world and give us a new life here, but He has a great plan for the future. For eternity!

The Bible says we are going to reign with Him. We're joint heirs with the Lord Jesus Christ, and we're going to spend eternity with Him! What is He doing now? He's preparing a home for us! It's been nearly two thousand years. What a home it must be! Eye cannot see nor ear hear, nor hath entered into the heart of man, what God has prepared for those who love Him!

BECAUSE OF THE PRESENT POSITION OF SATAN

There is a third reason why Christ must come: the present position of Satan. The most powerful being in all the world today, outside of God Himself, is the devil. And the Bible says, strangely enough, that he has access to heaven itself—to the throne of God. The

Bible says that he's the accuser of the brethren, night and day. He's called the anointed cherub—he's called the roaring lion—he's called the king of beasts. He's going about seeking whom he may devour. And at the temptation he showed Jesus all the kingdoms of the world, and he said in effect, "I will give you all of these if you will bow down and worship me" (Matthew 4:9). Jesus did not dispute him. Satan had the power to give Jesus the cosmos, the world system of evil. But, thank God, our Lord quoted Scripture, and that's one thing the devil can't stand! The Scripture defeats him every time.

In 2 Corinthians 4:4 he's also called "the god of this age." That means that he's the director of the false religions and philosophies of the world. The Bible says the whole cosmos (world) is under his control. What's going to transpire if something doesn't happen to Satan? Who's going to dispose of evil? Who's going to dispose of Satan? Humanity is helpless before him. Man is unable to chain him. The church cannot dethrone him. Legislation is impotent. The United Nations does not know how to handle him. They don't even understand that they're dealing with a spiritual power—an enormous power of evil in the world today.

Let's not forget one fact, however. There is One who is more powerful than Satan! This One defeated him two thousand years ago on the cross. The devil didn't want Jesus Christ to go to the cross because he was afraid of what Christ would do on the cross. He knew that when Christ died on the cross, He was bearing the sins of the whole world. And God was saying to mankind from the cross, "I love you. I want to forgive you of all of your sins. I want you to be My child and one day to join Me in heaven." And if Jesus had come down from the cross, we couldn't be saved. We couldn't go to heaven. That's why the devil didn't want Him on the cross. That's why they taunted Him, "If thou be the Son of God, come down from the cross." Satan suffered his greatest defeat at the cross and in the resurrection of the Lord Jesus Christ.

But the devil is still loose, still in charge of the cosmos, the evil that is in the world. All the injustices, all the wars in the world, the devil is promoting—all the crime, all the wickedness, all the terrible things that are going on. In his supernatural power, he has a supernatural plan, even to try to dethrone God.

There's only one person in heaven or earth who can deal with the devil, and He's coming back to deal with him. He's going to throw Satan into the bottomless pit and ultimately into the lake of fire. Then there will be no devil anymore. We're going to be freed from this terrible pull of evil and the satanic power that has controlled the hearts of men for so many centuries. That's why Christ has to come. He's the only One who can do it. The world right now is looking for a deliverer, as I read in one of our magazines the other day: "Oh, that the world had a deliverer."

Because of the Present Chaos in the World

And then fourth, Jesus must return because of the present chaos in the world—a world everywhere racked with pain, suffering, hunger, war, murder, lust, greed, hate, fraud, and corruption. Every possible form of human government seems to be failing. Each new one seems to be unsuccessful in dealing with our problems. The world is becoming more helpless and more hopeless as we enter this terribly involved and complicated computerized technological age. The Scripture says, "Say to them that are of a fearful heart, Be strong, fear not; behold your God will come with vengeance, even God with a recompence; he will come and save you" (Isaiah 35:4). Jesus Christ is going to save us from ourselves. There are many sociologists and scientists today who believe we have the capability to destroy ourselves. And we can. The human race has the power right now to destroy itself. But Christ is going to come. And just as man is ready to hurl those bombs at each other, He's going to come to set up His kingdom of righteousness and glory and peace and justice. What a world that's going to be!

Will you be ready?

BECAUSE OF THE DEAD IN CHRIST

The fifth reason Christ must come is the dead in Christ— those people who died believing in God and trusting Him. When I saw the film *The Holocaust*, I thought of all those people who were murdered by Hitler—many of them true believers. Thousands of people have suffered injustice, and killings, and all that has gone on in history, as believers in Christ and wondered why they had to die. Many must have wondered why they had to suffer for their faith. Jesus is coming back, and there's going to be a great resurrection. Believers are going to be raised from the dead! And then those who are alive and remain shall be caught up in the air, and so shall we ever be with the Lord. When is that going to take place? We don't know the exact day, but I believe it's drawing near. It's certainly two thousand years nearer than when He made the prediction.

Jesus left some signs behind for us to watch for. He said, first of all, there will be intellectual and mental confusion and disturbances throughout the world: "Upon the earth distress of nations, with perplexity . . ." (Luke 21:25). That word *distress* means tossed from all sides. And that word *perplexity* means no way out. We as a human race are going to reach a point where there's no way out.

THE WAY OUT

Jean-Paul Sartre wrote a book entitled *No Exit*, and he told us there is no exit from the human dilemma. No way out. I tell you, there is a way out. And that way is the Lord Jesus Christ.

Jesus also said there would be a collapse of morals just before He comes back. Jesus said, "Likewise, also as it was in the days of Lot; they did eat, they drank, they bought, they sold, they planted, they builded; but the same day that Lot went out of Sodom it rained fire and brimstone from heaven, and destroyed them all" (Luke 17:28, 29). Then He said, "Even thus shall it be in the day when the Son of man is revealed" (v. 30). "As it was in the days of Noah, so shall it be in the days of the coming of the Son of man" (Luke 17:26). In both instances, in Lot's day and in Noah's day, morals had collapsed, and moral fiber is collapsing all around us right now. The world is on an immoral binge such as it's never known in history. Jesus said just before He returns that will be the condition of the human race.

Third, Jesus also said there will be a falling away. That means that people who were believers will be falling away individually or collectively. And "many false prophets shall rise, and shall deceive many." Look at the false prophets we have today. Now "the Spirit speaketh expressly that in the latter times, some shall depart from the faith, giving heed to seducing spirits and doctrines of devils" (1 Timothy 4:1). There will be a falling away from true faith. Many have a false idea of God and see a caricature of Christianity. They are not really true disciples of Jesus Christ. They have already unwittingly fallen away—maybe not intellectually. They may still believe, but they've fallen away in the way they live. Your life justifies what you believe. Jesus says, "By their fruits ye shall know them." And the devil is still coming around and saying, "Yea, hath God said?" trying to make us doubt His holy Word. A lot of false prophets are coming around today and saying, "This cannot be trusted." I tell you, the Bible was inspired by God from cover to cover. It is God's holy Word. And there are those who are telling us, "Jesus Christ was a mere man," that He was not God. He is a God-man. Equally God and equally man. Filled with love for us, so much that He died for us.

A fourth point: Jesus indicated there would be an increase in lawlessness. He said that as lawlessness spread, men's love for one another will grow cold (Matthew 24:12). Newspapers are filled with these accounts right now. Have you ever heard of such terrorism all over the world? Terrorist activities are increasing in almost every country. Because of modern technology, people don't know how to cope with it. Jesus said in Luke 21:9, "Ye shall hear of wars and commotions," and that word *commotions* carries with it the idea of rebellion against all authority. We're seeing that in many parts of the world. Jesus said that would be one of the signs. And then He said there will be peace conferences. Paul wrote, "For when they shall say Peace and safety; then sudden destruction cometh upon them" (1 Thessalonians 5:3). The prophet Isaiah wrote, "There is no peace, saith the Lord, unto the wicked" (48:22). Never before have we had so many people seeking peace. The United Nations goes into one emergency session after another. The Congresses and the Parliaments of the world are searching for peace. Our secretary of state goes back and forth around the world seeking peace, trying to patch this little place here, and this place there. By the time he or she gets back to Washington, trouble has broken out somewhere else. Jesus said it would be like that: "Except those days be shortened, there should no flesh be saved: but for the elect's sake those days shall be shortened" (Matthew 24:22).

Then Jesus said that there would be a worldwide emphasis on evangelism and the proclamation of the gospel before He came back: "And this gospel of the kingdom shall be preached in all the world for a witness unto all nations; then shall the end come." For the first time in history, the gospel is now being heard by radio, by television, by literature, and by satellite in every part of the world. There's not a place that they could not hear the gospel. For the first time.

Now, what are we to do? How do we face this? First, we purify ourselves. The Scripture says, "Every man that hath this hope in him purifies himself." Do you have the hope of the coming again of the Lord Jesus Christ? Then you should live it—a pure life, a godly life, a surrendered life, a consecrated life. There's a sense in which we're sanctified when we receive Christ. There's a sense in which we grow in the grace and knowledge of Christ in progressive sanctification. But one day we shall see Jesus face to face, and total sanctification is when we're perfect, as He is perfect. We shall see Him as He is.

Second, we are to wait with patience. I know sometimes we get a little anxious and wonder if Jesus is really going to come back. The Scripture says, "For you have need of patience, for yet a little while, and he that shall come will come, and will not tarry" (Hebrews 10:37). He has appointed a day. God knows the day. It's all set. He will be back right on time—He won't be an hour late or an hour early.

The third thing we're to do is watch. That word *watch* means that we are to desire His coming. We are to be constantly thinking about His coming. At the beginning of this chapter I quoted the verse, "Looking for that blessed hope and glorious appearing."

The fourth thing is that we're to work. People say, "Well, Christ is coming back—let's quit all these activities that we're involved in." No! He may not come for a hundred years, or a thousand years. He may not come in our lifetime. Let's do our best to help reach our fellow man for Christ. His return should be our incentive toward work.

The last point: We're to be prepared. Are you prepared? "Be ye therefore ready also: for the Son of man cometh at an hour when ye think not" (Luke 12:40). The Scripture says, "By faith Noah being warned of God of things not seen as yet, moved with fear, prepared an ark to the saving of his house." That word *fear* means terrified. Yes! Some people are drawn into the kingdom of God by love and some come into it in terror. We have a right to be terrified because for those who know not Jesus Christ as their Lord and Savior, it means judgment; it means hell. We must come to Christ while we can.

19

Peace at Last

And God shall wipe all tears from their eyes; and there shall be no more death, neither sorrow, nor crying, neither shall there be any more pain. . . .
REVELATION 21:4

In this book we have been looking at what it means to be at peace with God. We now know what it means to be a Christian. We know the price that was paid to get these elusive things called peace and happiness. I know men who would write a check for a million dollars if they could find peace. Millions are searching for it. Every time they get close to finding the peace found only in Christ, Satan steers them away. He blinds them. He throws up a smoke screen. He bluffs them. And they miss it! But we Christians have found it! It is ours now forever. We have found the secret of life.

The word *peace* has been used often in the last forty or fifty years. We talk about peace, and we have many peace conferences; yet at the moment it seems that the world is heading toward anything but peace.

"The way of peace have they not known," the apostle Paul says concerning the human race (Romans 3:17). As we look around, we find that there is little personal, domestic, social, economic, or political peace anywhere. Why? Because we all have the seeds of suspicion and violence, of hatred and destruction within us.

Jesus said, "Blessed are the peacemakers" (Matthew 5:9). We are to try for peace. This does not mean pacifism. We are to work for peace. But Jesus also predicted, "Ye shall hear of wars and rumors of wars: see that ye be not troubled: for all these things must come to pass, but the end is not yet. For nation shall rise against nation, and kingdom against kingdom" (Matthew 24:6–7).

Peace can be experienced only when we have received divine pardon—when we have been reconciled to God and when we have harmony within, with our fellow man and especially with God. "There is no peace, saith my God, to the wicked" (Isaiah 57:21). But through the blood of the cross, Christ has made peace with God for us and is Himself our peace. If by faith we accept Him, we are justified by God and can realize the inner serenity that can come to man through no other means. When Christ enters our hearts, we are freed of that haunting sense of sin. Cleansed of all feeling of contamination and unfitness, we can lift up our heads secure in the knowledge that we can look with confidence into the face of our fellow men. "When a man's ways please the Lord he maketh even his enemies to be at peace with him" (Proverbs 16:7). Even more important, we know that we can stand before God in the hour of our death with this same feeling of peace and security.

In the Bible Jesus told us there is going to be war until the end of the age. He knew that human nature is not going to change without a spiritual new birth. He knew that the vast majority of the human race were never going to be converted to Him. The vast majority of the people of the world today are not "born again." So we always have the potential that violence will break out in a home, in a community, in the world.

There are three kinds of peace described in the Bible.

Peace with God

First, peace *with* God. "Therefore being justified by faith, we have peace with God through our Lord Jesus Christ" (Romans 5:1). "Having made peace through the blood of his cross . . ." (Colossians 1:20). There is a peace that you can have immediately—peace with God.

The greatest warfare going on in the world today is between mankind and God. People may not realize that they're at war with God. But if they don't know Jesus Christ as Savior and if they haven't surrendered to Him as Lord, God considers them to be at war with Him. That chasm has been caused by sin. The Bible says that all have "sinned and come short of the glory of God" (Romans 3:23). "Oh," people say, "I have joined the church. I have been baptized." But has Jesus come to live in their hearts? Not only as Savior, but as Lord?

It would be the greatest tragedy if I didn't tell you that unless you repent of your sins and receive Christ as your Savior, you are going to be lost.

"For God so loved the world, that he gave his only begotten Son, that whosoever [that "whosoever" is you] believeth in him should not perish, but have everlasting life" (John 3:16). It's not just head-belief. It's heart-belief too. It's total trust, total commitment. We bring everything to the cross where the Lord Jesus Christ died for our sins. He made peace with God by His death on the cross. If we turn our backs on Him and don't commit our lives to Him, we will have no hope in the future.

For one to have peace with God, it cost the blood of His Son. "With the precious blood of Christ, as of a lamb without blemish and without spot," said Peter (1 Peter 1:19). If I were the only person in all the world, Jesus would have died for me, because He loves me. And He loves you! His love is pouring out from the cross.

"MEET ME IN HEAVEN"

I read a biography of Queen Victoria, and I learned that the queen would sometimes go to the slums of London. She went into one home to have tea with an older lady, and when the queen rose to leave, she asked, "Is there anything I can do for you?" And the woman said, "Yes, ma'am, Your Majesty, you can meet me in heaven." The queen turned to her and said softly, "Yes. I'll be there, but only because of the blood that was shed on the cross for you and for me." Queen Victoria, in her day the most powerful woman in the world, had to depend on the blood of Christ for her salvation. And so do we. The Bible says that God is the Author of peace (1 Corinthians 14:33). God provided salvation through the cross. He made peace by the shedding of His blood. The war that exists between you and God can be over quickly, and the peace treaty is signed in the blood of His Son Jesus Christ.

Are you at peace with God? Or do the sins of your heart separate you from God?

THE PEACE OF GOD

The second peace spoken of in the Bible is the peace *of* God. Everyone who knows the Lord Jesus Christ can go through any problem, and face death, and still have the peace of God in his heart. When your spouse dies, or your children get sick, or you lose your job, you can have a peace that you don't understand. You may have tears at a graveside, but you can have an abiding peace, a quietness.

A psychiatrist was quoted in the newspaper as saying that he could not improve upon the apostle Paul's prescription for human worry. Paul said, "Be [anxious] for nothing; but in every thing by prayer and supplication with thanksgiving let your requests be made known to God. And the peace of God, which passeth all understanding, shall keep your hearts and minds through Christ Jesus" (Philippians 4:6–7). Be anxious for nothing. How many times do you and I fret and turn, looking for a little peace? God's peace can be in our hearts—right now.

Colossians 3:15 says, "Let the peace of God rule in your hearts." Some of you believe that you know Jesus Christ as your Savior, but you haven't really made Him your Lord. You're missing the peace of God in your struggles and turmoils and trials and pressures of life. Is the peace of God in your heart?

We are all familiar with the transformation that took place in Saul on the road to Damascus, when Christ entered his heart and changed him from one of His most destructive enemies to one of His mightiest advocates. Many equally dramatic changes in human personalities are taking place today, and they are being brought about by the self-same means that transformed Saul into Paul—birth again through Jesus Christ!

There is no human philosophy that can achieve such changes or provide such strength. This mighty strength stands ready to be available at your beck and call at all times. God said, "Fear thou not; for I am with thee: be not dismayed; for I am thy God: I will strengthen thee; yea, I will help thee; yea, I will uphold thee with the right hand of my righteousness" (Isaiah 41:10).

Whatever the circumstances, whatever the call, whatever the duty, whatever the price, whatever the sacrifice—His strength will be your strength in your hour of need.

There are physical benefits that accrue from Christian living. Sin and the sense of inner unworthiness impair physical and mental well-being. The sense of physical impurity and physical immorality, the sense of hatred directed toward our fellow men, the awareness of our own inadequacy and frustration and our inability to achieve the goals to which we aspire—these are the real reasons for physical and mental illness. The sense of guilt and sin that natural man carries within himself renders him unfit for the performance of his duties, renders him sick in both mind and body. It was no accident that Jesus combined healing with His preaching and teaching when He was on earth. There is a very real relationship between the life of the spirit and the health of the body and mind.

Peace with God and the peace of God in a man's heart and the joy of fellowship with Christ have in themselves a beneficial effect upon the body and mind and will lead to the development and preservation of physical and mental power. Thus, Christ promotes the best interest of the body and mind as well as of the spirit, in addition to inward peace, the development of spiritual life, the joy and fellowship with Christ, and the new strength that comes with being born again.

There are certain special privileges that only the true Christian can enjoy. There is, for example, the privilege of having divine wisdom and guidance continually. The Bible says, "If any of you lack wisdom, let him ask of God, that giveth to all men liberally, and upbraideth not; and it shall be given him" (James 1:5).

Also the Christian has a sense of true optimism, the assurance that according to divine revelation everything will turn out well in the end.

The Christian also has a world-view. This world-view sets forth God's purpose and the end toward which all are proceeding. It assures us that in spite of men's war upon each other and in spite of the destructive forces of nature which seem to hold us in their grip, God is still on the throne and in command of everything. Satan himself is held back by God's power and given an opportunity to exercise his evil influence only as God sees fit and only as long as God sees fit to let him do it. The Scriptures teach us that God has a definite plan for each period of history, for every nation, and for every individual. The Scripture discloses God's plan for the return of Christ when His kingdom shall be established, as we have already seen. Thus, for the Christian, life has a plan and an assurance that God will ultimately triumph over all unrighteousness.

In summing up the superiority of the Christian life over all other ways of living we cannot overlook the advantage that the Christian will have for all eternity. Job said, "If a man die, shall he live again?" (14:14). He answered his own question when he said, "For I know that my Redeemer liveth and that he will stand at the latter day upon the earth" (Job 19:25).

What a prospect! What a future! What a hope! What a life! I would not change places with the wealthiest and most influential person in the world. I would rather be a child of the King, a joint-heir with Christ, a member of the Royal Family of heaven!

I know where I've come from, I know why I'm here, I know where I'm going—and I have peace in my heart. His peace floods my heart and overwhelms my soul!

The storm was raging. The sea was beating against the rocks in huge, dashing waves. The lightning was flashing, the thunder was roaring, the wind was blowing, but the little bird was asleep in the crevice of the rock, its head serenely under its wing, sound asleep. That is peace: to be able to rest serenely in the storm!

In Christ we are relaxed and at peace in the midst of the confusions, bewilderments, and perplexities of this life. The storm rages, but our hearts are at rest. We have found peace—at last!

FUTURE PEACE

The third peace the Scriptures mention is *future* peace. The Bible promises that there will be a time when the whole world is going to have peace. It seems that the world is heading toward Armageddon. In Revelation 6:4 John the beloved apostle says there's a red horse, "and power was given to him that sat thereon to take peace from the earth." We're not going to have peace—permanent peace—until the Prince of Peace comes.

And He is coming. One of these days the sky is going to break open and the Lord Jesus Christ will come back. He will set up His reign upon this planet, and we're going to have peace and social justice. What a wonderful time that's going to be!

Isaiah predicted, "The government shall be upon his shoulder: and his name shall be called Wonderful, Counselor, The mighty God, The everlasting Father, The Prince of Peace. Of the increase of his government and peace there shall be no end" (Isaiah 9:6–7). Think of it: no fighting, no war, no hatred, no violence. It will all be peace.

To Be with Christ

Do you know Christ? Are you sure He's in your heart? Perhaps you have been thinking, *I want to be sure I have peace with God. I want to be sure that I'm ready for death. I want my sins forgiven. I want my guilt removed. I want to be with Christ when He comes and sets up His Kingdom.*

It's all yours, and it's free. You don't have to work for it. "For by grace are ye saved through faith; and that not of yourselves: it is the gift of God: not of works" (Ephesians 2:8–9).

Give your heart and life to Christ now. Do not put it off.

20

THE DAY AFTER

It is appointed unto men once to die, but after this the judgment.
HEBREWS 9:27

A few years ago, one of the television networks aired a program called "The Day After." At the end, it was as if the entire earth was a cemetery littered with corpses. For millions, this picture was a disturbing and traumatic experience.

If imagining such a possible nuclear winter experience would cause millions to think of their future, how much more so should the fact that however the end may come for them, the real "day after" for those who reject Christ is not this grim oblivion but even worse judgment and eternal hell, which would make the TV portrayal seem like a picnic in comparison!

But your future does not hinge on the world situation, however grim it might become. It depends on what happened two thousand years ago at the cross and your acceptance or rejection of the Prince of Peace.

In updating this book, it has been our prayer that you will not delay finding the end of your Quest a moment longer. The time is far shorter than it was when this manuscript was originally written. Few of us know for certain when death will come for us. Make your peace with God today.

O God, I am a sinner; I am sorry for my sin; I am willing to turn from my sin. I receive Christ as Savior; I confess Him as Lord; I want to follow Him and serve Him and others in the fellowship of His church. In Christ's name, Amen.